NATIONS OF THE MODERN WORLD

ARGENTINA   H. S. Ferns
Professor of Political Science,
University of Birmingham

AUSTRALIA   O. H. K. Spate
Director, Research School of Pacific Studies,
Australian National University, Canberra

CEYLON   S. A. Pakeman
Formerly Professor of Modern History, Ceylon
University College; Appointed Member, House of
Representatives, Ceylon, 1947–52

CYPRUS   H. D. Purcell
Lecturer in English Literature,
Queen's University, Belfast

EAST
GERMANY   David Childs
Lecturer in Politics, University of Nottingham

MODERN EGYPT   Tom Little
Managing Director and General Manager of
Regional News Services (Middle East), Ltd., London

ENGLAND   John Bowle
Professor of Political Theory, Collège d'Europe,
Bruges

FINLAND   W. R. Mead
Professor of Geography, University College, London;
Formerly Chairman, Anglo-Finnish Society

MODERN
GREECE   John Campbell
Fellow of St. Antony's College, Oxford
Philip Sherrard
Assistant Director, British School of Archaeology,
Athens, 1958–62

MODERN INDIA   Sir Percival Griffiths
President of the India, Pakistan and Burma
Association

MODERN IRAN   Peter Avery
Lecturer in Persian and Fellow of King's College,
Cambridge

ITALY	Muriel Grindrod *Formerly Editor of* International Affairs *and* The World Today *Assistant Editor of* The Annual Register
JAPAN	Sir Esler Dening *H.M. Ambassador to Japan, 1952–57*
KENYA	A. Marshall MacPhee *Formerly Managing Editor of* The East African Standard Group; *producer with British Broadcasting Corporation*
LIBYA	John Wright *Formerly of the* Sunday Ghibli, *Tripoli*
MALAYSIA	J. M. Gullick *Formerly of the Malayan Civil Service*
MOROCCO	Mark I. Cohen and Lorna Hahn
NEW ZEALAND	James W. Rowe *Director of New Zealand Institute of Economic Research, Inc.* Margaret A. Rowe *Tutor in English, Victoria University, Wellington*
NIGERIA	Sir Rex Niven *Colonial Service, Nigeria, 1921–59; Member of Northern House of Assembly, 1947–59*
PAKISTAN	Ian Stephens *Formerly Editor of* The Statesman *Calcutta and Delhi, 1942–51; Fellow of King's College, Cambridge, 1952–58*
SOUTH AFRICA	John Cope *Formerly Editor-in-Chief of* The Forum; *South African Correspondent of* The Guardian
SUDAN REPUBLIC	K. D. D. Henderson *Formerly of the Sudan Political Service; Governor of Darfur Province, 1949–53*
TURKEY	Geoffrey Lewis *Senior Lecturer on Islamic Studies, Oxford*
THE UNITED STATES OF AMERICA	H. C. Allen *Commonwealth Fund Professor of American History, University College, London*
WEST GERMANY	Michael Balfour *Reader in European History, University of East Anglia*
YUGOSLAVIA	Muriel Heppell and F. B. Singleton

NATIONS OF THE MODERN WORLD

ARGENTINA

ARGENTINA

By

H. S. FERNS

FREDERICK A. PRAEGER, *Publishers*

New York · Washington

BOOKS THAT MATTER

Published in the United States of America in 1969
by Frederick A. Praeger, Inc., Publishers
111 Fourth Avenue, New York, N.Y. 10003

Library of Congress Catalog Card Number: 68–9438

Printed in Great Britain

To the memory of my friend

Tryggvi Julius Oleson

Preface

IT IS the purpose of this book to provide for those having little or no knowledge of Argentina an introduction to a fascinating and troubled community which has in the past twenty years or so seemed to fall below the horizon of European experience – the sort of book I wish I could have come upon thirty years ago when I first decided to study Anglo-Argentine history. For nearly three-quarters of a century, roughly from 1870 to 1945, Argentina was a country of enormous economic importance to Britain – as a place of capital investment and as a source of food and raw materials, but there was always during that time an odd contradiction between the material importance of Argentina to Britain and the widespread ignorance in Britain of Argentina. One explanation is fairly obvious. The British government's policy of non-intervention in the political affairs of Latin America and the steady adherence until 1932 to the *laissez faire* conduct of international economic relations ensured that political conflicts hardly existed. The combination of political ambition to cut a big figure in the world, fear of foreign encroachment on British preserves, and the impulse to improve, reform, and modernize, which motivated the British imperial presence in Asia, Africa, and the Middle East, were mercifully absent in South America.

It is not surprising, therefore, that the limited British interest in Latin America – important as it was in an economic sense – failed to generate much intellectual concern with Argentina or any of its neighbours. British and Anglo-Argentine businessmen knew a great deal about Argentina, and the rest of the community knew nothing or next to nothing. This was a great pity, and serves to explain why, when circumstances changed with the onset of World War II, Argentina was quickly forgotten and the great Anglo-Argentine interest was much diminished and all but destroyed without a pang, without a protest, and without a thought.

That destruction has had a curious consequence. Interest in

Argentina and in Latin America generally has begun to revive. British universities, which are seldom more than twenty years behind the times, have begun to interest themselves in Latin America. This book is a product of that interest, but it is not an academic book. Its purpose is to arouse interest beyond the limits of universities. Its aim is not to be definitive but to be argumentative. Having regard to the state of knowledge about Argentina and being about Argentina it could scarcely be otherwise; for the attraction of the Argentine community resides in the fact that nothing is settled about Argentine life and there one encounters political, economic, and moral problems on the manageable scale which used to distinguish the north Atlantic world before super-power, super-industry, and super-advertising took over. This book will have accomplished its purpose if it encourages people to read other and better books about Argentina.

The information upon which it is based has been gathered from works of recognized scholarship by both Argentines and foreigners, from official publications, from newspapers, and from personal observations and discussions. But the interpretations of what I have read, seen, and heard are my own. I do not expect many of my Argentine friends will agree with everything in this book and some may very well agree with nothing in it. To all of them I am grateful for the kindness and help they have given to one who regards the Argentine Republic as his *autre pays*, and therefore not entirely outside Argentine argument.

Birmingham, England   H.S.F.

July 1968

Contents

Maps

List of Illustrations

Acknowledgements

ACKNOWLEDGEMENT for kind permission to reproduce illustrations is made to the following, to whom the copyright of the illustrations belongs:

Mike Andrews: 1
Camera Press Ltd: 5, 8, 10, 11, 19, 26, 27
Sara Facio and Alicia D'Amico, Buenos Aires: 12, 13, 14, 15, 16, 17, 18, 20, 21, 22
Keystone Press Agency Ltd: 25, 28
Paul Popper Ltd: 4, 9, 23, 24

Introduction

FOR THE past twenty-five years the Argentine community has been seriously disturbed. The degree of this disturbance can be measured in a variety of ways. Under the terms of the constitution of 1853 Argentina should have elected four Presidents during this period. In fact there have been ten Presidents. One lasted two days and one held office for ten years: four years longer than the term prescribed by the constitution. Of these ten Presidents only four were elected: Perón (once under the terms of the constitution and once under the terms of a constitution of his own devising), Frondizi, and Illia. Although Perón lasted through one term as an elected President, he and the two other elected Presidents were overthrown by military violence. In addition one basic political change (the restoration of Perón to the Vice-Presidency in 1945) was made in response to mass demonstrations and the occupation of central Buenos Aires by riotous mobs, and there were five unsuccessful outbreaks of military violence.

Another way of measuring malaise is economic. Twenty-five years ago the Argentine standard of living was among the highest in the world: below the United States, Canada, Britain, and Sweden, but above European standards and comparable with that of Australia. Even in 1950 the *per capita* gross national product of Argentina was above the world average: 88 as compared with 77. Since then the *per capita* gross national product of the world has increased from 77 to 128, but Argentine economic performance has fallen well behind the world as a whole. Measured on the scale stated it has never been above 104, and was only 99 in 1966. While the rest of the world, and particularly the advanced nations, have moved ahead rapidly in economic terms, Argentina has moved slowly and spasmodically forward and during five years since 1950 has actually gone backward.

The malaise of the Argentine community is visible in the streets and in the countryside. Buenos Aires, planned on an ample scale on lines more magnificent than the Paris of Louis Napoleon or imperial Berlin, is a shabby city which has grown enormously without renewing itself, replicating for mile after mile suburbs as unimaginative as the worst in Europe or the United States. Rosario, which grew as fast as any city in the world before World War I and was a prosperous community, looks today old and tired and bedraggled. The same is true of Tucumán. This depressing impression is only relieved by the trimmer, livelier, optimistic, and proud atmosphere one encounters in Córdoba, Salta, Jujuy, and Mendoza.

This malaise, whether political or economic or visual, is not something inevitable which springs from the facts of nature and human nature like the poverty of India or the social distress of north-eastern Brazil: problems for which the explanation is easier than the remedy. Argentina has few problems rooted in the hardness of the environment or the physical and socially generated incapacities of the people. For two centuries both visitors to and inhabitants of the territory now known as Argentina have been excited by the possibilities of the region as a habitation for men, as a place for producing wealth, and as a foundation on which a civilized community can be erected. And this enthusiasm has been justified as often as it has been disappointed. From 1860 to 1930 Argentina grew rapidly with few interruptions from being an obscure and backward corner of a remote continent into a major factor in the world market for food products and industrial raw materials like wool and linseed. On this foundation there grew up a civilized society, perhaps in some aspects only a copy of European luxury and perhaps, too, unnecessarily showy and sybaritic, but also informed by healthy conceptions of the public good manifest in a system of universal education, public amenities, and popular abundance.

Argentina has good natural resources and the Argentines themselves are a strong, healthy, intelligent, and capable people. They possess a territory of over one million square miles. Much of this territory is economically usable, and more than half lies within the zone of benign climate where warmth and water and good soil render the production of abundant food, both vegetable and animal, easy and at first sight almost effortless. If food is abundant, fuel is less so. The known Argentine supplies of coal are poor, hard to mine, and badly located in relation to the main centres of population. Petroleum is sufficiently abundant to meet growing needs, but problems of production and distribution together with a restricted range of quality in the natural crude, have combined to render Argentina less than self-sufficient. Hydro-electric potential is good, but the main waterflows are remote from centres of population. Heavy capital investment for necessary flood control and power production on the Paraná river system would have a revolutionary effect on power supplies. Gas supplies are good, and pipelines from the fields in the north-west and the south now provide the main cities with cheap gas for domestic heating and industrial purposes. Known mineral resources are not good, and Argentina particularly lacks abundant supplies of basic industrial ores such as iron, bauxite, and base metals. Forest resources are good.

In any estimate of a community's resources, location is an important consideration. The main centres of Argentine population in the basin of the Plata-Paraná river system have excellent connections by cheap water transport with one another and with the rest of the world. Bulky resources such as ore and coal which Argentina lacks within its national territory are, in the absence of political obstacles, abundantly available in Brazil, Bolivia, Nigeria, the United States, and Canada. Argentina's position on the rim of the Atlantic Ocean is a good one. The British naval officer who thought Buenos Aires worth seizure truly observed over a century and a half ago: 'Buenos Aires has the best commercial situation in South America, so centrically [sic] situated as to be within 60 or 70 days sail of all the considerable trading countries...' Discount these times by a factor of five, and Commodore Popham's generalization is still true.

Considered in terms of people Argentina is unlike other Latin American nations, which are communities containing within themselves minorities outside modern civilization: minorities of Indians dwelling within tribal or what we call primitive social structures or Indians and mixed races living on the fringes of civilized society without the necessities and amenities of civilized life such as sanitation, homes, education, regular employment, and the means of rationally protecting and forwarding their interests as human beings and citizens. Argentina more closely resembles the nations of western and northern Europe than even the United States, for Argentina contains no significant minorities denied or unable to obtain the minimum well-being of a civilized community. The native races have long since been exterminated or absorbed into the dominant society, and the immigrant stock absorbed during the past century is predominantly European. In the absence of conscious and intelligent action the influx of people from Paraguay, Bolivia, and Chile may eventually create a problem (the growth of *villas miserias* are a physical sign of the possibilities) but there is much present evidence that the Argentine community is a homogeneous body of men and women speaking the same language, living within a culture comprehensible and open to all, and enjoying a sufficiency of common opportunities for health and education to prevent the growth of almost unbridgeable social gaps which we discern in societies where mass illiteracy, the legacies of slavery and caste systems render social co-operation, economic integration, and human brotherhood, if not impossible, at least extremely difficult. It is by no means certain that Argentina will not sink to the condition of Brazil or the United States and be faced with comparable problems. This possibility worries some Argentines who, conscious of too much past boasting of advantages, know that Argentina has been too heedless of the artificiality of all good fortune and has insufficiently cherished the talents and opportunities God has given them.

Objectively considered the difficulties of Argentina are connected with wealth not poverty: a natural wealth of resources, of sun, of water, and of climate. Save in the southern regions and in parts of the north and west, the Argentine environment offers more gifts than a challenge. In Canada, in most of the United States, and in most of Europe, nature has disciplined man so that social co-operation, devotion to problem solving, which we call technology, and prudence have become the characteristic habits of the people living there. It is otherwise in Argentina. Not only is much of Argentina naturally rich, but it was colonized by Spaniards: a difficult conjunction of factors. The Spaniards came to America as conquerors and missionaries. They performed prodigious labours in a rugged and forbidding world of mountains and jungles, but the problems they faced and overcame were not problems of production and adaptation to environment. The Indians had solved these problems. The Spaniards directed themselves to the problems of government, exploitation, and conversion to Christianity. The Spaniards transformed America, but they did not make it an easier place to live in. Quite the contrary. In the main centres of their power in Mexico

and Peru the native peoples experienced the destruction of part
of their apparatus of living, which produced severe declines in
population.

But in the regions of the Río de la Plata the Spaniards encountered circumstances different from those they found in Mexico and
Peru, and different also from those in the interior of modern
Argentina. On the great pampas the Indians were hard to catch and
harder to keep. In the great river basin of the Plata-Paraná system
and on its immense adjacent plains, a community of Spaniards
developed which was in all its fundamental, political, social, and
economic characteristics very unlike the societies which were created
by Spanish conquest and colonization elsewhere in America. Abundance of cattle and horses and seemingly limitless pastures produced a race of mounted nomads and hunters more resembling
the Bedouin or the Indians than the society of cities, plantations,
and mining camps of the Spanish empire. The abundance of the
plains provided for the existence of a free and undisciplined people
and all the bonds of hierarchy and authority were relaxed. One of
the first British ministers in Buenos Aires described the society of the
pampas as one of the 'Democracies of the purest, but of the lowest
descriptions'. General Juan Manuel Rosas, the greatest *caudillo*
of the plainsmen and the strongman of Argentina from 1829 to
1852, observed in a similar vein, 'There is no aristocracy here to
support a Government. Public opinion and the Masses govern . . .
and if I do not in some things give way . . . I am lost.'

The consequences of natural abundance on social habits as well
as political structure were very early noticed by foreigners. One
high British officer who participated in the British invasion of the
Viceroyalty of the Río de la Plata in 1806–07 remarked: 'The
people of this Country have been totally misrepresented. They are
slothful to the last degree, and obtain food at so easy a rate that
they will not labour.' As soon as they learned of the possibilities of
rude ease and savage freedom afforded by the plains, British soldiers
went A.W.O.L. in large numbers, and they were as hard to catch
and to keep as the Indians or the gauchos. Spanish soldiers were no
different. It was estimated that it took only two years in the regions
of the Río de la Plata to dissolve a Spanish regiment. English
workers were likewise influenced. An early English mine manager,
Sir Francis Bond Head, reported that 'In Cornwall the miners are
subjected to a code of most admirable local regulations, which

encourage competition and industry, and leave the idle to starve: – in South America, the miners are away from the force of all these regulations, and a high fixed salary, with cheap wine and provisions, discourage competition and labour.'

In the presence of these circumstances those who aspired to replicate European civilization on the shores of the River Plate encountered very difficult problems. One of the early Argentine revolutionary leaders, child of the Enlightenment and a worshipper of Progress, Rivadavia, grappled with this problem along two lines: to import people, preferably from northern Europe, who had well-developed habits of industry; and to build up a powerful centralized administration backed by a professional army. He failed. The great liberal reformer of the mid-nineteenth century, Sarmiento, believed like Rivadavia that barbarism would only yield to civilization if the gauchos were swamped by European immigrants, and all educated in habits of industry and civil and military discipline. In fact this happened. Railways, immigrants, and a professional army were the means of bringing into subjection the gauchos and destroying the Indians, so that peace and order supervened, and a structured society on the European pattern emerged.

But even so, the richness of the environment still exercises its influence and still shapes the character of Argentine society. A Canadian pioneer, for example, was obliged to work hard and co-operate with his neighbours or he froze or starved. A modern Canadian living in a gas-fired, super-insulated house, moving about in a heated motor-car over scientifically cleared roads, is even less free to indulge a disposition to individualism and primitive self-expression than his ancestors. Not so an Argentine. Maybe material life in Argentina could be better than it is. Maybe the telephones could be made to work right, and the trains might be cleaner and more often on time. But on the other hand no one is likely to starve if the gross national product fails continuously to rise. Nor are the Argentines engaged in power struggles with their neighbours so that they have to have the most up-to-date technology. The result is an agreeable life enlivened by expansive debate, virile individualism, and sensuous and melancholy contemplation of mankind's depravity and capacity for self-defeat. As one very intelligent Argentine remarked to the author: 'If I have to choose between a society with a good telephone system, racial tensions, and do-good wars in Asia, Europe, Africa, and the Caribbean then I opt for Argentina. It is better to have a good conscience than to get a right telephone number. Certainly we have our problems, *pero que si?'*

Valid as this remark is, we are bound to come back to the sense of malaise which afflicts Argentina, and manifests itself in political instability and economic stagnation. The Argentines are very much themselves, but they have developed within a very old tradition which is moral, rational, and religious. To them the problems of how to live and to what purpose is never far from their thoughts. The Spanish disposition to burning faith and rigid and general logic, which has led so often to heroism and absurdity, conflicts in the Argentine with an equally strong disposition to sensuous indulgence and spontaneous and individualized feeling, which has often led to pleasure and confusion. As a consequence of tradition and circumstance the Argentine is concerned, puzzled, and seeking a way out of a dilemma: a dilemma which presents itself as knowledge that, given his abilities and his resources, he would do better than he actually does; that given the guiltless innocence of his nation, he could play a bigger part in the world than he does.

Writing in the mid-nineteenth century, the great liberal reforming President, Domingo Faustino Sarmiento, generalized the dilemma as a choice between barbarism and civilization. He, of course, was for civilization, and worked strenuously all his life to educate, enlighten, discipline, and beautify the community. He even endeavoured to banish the *poncho* in favour of the frock-coat. But he, like great men before and since, was not able to overcome the dilemma, and fix the Argentine community on the one sure path of progress admired by the Victorians and best exemplified by Britain, the United States, and Germany. The possibilities of the Argentine environment are too numerous, the choices too attractive for any to be unalterably made. Argentina is too far away to suffer the pressure of external politics. Even nuclear fall-out does not affect very much of Argentina. Argentina is the last Garden of Eden, for there man is free and innocent, yet he has knowledge and knows the corruption of the flesh and of civilization. Hence his confusion and malaise.

Chapter 1

The Spanish Colony

ARGENTINA IS A SPANISH adjective meaning silvery. It was first used as a description of a political community in the abortive constitution of 1826, the object of which was to establish a central government of the Argentine Confederation, a group of states or provinces which had emerged from the revolutionary overthrow of the Spanish Viceroyalty of the Río de la Plata. Argentina thus emerged as a more elegant equivalent of the name which the Spaniards had given first to the great river flowing out of the continent into the south Atlantic, the Río de la Plata, and then to the immense Viceroyalty created in 1776 by the reforming Spanish Bourbon, Charles III. The River of Silver, the Río de la Plata, described nothing but a Spanish dream, for its waters muddied with the silt off vast plains and the decaying vegetation of enormous forests, did not answer to such a description, nor did the river flow from or through regions rich in mines of silver.

Mountains of silver indeed there were in Mexico and Peru, and these were the goal and foundation of Spanish power in the Americas. Not so in the region to be called Argentina. The first Spaniards arrived in 1516 under the leadership of Juan Díaz de Solís. Unlike Cortes, de Solís encountered no civilized community of Indians which he could divide and conquer. Quite the contrary. The Indians were poor, primitive, and savage, and they ate him. Sebastian Cabot, then in the service of the Spanish Crown, had better luck. He navigated the river as far north as the spot where the city of Rosario now stands. He believed that the river led to the place where silver was supposed to be, and he named it the Río de la Plata. In 1535 Pedro de Mendoza founded Santa María de Buenos Aires, but again the Indians drove the Spaniards away, this time up river, where in the forests of Paraguay they encountered fuel, building materials, and Indians living a sedentary life as cultivators and food gatherers. Here they founded Asunción, a strong point whence they could convert and exploit the country and its people.

25

The centre and heart of modern Argentina is this city of Santa María de Buenos Aires, which died at birth, and after rebirth in 1580, remained for nearly two centuries the least of cities in an empire that could boast of great centres of civilization and power like Mexico, Havana, Lima, Quito, and Santa Fé de Bogotá. Of the principal modern Argentine cities most were founded before Buenos Aires was permanently established by Juan de Garay: Santiago del Estero in 1553, Corrientes and Paraná in 1558, Mendoza and San Juan in 1562; Tucumán in 1565, Córdoba and Santa Fé in 1573. Buenos Aires was almost the last of the colonial foundations, and until the middle of the eighteenth century was of no importance compared with Asunción in Paraguay and Córdoba or Mendoza or Tucumán in what is now western and north-western Argentina.

Other great cities on the western side of the Atlantic like New York, Philadelphia, Boston, Montreal, or Bahía were of importance from their first foundations and grew as their hinterlands developed. The fact that Buenos Aires differed so markedly in its history deserves some explanation. In a sense the word for silver was justified in respect to colonial Argentina, for, though there were no silver mines in its territory, its economy owed its development and part of its prosperity to the market opportunities provided by the Andean silver-mining communities, particularly at Potosí in what is now Bolivia. The mining centres existed in a high and harsh region where many of the means of life and industry had to be supplied from elsewhere. Wine, cereals, sugar, textiles, and mules were produced in the Andean foothills of what is now Argentina and sold in the colonial mining towns. That the Spanish plantation owners and merchants were able to do this owed much to the existence of a labour force in the shape of Indians experienced in cultivation and domestic crafts and industries.

Buenos Aires in the seventeenth and for part of the eighteenth centuries stagnated on the distant edge of these developments in the Andes. The Spanish Crown was interested principally in the flow of bullion, for it was from this source that the government in Spain derived most of the benefits of its empire in the Americas. For reasons of security and the protection of vested interests connected with the production of bullion in the Viceroyalty of Peru, the routes to Spain did not lie through Buenos Aires, and the Spanish government prohibited or discouraged trade by way of the Río de la Plata. Quite apart from the man-made obstacles erected in the service of a larger policy, there were many natural impediments to the growth of communities on the great prairies or pampas lying between both flanks of the great rivers of the Plata-Paraná system. Supplies of labour were scarce, and Indians who could be reduced to discipline and put to work were non-existent. The subsistence farming of cereals and vegetables was possible, but there were no markets in this remote desert to encourage expansion. There were no supplies of exotic staples such as spices and dyewoods, and sugar did not flourish so far south. The natural fauna except the ostrich yielded nothing marketable abroad, and so Buenos Aires could not at first rely for commercial growth and prosperity upon the harvest of hunters as did New York and Montreal.

And yet the presence of the Spaniards unintentionally laid the natural basis for the transformation of the deserted pampas into a treasure house of riches. Cattle and horses brought to America by the Spaniards found on the endless pastures of the humid pampas an environment ideally suited to their proliferation. Grass and water were there under a sun which heated without killing. A new dimension was then added to human life in the shape of an improved food supply and new means of movement. The Indians, the half-breeds, and the Spaniards were all affected in diverse ways. Prodigiously fleet of foot as were the Indians of the pampas (they could run as fast as ostriches), horses rendered them more mobile and constituted for them a revolution which strengthened their grip on the pampas and extended the range of their power. For the half-breeds and the labouring Spaniards horses were a means of escape from agricultural employment on to the open pampas where they could hunt their food, and find in hides the trade goods sufficient to supply their simple wants. To the Spanish townsman cattle meant an exportable staple – hides which he could buy from the hunters and Indians or obtain by contracting with the gauchos to have the cattle rounded up and slaughtered. Thus was the *civilización de cuero* – the leather civilization – born.

The conjunction of immense herds of cattle, of vast open spaces, of savage Indians and near-savage gauchos, and of a class of Spanish merchants connected with European markets constituted a combination unique or nearly unique in the Spanish empire, and one which fitted into none of the categories of social structure known to the Spaniards. In Mexico, Peru, Chile, and in the sub-Andean regions of what is now Argentina as well as in Paraguay and what is now modern Ecuador, the Spaniards were able to adapt institutions of labour service long established in Spain to American circumstances, and some of the Indians' own institutions of labour service resembled those of the Spaniards so that the Spaniards, once they broke the Indian political power, were able to take over Indian society without too drastic a reorganization and without the invention of new social institutions and political practices. In areas like the Caribbean where the Spanish conquest and colonization *did* mean total disaster for the Indians – either through the diseases they brought and reinforced with unhygienic Christian prejudices against bathing and exposure of the body to the germicidal sun, or by the social disorganization they promoted – the ancient Mediterranean labour institution of gang slavery was revived and supplied by Africans whose tribal institutions made adaptation to slavery easier than in the case of the Indians. In the Río de la Plata, however, an absolutely new set of circumstances came into being. The history of the region in modern times from the beginning of the seventeenth century is concerned mainly with the efforts of men to evolve, adapt, and incorporate from outside institutions and techniques which made possible life and growth. Some of the Spanish institutions failed completely; others endured. For example, the labour service system of the *encomienda* which enabled landlords or state institutions to command the labour of Indians never established itself on the region of the Río de la Plata. Nor did the *mita* system of forced labour. The explanation is simple. The Indians were hunters, not husbandmen and craftsmen, and they were dispersed and mobile. Slavery, too, never established itself as a major institution for organizing work. Under the terms of the Treaty of Utrecht in 1713 the English were given the right to import slaves and to this end established a factory of the South Sea Company in Buenos Aires, but gang slavery on plantations never developed because the region was too cold for sugar and the types of cotton then used. The slaves imported under this arrangement with the British tended to become house servants, craftsmen, and fetchers and carriers in Buenos Aires itself. And slaves like others could always lose themselves on the pampas, and turn into gauchos. The social pressure necessary for hierarchically structured institutions, exploitation, and an elaborate division of labour was absent.

None the less some institutions brought from Spain survived and even gradually began to flourish. Trade as an institution for social co-operation developed: hides traded for small iron and steel wares, for textiles, and for *yerba maté* (known as Paraguayan tea). The *cabildo* for the government of the town functioned. The Spanish agents of government were able to exist, even though there was little which needed the authority of government. The Church took root, and the more rational and enterprising branch of the Church, the Society of Jesus, enjoyed a limited success in showing what could be accomplished in the way of organizing a community of agriculturalists and craftsmen on the basis of slavery. Moreover, the Church imparted to the gauchos a vague ideology, which gave them, dispersed as they were, something besides language and barter to bind them to the townsmen who lived by trade and bureaucratic tolls levied on trade.

The institution of property – the control of resources by an individual, or a family or a corporate body – was imported along with all the other social artefacts of the Spaniards. As early as 1589 an endeavour was made to mark out land as the possession of heads of families. In 1608 the *cabildo* of Buenos Aires ordered the survey of land and the allocation of farmsteads and ranches. A land register was established, and severe penalties were prescribed for the unauthorized slaughter of animals on lands registered in the name of grantees. So long, however, as the cattle were numerous and the men few there was no means of working a ranch except by inducing the people who lived by killing cattle for food to come to the owner's land, round up the cattle, slaughter them, and stake out their hides to dry. Thus, a free contractual relationship developed between the merchant-rancher and the worker-gaucho. With the Indians a straight trading relationship existed. Thus, in colonial Río de la Plata there developed a society which in its most fundamental aspects was egalitarian, open and free in a way not to be found elsewhere in the world at that time, save on the frontier of the British colonies in North America.

The growth and transformation of this society was stimulated by the expansion of international trade. After the Treaty of Utrecht and the replacement of the inbred, decadent, and wholly incompetent dynasty of the Habsburgs by the more energetic Bourbons, both the Spanish government and foreign traders such as the English began to explore more actively the possibility of expanding trade between Buenos Aires and the rest of the world. Hides were one commodity that could be readily sold in Europe and would keep well enough to stand the long voyage and irregular shipping service between the River Plate and the rest of the world. Demand increased, and this profoundly affected every aspect of life on the pampas. So long as there was a balance between men and animals, so that men did not slaughter in excess of the cattle's reproductive capacity, a system of free slaughter was viable (whether for individual use or on a contractual basis for a merchant or landowner did not matter). Once, however, the rate of slaughter rose so high as to affect adversely the reproductive power of the herds the system was in crisis, and some resolution was necessary. Félix de Azara, the eminent Spanish naturalist, author, and civil servant, estimated that in 1748 the herds on the pampas under the jurisdiction of Buenos Aires amounted to 48 million head. This total had fallen by 1780 to 6½ million.

The resolution of this crisis involved a steady increase in the authority of government and the development of control mechanisms over both men and animals. The system of property imported from Spain was increasingly endowed with some meaning. Cattle were marked off by a system of branding. The sale of unbranded hides and the unauthorized sale of branded hides was punished by law. The identification of herds with a particular owner, endeavours to confine them to a defined pasture, and attempts to prevent indiscriminate slaughter by all comers, meant that some individual with the backing of authority had an interest in and a motive to preserve the cattle and rationally regulate their exploitation for food and hides. Implicit in the sorting out of the cattle and their identification with particular *estancieros* (ranchers) was a sorting out process of men which aimed at their transformation from free hunters into ranch cowboys. The distinction was made between the *gaucho vagabundo* or *gauchomalo* and the gauchos who were employed and possessed a *libreta* or pass signed by a Justice of the Peace indicating that the possessor was employed and free to travel and move about lawfully. Finally in order to reinforce this new order designed to conserve resources, a frontier force of rural police – the *Blandengues* – was organized for the purpose imposing some control on the Indians and confining them to the areas more remote from Buenos Aires.

The establishment of the control mechanisms thus described was not the work of a precise moment in time. The institution of landed property was there from the first moment of the Spaniards' coming, but the creation of a viable social framework, the rational use of resources, and employment of labour in the production of market-able commodities were the slow result of adaptation, trial, error, failure, and success. Some of the changes described were not effected until after the revolution, and the revolution undid for a long space of time much that had been achieved in colonial times. The Spanish colonial authorities moved slowly and achieved much. Compared with the near-anarchy which followed upon the revolution, the pro-gress towards orderly production was remarkable. We have to keep this in mind in order to grasp the fundamental issues not only of the revolution but of the civil wars and the great consolidation of revolu-tion associated with the name of General Juan Manuel Rosas.

The tensions arising out of endeavours to find a way out of the crisis in the relationship between man and cattle imparted a distinc-tive character to the politics of the pampas. So long as the colonial authorities were able to maintain their control these tensions were masked, and the conflict, which could be discovered in the souls of individuals as well as in society, between the love of savage freedom and the deep need for a social bond, was never clearly defined. So long as the resources of the pampas were exploited by townsmen who bought and sold hides, and employed gauchos for the great slaughters, the open country was, indeed, a disorderly, inchoate, and individualist society. In colonial times even after the cattle industry had undergone considerable development there were comparatively few landowners. Late in the colonial period there were only 327 landowners in the jurisdiction of Buenos Aires and of these only 141 lived outside the city. In the 1790s the Viceroy authorized large grants of land in the vicinity of the Río Salado east and south of Buenos Aires on the understanding that the grantees lived on their lands and showed themselves capable of defending them from the Indians. But it was no easy task to reconcile the need for a social bond with the love of savage freedom. Those who most benefited from social organization and most needed it tended to congregate in Buenos Aires. Those who did not were plainsmen. The social distance, the antagonism of interest, and the inadequacy of com-munity sense to which these circumstances gave rise provided the substance, as in some measure they still do, to the politics of the region. Once Spanish authority was broken the survival and reputa-tion of leaders depended upon the capacity to express and in some degree to contain the feelings excited by this condition in which men found themselves on the pampas.

The emergence of colonial Argentina as a community capable of independent life in the world of principalities and powers owes much to the antagonisms and tensions of international politics. Just as the first world-wide confrontations of European imperialist states, which we call the Seven Years War between France and Britain, served to transform the British colonies of North America, so the confrontations of the British and Spanish empires after the Seven Years War stimulated a transformation of the Spanish empire. In the region of the Río de la Plata this led to reorganization and development in which we can discern the shadow of independent nations about to be born.

At the end of the Seven Years War in 1763 there were three major European empires in the Americas, and there was no part of the Americas that European powers did not claim entirely and control in some degree. The British, the Spanish, and the Portuguese crowns were the principal claimants, while on the margin there were the French, the Dutch, and the Russians. In this power structure the region of the Río de la Plata occupied an inconspicuous place, but after 1763 it became increasingly a focal point of inter-imperialist rivalry between Spain and Portugal. In this confrontation, Portugal had the backing of Britain, for the British had a close political and a comparatively free and beneficial commercial relationship with Portugal. In the River Plate area the Portuguese had established Colonia do Sacramento on the east bank of the Río de la Plata, faintly visible on a clear day across the great estuary from Buenos Aires, and further up the river than the Spanish fortress at Montevideo. The eastern pampas beyond the Río Uruguay had become debatable territory not clearly under Spanish or Portuguese control, while further north the Portuguese *bandirantes* continued to press upon the Spanish province of Paraguay as they had done for more than a century. Colonia was a particular danger not on account of its military character but because it was a way into the Spanish dominions for illegal trade and a way out for illegal shipments of bullion and hides. To achieve the control which the Spanish Crown considered indispensable for the solution of the problems of the area, a firm decision about who ruled in the Río de la Plata was necessary and to this the government of Charles III of Spain turned its attention. During the space of twenty years two able men, Pedro de Cevallos and Juan José Vértiz y Salcedo, occupied the post of governor of Buenos Aires, while it was a part of the Viceroyalty of

Peru. Both of them saw clearly what was required and meditated deeply on how to do it. In their view a military solution required an economic, political, and financial reorganization of the area so that the necessary military effort could be sustained and brought to a successful conclusion. When the favourable moment for action came this total reorganization was put into execution.

The principal factor in the emergence of this favourable moment was the British difficulties with their colonies in North America. A lesser factor was the friction between Britain and Portugal arising out of the Portuguese endeavours to free themselves from too great a British penetration of their economy. The major and the minor factors combined to limit the British capacity and willingness to support Portugal in a confrontation in America. When this was clear (and the British minister in Madrid made it clear by stating that his government regarded the situation in the Río de la Plata as simply a boundary dispute), the Spanish government commissioned Cevallos in 1776 to act militarily and responded positively to his demand that the resources of the mining regions of the Andes be put at his disposal.

As a military commander Cevallos won quick and decisive victories. The Portuguese were cleared out of Colonia do Sacramento, and the Uruguayan pampas passed into the control of Spain. At San Ildefonso in 1777 the Portuguese agreed to a boundary settlement which removed them from the River Plate and stabilized the boundaries of Paraguay. Of equal significance was the swift administrative and political action of Cevallos in incorporating the mining regions of what is now Bolivia, and creating a new Viceroyalty the centre of which was Buenos Aires. This the Spanish Crown proclaimed. A common market was created of which Buenos Aires was the centre, and export trade in bullion through Buenos Aires became legal, and likewise the coining of bullion as money. Customs barriers among the provinces of the new Viceroyalty came down and the whole region was free to trade with Spain through Buenos Aires.

Looking back over the history of the Argentine community one can observe a rhythm or pattern of development; of periods of stagnation, crisis, bewilderment, and frustration; of transformation; and of periods of brilliant new development, of freshness, expansion and optimism and wealth, and then depression and so on. Such is the manic pattern, and in this period of the Viceroyalty from 1776 to the revolution the Argentine community experienced its first period of brilliance, of change, and of fruitfulness. The mean provincial town of Buenos Aires became a city and the metropolis of a vast region. Ritual and superstition were obliged to yield a place to rational speculation and the romantic imagination of sentiments and societies unknown. Theatres, newspapers, street lighting, and vaccination came to the River Plate. The Viceroy silenced a priest who denounced the impropriety of women witnessing the art of Lope de Vega. With astonishing rapidity what had long been inchoate became actual.

This cycle of fruitfulness was based upon improved opportunities to trade, improved methods of work, and a wider range of productive activity. It was, of course, a great benefit that the mining regions of the Andes were brought within the economic system of which Buenos Aires was the centre and connection with the world overseas. What was of even more consequence and of great long-run importance was the improvement of pastoral production. Not only were the herds of cattle and horses brought under control and the indiscriminate slaughter of animals checked, but a more intensive economic use of the animals was developed. A system of slaughtering in *saladeros* was much expanded, and dried and salted meat, hair, bones, and grease were added to the list of animal products entering the market. In terms of organization the *saladeros* were industrial establishments producing for a large impersonal and international market, and, although they did not involve the use of power-driven machines, they were based on a rationalized division of labour and a wage system of paying workers. Furthermore the workers with animals were not *peóns* tied to estates, but men whose relations with their patron or employer cannot be described either as dependent or independent. Rather, it was relationship in a delicate balance between diverse strengths: on the one side the backing of political authority, contact with the outside world, education, and comparative wealth; on the other the authority of numbers, a tradition of personal independence based on physical strength and skill, an ability to live close to nature, and the strategic advantage of being able to escape authority and/or join the Indians.

Students of the revolution which brought political independence to the Argentine community, tend to suggest that this event was the consequence of stagnation which characterized the economy and politics of the Spanish regime. This is not so at least in the Viceroyalty of the Río de la Plata. It is doubtful whether revolution anywhere is produced by stagnation and the doubt is particularly strong in the case of the Río de la Plata. Here was a large community of interconnected regional centres: but large in the sense that it was geographically so and described thus because it embraced several diverse elements. It must be remembered that at this time less than half a million people occupied a region nearly half the size of the continental United States of America and containing as much land as Europe west of the Elbe River. Of these 70 per cent lived in the Andean and sub-Andean regions, and only 30 per cent in the *Litoral*, the plains running down from the hills to the sea and through which the great rivers flowed. Trade, government, and common language and religion bound these people together as a community, and distance and economic and social differences separated them.

A brief description of their government in late colonial times will throw some light on the character of their society. The government was an absolute monarchy, and the Viceroy governed as the representative of the Spanish King in a portion of South America, the boundaries of which had been devised in Spain by the Council of the Indies. While the Viceroy possessed the ultimate authority in the territory and its community, responsible only to his master in Madrid and he in turn only to God, he was not a tyrant whose arbitrary decisions and casual whims had easy effect upon those who were his subjects. Quite the reverse. A Spanish Viceroy governed according to law, and these laws were numerous and detailed. The Spanish empire provides a striking example of the consequences of attempting to manage too exclusively the affairs of society by means of a university-educated bureaucracy of high-minded men trained in morals and logic and devoted to stating everything they conceived ought to be done in precise written form and then requiring written reports on everything that had been done. The Viceroy was in a sense the first bureaucrat, as strong and immobile as the machine of which he was the crown gear. He was, of course, moved by other lesser gears and cogs, and these were meshed together in bodies which united the functions of legislating, executing, and judging so that the making of laws in the Viceroyalty, their enforcement, and their interpretation in particular instances were carried out by men each of whom might have differing kinds of knowledge and different functions such as that of lawyer or accountant or soldier, but who none the less performed all the acts of government as groups. The Viceroyalty of the Río de la Plata was established in 1776, and during

the whole of its history its government operated with the assistance of officers unknown in the Spanish empire before the middle
of the eighteenth century. These were the intendants, a species of
business manager, first invented in France and imported into Spain
by the Bourbon Kings. In their powers and duties they bore some
resemblance to the French Prefect of today. Their purpose was to
provide a more mobile element in the rigid Spanish system, and
to make possible a quicker and more personal response by leaders to
social, economic, and administrative needs than was possible under
the bureaucratic system of law-making, reporting, reading, and doing nothing which so effectively diffused responsibility, entrenched
the past, and neglected the future.

The monarchical form of government, however, had certain
advantages in the circumstances of colonial society. It solved for
them the difficult problem of determining for themselves who
governs and on what terms. When we consider that the destruction
of the Viceroyalties in the revolution was followed all over Spanish
America by political struggles over constitutions and offices, in some
instances bloody and prolonged down to the present day, we are
bound to regard the institution of monarchy with the same respect
accorded to it by revolutionary heroes as eminent as San Martín
and Pueyrredón. The higher personnel of government in the Viceroyalty of the Río de la Plata as in the other Viceroyalties were selected by the government in Spain. The Viceroy, the intendants, and
the *audiencias* (which was the name for the council combining the
functions of legislature, executive, and judiciary), were appointed by
the Crown and all but a very few were peninsular Spaniards. In
order to preserve the highest office of government as nearly as possible free of local influence, impartial in judgement, and dependent
on the King in Madrid, the Viceroys were appointed for only seven
years, they were forbidden to marry or establish family relationships
in their dominions, and upon the termination of their office their
conduct was subjected to a close retrospective scrutiny by the
bureaucrats in the service of the Crown.

The only instruments of government normally and generally in
the hands of men born and rooted in the Viceroyalty were the
cabildos, or city councils. The method of appointing the governing
bodies of the cities of Spanish America (and the Spanish empire was
predominantly organized on the basis of cities) varied from the
practice in a few instances of election by householders through

appointment by the Crown to purchase and inheritance of the office of *regidor* (town councillor). The *cabildos* elected their own officers such as the *alcalde* or mayor, but just as in Spain not much was done without royal approval, so in the Río de la Plata the town councillors and *alcaldes* were seldom selected, elected, or appointed without the direct or indirect exercise of royal authority. None the less the *cabildos* were municipal institutions in which creoles played an active part, and they were one formal institution of government in which the creoles had the opportunity to undertake public responsibility and exercise authority.

There was one other, and this was of recent creation in the Río de la Plata: the *consulado*. The *consulado* was an ancient institution of peninsular Spain, and it had been brought to the New World in the sixteenth and seventeenth centuries, but not to Buenos Aires. In medieval Spain the *consulado* was a species of municipal institution belonging to the merchants and particularly those engaged in maritime commerce, and its purpose was the settlement of disputes arising out of trade and commerce according to the conventions and laws of mercantile intercourse. Like the *cabildos* the *consulados* had been drawn into the system of absolute government, and their officers, although merchants, were royal appointees. At the same time the *consulado* had the character of a guild or trade union or chamber of commerce inasmuch as its total membership embraced all but the pettiest traders of the community. The *consulados*, as they existed in Lima and Mexico, were judicial bodies concerned with the application of commercial law by their officers to members.

In response to the demands of some merchants in the Viceroyalty and to the growing economic importance of Buenos Aires in the 1780s, the Spanish government decided to set up a *consulado* in the Río de la Plata with its centre in Buenos Aires and with a jurisdiction extending over the whole of the region. Had the *consulado* of Buenos Aires been designed simply as a judical body on the ancient pattern, it might not have deserved attention in a brief book on Argentina, but, instead of following ancient precedent, the government gave to this *consulado* new and extensive duties of a non-judicial kind. It was, for example, charged with the duty of protecting and developing commerce and by all possible means increasing agricultural production, improving techniques, introducing machines and improved tools, stimulating inter-regional trade, improving technical and commercial education, building roads, planning land settlement, and even cleaning and lighting the streets and improving harbours. It was almost as if in the *consulado* of Buenos Aires the Spanish Crown was establishing a new type of government or at least a government department of a kind unheard of in the extent of its responsibilities for economic development.

Like the *cabildos*, this new instrument of government was locally based and drawn from the community in the Río de la Plata, and it was self-generating and, under the authority of the Crown, self-governing. The first Prior appointed in 1794 was a peninsular Spaniard and peninsular Spanish merchants were, of course, members as were all merchants, but there was nothing in the system of choosing the Prior, the Consuls, and the Council of Twelve by lot which precluded the election of creoles to these positions of authority. The first secretary was a creole, Manuel Belgrano, later a revolutionary soldier and one of the founding fathers of the Republic.

The creation of the *consulado* in 1794 came at a most fortunate time, for this was the eve of the tragedy of the Spanish empire under the impact of the French Revolution and the international rivalry of the great powers. As the Spanish Crown entered upon its time of terrible trouble in Europe there came into being in Buenos Aires an institution which organized and concentrated the most powerful and fastest growing interest in the Viceroyalty and at the same time gave it an autonomous life. It is not accidental that among the officers of the *consulado* even more than of the *cabildo* were to be found many of the men who made the policies of the community in response to economic blockades, invasion, and the dissolution of power in Spain: in short the men who endowed the community in the Río de la Plata with an autonomous life and who became the ruling élite of what eventually became Argentina. A few names selected from those associated with the work of the *consulado* suggest both wealth and power which endured for long and still endures in Argentina: Álzaga, Anchorena, Martínez de Hoz, Arana, Agüero, Larrea, Ramos Mejía. And they suggest, too, the revolution: Belgrano, Moreno, Rivadavia.

In comparing the history of the Latin American nations with the English-speaking nations of America it is part of conventional wisdom to say that the Spanish-speaking peoples had no political experience previous to the revolutions which separated them from their mother country, and that this lack serves to explain in part the troubled political life of Latin American communities. There is a certain amount of truth in this observation, but it is important to know what in particular is true about it. The communities of Latin America had a political life like any community inasmuch as they differed, argued, and intrigued about personalities, policies, and privileges. Close students of Spanish colonial government are impressed and sometimes overwhelmed by the remains of dead quarrels, the workings of pressure groups, and the fierce struggles which occupied the attention of colonial governments and not least the government of the Río de la Plata. What the people in Spanish Viceroyalties lacked and the people in the British colonies in North America had was experience in selecting legislators and making laws which, within limits, ordered the affairs of society. When the authority of the Spanish Crown collapsed and the Latin American communities were confronted with the task of finding for themselves a body of legislators, an executive, and judges they adopted systems of representation based on election, but these systems were simply ideas and not long-established practices and conventional solutions of basic political problems. Because they were ideas, not social practices like marriage, or property-owning, or going to mass, they had no more general compulsive value than any other set of ideas might have. The conventional practice of the Spaniards in respect of the selection of political authority involved the creation of authority by some agency *outside* the community so that, when this had to take place *inside* the community, something more like the Hobbesian state of nature supervened than was the case in the British colonies after the defeat of the British Crown. In short the system of monarchy as it had been applied in the Río de la Plata was not a flexible system nor was it a locally self-renewing system.

Although the community for which this system provided authority and government was not numerous and was much scattered, it embraced a wide variety of social relations. In the sub-Andean region of the west and north-west the Spaniards had displayed, at their best, capacities for colonization and amalgamation with the native Indians. The process by which a Spanish-speaking, Catholic civilization came into being was slow and peaceful, and the institutions of the Indians and the Spaniards were fitted together so that society was not afflicted by the guilt and resentment so often the consequence of violence and injustice. The races, too, mixed, and in the streets of Salta, Jujuy, Mendoza, and Tucumán, and even in the great industrial city of Córdoba, one can see today the evidence

in the black hair, the brown complexions, and the strong bodies of
the Indo-Europeans who were the first Argentines. The economy
created by the Spaniards on the basis of the Indian cultivators and
shepherds depended for its prosperity upon an interchange of its
products with the mining regions of Peru and more distantly with
Europe, but in its essentials it was self-sufficient, producing its own
food, clothing, and handicrafts. In Mendoza and San Juan bits
of the desert were made to yield food and wine by irrigation and
hard work. It was this solid self-sufficient base laid in colonial times
which enabled the interior regions to survive if not prosper amid
the disasters which attended the shattering of Spanish power, and
it was, too, one of the bases which made successful revolutions
possible. In these regions the society was hierarchical and paternal,
grown in accord with ancient patterns both Spanish and Indian.
Religion dominated the lives of the people not as dogmas but as part
of the response of men and women to the magnificence, the terror,
and the loneliness of the vast deserts, mountains, *sabanas*, and
forests. Seeing these regions and scanning their history one can
understand why some modern Argentines, bewildered, frustrated,
and defeated by the complexities of industrial and international
society, are romantically tempted to seek for what they call *autenticidad* in the interior of the country and its people.

   The Spanish, Catholic communities of the interior grew up during the sixteenth and seventeenth centuries and developed
simultaneously with other Indian-based communities in the forests
of Paraguay and in the mountains of what is now Bolivia. These
communities were part of the Viceroyalties of the Río de la Plata,
and what they produced constituted important factors in the trading system of the Viceroyalty. The Andean mining regions were in
many respects the economic heart of the Viceroyalty, for the bullion
produced there remained till the revolution the most important
means of paying for imports and for financing the state. The mining
regions, too, provided the best market for the food, textiles, and
animals produced in the interior regions which we have described.
But in the mining areas social relations were altogether harsher than
they were further south. The mines required labour, and this, no
matter what the system of recruitment, was basically forced labour
and largely unremunerated. Although recruitment as a species of
labour tax was an Indian practice, in Indian society such duties
were performed for public and religious purposes and did not re-

present a continuous drain on Indian manpower for purposes having no relation to their social needs and religious practices. The Indians generated the means or the will only once to resist this system, as they did when the descendant of the Inca, Tupac Amaru, led a revolt in 1780, but such a society lacked the solidarity of that which had come into being in Salta or Mendoza or Córdoba further south; and it is not surprising that with the coming of the revolution the traditional bullion production declined and eventually disappeared, and the region never became part of the Argentine community.

In Paraguay, on the other hand, the Indians found in the Spaniards and particularly in the Jesuits protectors from the slave-hunting Portuguese *bandirantes* who raided the forests in search of workers for the sugar plantations and mines of Brazil. There another type of paternalistic society developed in which the Jesuits played a considerable role as organizers and leaders. This society was basically self-sufficient, but its prosperity depended on the sale principally of *yerba maté*, or Paraguayan tea, which was widely consumed elsewhere in the Viceroyalty and whose alkaline properties seem to have had some importance for a people like the gauchos who lived on an almost exclusively protein diet. In 1768, a few years before the establishment of the Viceroyalty, the Jesuits were expropriated and expelled, an event somewhat resembling the seizure of the monasteries in Tudor England. The properties of the Jesuits passed into secular hands and ceased to be collective organizations under authoritative direction. The new owners included many from outside Paraguay, and their endeavours to exploit their properties seem to have had a disturbing effect upon social organization and to have been a factor in the determination of the Paraguayans to cut themselves off from the outside world once the Spanish power was no longer able to exert itself.

Although the community on the pampas and on the banks of the great rivers numbered fewer people than those in the interior it had become during the period of the Viceroyalty the growing point of the southern part of South America. The character of this community was outward-looking and expansive, and in its social structure it was in practice, if not in theory, more egalitarian and flexible than elsewhere in the Spanish empire. Both the nature of the productive arrangements on the *estancias* and in the slaughtering places and the position of Buenos Aires as a trading centre of an immense region rendered the society predominantly mercantile in character.

It is not accidental that in the late eighteenth century the discussion of economics was as lively and sophisticated in Buenos Aires as it was in western Europe. Adam Smith attracted as much attention on the banks of the River Plate as he did on the banks of the Thames and just as soon. Young men like Labardén, Belgrano, and Moreno considered general questions of economic policy in a fresh and original manner, and were concerned to discover the means of advancing the development and welfare of their society.

Speculation on economic policy tended bit by bit to reveal the situation and the needs of this outward-looking and dynamic community, and to suggest that it did not fit harmoniously into the Spanish imperial structure. The imperial system of Habsburg Spain had been – commercially speaking – extremely restrictive, partly in the interest of privileged cities and groups in Spain, partly on account of the need to concentrate activity and defend it from marauders and jealous foreign powers, and partly in order to distribute economic benefits in the direction of the Crown and the Court. Under the Bourbons there had been a great liberation and at the same time a tightening-up of regulations *vis-à-vis* foreign states. During the entire history of the Viceroyalty of the Río de la Plata, its commerce functioned under a system of free trading inside the Spanish empire, which enabled goods to flow back and forth through Buenos Aires to a large number of ports in the Spanish dominions in Europe and overseas. Thus the market area of Spanish enterprise was enlarged, while at the same time efforts were made to limit the penetration of foreign commodities into this market and to reduce contraband trade. This policy served well enough so long as Spain was at peace and the Spanish economy was expanding as it was during most of the eighteenth century.

When, however, the revolutionary and Napoleonic War broke out in Europe and Spain became involved, the commercial problems of Buenos Aires and its hinterland became acute. The predominant interests in the *Litoral* depended, if not for their existence, certainly for their increase and their welfare, upon the maintenance and expansion of buying or selling locally and overseas. For them a world market was theoretically a great advantage, and this is how some of them began to see their situation. But the communities in the interior were not so placed. They were more self-sufficient. The *vignerons* of Mendoza, the weavers of Tucumán, and the mule breeders of Salta had an interest in maintaining the markets of the

Viceroyalty, and they were not too happy even about a commercial system which enabled Spanish wines, fabrics, and cutlery to be sold freely in the *Litoral*. To the commercial interest in Buenos Aires buying and selling was essential, and the more the better no matter where the goods might come from. The only real division in the *Litoral* commercial interest was between the creole merchants and the Spaniards, the first group jealous of the advantages which the second enjoyed in a system of commercial regulations designed to maximize the Spanish place in the system and minimize foreign intrusion.

Such then was the community in the Río de la Plata and its government when the mounting disruption of the French Revolution put at risk and eventually overwhelmed the Spanish Crown and destroyed its authority in America.

Chapter 2

The Birth of the Argentine Nation

WHEN THE FRENCH REVOLUTION broke out in 1789 the Spanish empire was at peace, and in the Viceroyalty of the Río de la Plata a busy atmosphere prevailed. Compared with what had gone before and what was to come, the state of society and of the economy can be described as well balanced and progressive. Political problems there were, but none of them of excessive dimensions or of such a character that they could alarm even the most pessimistic. Anything which we today would identify as an independence movement did not exist, was not even vaguely an idea in anyone's head, nor were the institutions of society in any way under fundamental attack. And yet this was the eve of a time of troubles which witnessed blockade, invasion, revolution, and finally the total dissolution of the bonds of empire, the creation of independent, republican institutions, and social changes of a confusing and diverse nature.

The origin of these troubles lay outside the Río de la Plata. The creation of an independent Argentine community was a response to them; a means generated in the community of dealing with disasters they never made. Although the Argentines have a strongly intellectual disposition, a love of general ideas, and a propensity to moralize, their independence was not a product of translating ideas into reality. Rather, it revealed a practical capacity for direct response to events, a talent for meeting a challenge grounded in pride and vitality. This combination of pride and practicality is something foreigners have to reckon with in dealing with Argentines, and it was never better manifested than in the epoch when the Argentine Republic was born.

From 1789 until 1796 the Spanish Crown stood firmly in opposition to the French revolutionaries. In the spring of 1793 the French revolutionary armies attacked Spain. Spain joined Britain in alliance against France, but, like the others who sought to resist the revolutionary forces, Spain was invaded and then lured to the bargaining table to repair disaster by diplomacy rather than by the armed resistance of the people. In 1795 the Spanish Crown made peace with the French, giving away Santo Domingo in return for the withdrawal of French forces from Catalonia, Navarre, and Roussillon. This was fair enough, and to this point no serious damage had been done.

In 1796, however, the Spanish leadership, now in the hands of Manuel Godoy, the Prince of Peace, decided to join the war on the French side. Within six months the Spanish fleet, along with that of the French, was smashed off Cape St Vincent by the British Royal Navy. The island of Trinidad was snatched from Spain with the loss of only one British soldier. The consequence of war with Britain was serious in Buenos Aires. The British blockade cut exports from Buenos Aires from $5\frac{1}{2}$ million pesos in 1796 to less than half a million in 1797. To meet this circumstance the Spanish government authorized trade with neutrals, and thus the first breach was made, albeit temporarily, in the exclusive Spanish system of trade.

When a temporary peace came in 1802 the position of Spain did not yet seem perilous. The vast Louisiana territory had been transferred to France in return for some territorial gains in Italy. Portugal had been attacked, detached from her alliance with Britain, and was being prepared for partition between French interests and the Prince of Peace. Trinidad had been lost, but Minorca had been gained. In the Viceroyalty of the Río de la Plata all seemed well except for the fact that the decree permitting trade with neutrals had split the economic community of Buenos Aires roughly into two parties: those who wanted to maintain and extend freer trade and those who wished to keep the restrictive system centred on Spain.

War between France and Britain was resumed in May 1803, but until Britain was joined by Russia, Austria, and Sweden in the late summer of 1805, Spain was at peace. As allies of France the Spaniards were now involved. Napoleon abandoned plans to assault England and turned on his continental enemies with devastating effect. The battles of Ulm and Austerlitz followed before the year was out. But Britain, too, was capable of delivering a terrible blow. At Trafalgar the fleets of France and Spain were destroyed, and for Spain this was disaster indeed. The Spaniards, having an empire overseas to defend, had put much effort into reviving and perfecting their naval power. Communication and trade between Spain and

the Americas lay open to British assault, and the Royal Navy, need-
ing no longer to concentrate its main strength on the coasts of
Europe, was freer than heretofore to range the oceans of the
world looking for the friends of Napoleon Bonaparte.

It was this circumstance which quickly affected the Viceroyalty
of the Río de la Plata. Taking advantage of this new freedom of
movement and determined to ensure more completely the security
of the sea routes to the Far East, the British government despatched
a combined force of the Royal Navy and the British army to
southern Africa to take possession of the base at Cape Town belonging to the Dutch ally of Napoleon, the Batavian Republic. This
operation was executed with speed and economy. In fact the British
forces were larger after the operation than before; for by a ruse they
lured into the harbour of Cape Town a French ship loaded with
British prisoners-of-war, and these were added to the strength of the
British troops. At the same time food supplies were short on account
of a drought and perhaps because of political hostility on the part of
the Boer farmers. To meet this emergency the commander of the
naval forces, Commodore Sir Home Popham, resolved to cruise on
the coast of South America in search of flour and other supplies.
This decision was the germ of the enterprise which marked the beginning of the end of the Spanish empire in South America.

Commodore Sir Home Popham was no ordinary British naval
officer. Technically he was one of the ablest, most imaginative, and
successful officers in the service. His feats of navigation, his contribution to the improvement of signalling, his mastery of combined
operations justified both his promotion to high rank and his membership in the Royal Society. But he was also a politician and diplomat.
He had been convicted of corruption by a court martial, and had
forced a reversal of the decision and at the same time succeeded
in hanging round the neck of Admiral Lord St Vincent the charge
of having victimized an officer. He had negotiated with Arab
princes and the Czar of Russia. And he had connections in the
British Cabinet and the City of London.

On several occasions he had discussed with high politicians like
Henry Dundas, Viscount Melville, and with merchants in the City
the possibility of seizing or liberating the Spanish colonies in the
expectation that diminishing the power of Spain would be good for
British business. None of these discussions had produced a policy on
the part of the British government and, much less, planning and

orders for an attempt against the Spanish dominions overseas. Although Spain had long been Napoleon's ally against Britain, the British government, aware of the uncertain position of Spain and unimpressed by the Spanish contribution to French military strength, had been reluctant to adopt a strenuously hostile policy towards Spain. In any case the struggles against the French revolutionaries in the Caribbean had cost so dear that prudence alone suggested that an extension of the war into South and Central America might very well be fatal. Thus, no assault had been planned against the Spanish empire. Trinidad alone had been seized, an act which in no way impaired the Spanish position in Cuba and on the Main.

Sir Home Popham, however, decided to make policy on his own account. He managed to persuade the commander of the ground forces in Cape Town to make available the 71st Regiment of Foot, some artillery, and dismounted dragoons; in all less than one thousand men. To these he added about 900 artillery, dragoons, and marines when he reached St Helena. After an easy passage across the south Atlantic this force appeared in the River Plate on 8 June 1806. It by-passed the Spanish strong-point at Montevideo and proceeded to Buenos Aires. An assault by sea was impossible because the shallow waters of the vast muddy river prevented heavy ships from coming within cannon range of the Fort, the seat of Spanish Viceregal authority. On 25 June Popham quickly put a combined force ashore at Quilmes some 8 miles from the city. By a landward assault he took the town three days later having suffered only one man killed and twelve wounded.

From this rape the Argentine Republic was born. This violation of a sheltered child of Spain not only revealed the weakness of the parent, but wakened in the colony the resources of independent life. Within six weeks Popham's force were prisoners-of-war. By August 1807, a large British expeditionary force had been compelled to surrender. On 25 May 1810, a locally appointed committee took power from the Spanish Viceroy. After that date no agency of Spanish power ever again exercised authority in Buenos Aires nor in any but a corner of the Viceroyalty of the Río de la Plata, and there not for long. But the day independence was born was the day the Spanish Viceroy, the Marquis of Sobremonte, fled from his capital city. Thereafter men loyal to Spain, like the Spanish commander Liniers, or the merchant and *alcalde*, Álzaga, or the Viceroy Cisneros, played leading parts in the great events of their time, but in fact the initiative in policy formation and in political action had passed to the creole community. Henceforward their interests, their ideas, and their problems became the substance of politics, and the governments they generated represented them in the larger international community of nations.

This happened unself-consciously. The idea of independence from Spain was neither prevalent nor popular. Popham and his admirers in London had been led to believe that the creoles were longing to be free, and nothing shocked them more than the discovery that the idea as distinct from the practice of independence was of no account in the community of the Río de la Plata. Independence as a political objective grew out of, and did not precede, the response to the British invasion. This response established, too, the pattern and mode of Argentine politics – a pattern and mode which can still be discerned in modern Argentina.

When the Viceroy fled from Buenos Aires and allowed it to pass without serious resistance into the enemy's hands, he headed for the interior, the traditional and oldest centre of Spanish power, there to organize a force along conventional lines to drive out the enemy. He sent orders to Montevideo to despatch troops to the interior. But he had lost control, and the initiative had passed to the people. It is easy to sentimentalize about the people, and Argentine rhetoricians do this without restraint. More precisely defined this was, however, a fact capable of operational description. Neither the professional officers, nor the mercantile interests, nor the landed interest, nor the simplest householders, nor the clergy waited on the Viceroy or the government in Spain to save them. Nor did they resolve to accept the fact of conquest. They struck out for themselves to liberate their city and the pampas and the great river which flowed through them. This is the political fact beyond all other facts in the history of Argentina: a union for action of the people of the city and province of Buenos Aires.

In this stage the heroes of the hour were loyal supporters of the Spanish Crown: Santiago de Liniers, Martín de Álzaga, and Juan Martín de Pueyrredón. Of these three the first two perished in the revolution on account of their actual or alleged devotion to the Spanish connection; the third became a hero of the independence. But at this moment they acted independently without, or in disobedience of, the orders of the Viceroy, and they acted to mobilize the whole community for action. Their leadership only matched the zeal and invention of the people. A Catalan, José Fornaguera, for example, proposed the day after the capitulation to organize a secret band of experts with the knife whose task it would be to slaughter Englishmen wherever they found them. A plan to transport reinforcements from Montevideo in small ships capable of navigating in the shallow waters beyond the reach of the English warships was undertaken. The gauchos and the Indians were mobilized to help, and so it went, swiftly, often chaotically but energetically.

Simple enthusiasm is, of course, insufficient against well-disciplined, well-equipped armed forces. It must be remembered that the British troops were commanded by Brigadier William Carr Beresford, who became one of Wellington's Field Marshals, and that the ships in the river were comparable by the standards of the time with those which stand off the coast of Vietnam today. The man who brought organization and experience to bear on the problem presented by British military and naval power was an unlikely hero: an ageing Frenchman who had served in the Spanish navy for many years honourably but without distinction. Captain Santiago de Liniers y Bremond was a port captain at Ensenada and the man in command of the fortifications there. He was married to the daughter of a well-to-do creole merchant and landowner, Martín de Sarratea. For twenty years or more he had navigated the waters of the River Plate, and this was the key to his success, for he knew the characteristic patterns of the winter gales in the vast shallow estuary. Because he was neither a Spaniard nor a creole he was not covered by the terms of the Spanish surrender, and he was in Buenos Aires the day after the capitulation. On 1 July he went to mass, and found that the spirit had departed from the service, whereupon he swore to the Virgin of Rosario that he would rescue her from captivity. This together with a conversation with Martín de Álzaga, the *alcalde de primer voto*, appears to have persuaded him to disobey the orders of Sobremonte to despatch troops from the north shore to the interior. Instead he gathered together some 500 men and artillery, and, while the British ships were immobilized by gales, he got them across the river upstream from Buenos Aires. Thus, enthusiasm was reinforced by disciplined fire-power.

Meanwhile Pueyrredón had aroused the countryside, and the gauchos rallied to him – ill-equipped in terms of guns but mobile, skilful in the use of the *bolas* and the knife, and capable of harassing to death any military formation not heavily concentrated and well protected by musketry and shrapnel fire. Militia formations came to life, and the Regiment of the Patricios was born. At the same time the citizens made each of their flat-roofed, blank-walled houses into fortresses from which the 'secret army' of knifemen could operate.

The British forces taken all together were undoubtedly superior to the Spanish in fire-power, in organization, and in military experience. Their situation was none the less unhappy. They had absolutely no political support in the community, and in a self-denying ordinance Beresford had announced that he had no intention of appealing to the slaves and Indians against the Spaniards. Furthermore, their heaviest weapons, the naval cannon, were dispersed in the ships in the river and immobilized by the heavy gales and the shallow waters which prevented them from covering the troops in Buenos Aires. The troops themselves were superior to the Spanish forces in terms of trained men, but they could not give battle in the open because the rains had rendered the approaches to the city a great sea of mud. In these circumstances Liniers' forces closed in, firing down the straight narrow streets and assaulting the troops from the rooftops. The British enjoyed some success, but injuries inflicted on them were too great. On 12 August 1806, Beresford agreed to surrender on the understanding that he could re-embark his troops and depart. It was symptomatic of political change that Liniers was unable to keep to this agreement. Popular pressure obliged him to march the British force to a place of imprisonment and safety away from Buenos Aires.

The political meaning of the successful resistance to the British soon became evident. Liniers had been a simple port captain. Now he was a hero, the embodiment of the general will and the general power, and the only man capable in some degree of exercising authority. The only organ of government still functioning in the city was the *cabildo*. In order to consider the many immediate problems of the liberation the *cabildo* summoned a 'General Congress' to meet on 14 August. To this they invited the leading ecclesiastics, officers of the Viceregal government such as the *oidores*, members of the *cabildo* and councillors of the *consulado*, some leading merchants and landed proprietors, and men from the professions of law and medicine. Altogether ninety-eight persons were invited of which not more than twenty were creoles. Outside the *cabildo* where the meeting was held a crowd of 4,000 had assembled crying 'Long live the King. Death to Traitors'. The crowd pressed into the building and at their head were some professional men who had not been invited, including Juan Martín de Pueyrredón and Manuel José de Labardén. These last demanded that the Viceroy be divested of his military authority and that Santiago de Liniers be made Commander-in-Chief. This proposition was debated, and after considering what the Laws of the Indies had to say on this unusual proposal (which was not much), it was decided to despatch a delegation consisting of the *fiscal*, the regent of the *audiencia*, and the *syndic-procurador* of the *cabildo* to the Viceroy to examine the problem and tactfully suggest that he step down.

This Sobremonte was not disposed to do, but a bishop persuaded him that he ought to give Liniers the command as a reward for his services pending royal confirmation. Thus the first instance of popular pressure in the direction of locally based decision-making was accomplished.

Troubles with the English were not at an end. When news of the seizure of Buenos Aires reached London the government were indignant at action taken without orders and to the prejudice of high policy. Popham was removed from his command and summoned home. Public opinion, particularly in mercantile circles, was, on the contrary, enthusiastic about the new acquisition. Popham faced a court martial while the City of London voted him a jewelled sword. The Prime Minister, Lord Grenville, was dismayed at the prospect of further dispersing British troops around the world while Napoleon tightened his grip on Europe, but in the interest of conciliating the mercantile groups it was decided on nothing less than the dissolution and perhaps acquisition of the Spanish empire. A pincer movement to snap up Mexico was planned. Chile was to be taken over, etc. Then the news arrived in November 1806 that Buenos Aires had been taken back by its inhabitants. The troops destined for Chile were redirected towards the River Plate, and an expeditionary force of 12,000 was prepared to reconquer Buenos Aires.

The British assault on Montevideo proved to be another nail in the coffin of the Spanish empire. Under the command of General Sir Samuel Auchmuty, the British forces took Montevideo, not with the ease with which they had occupied Buenos Aires but with professional skill and heavy casualties. In its fall Sobremonte played a disastrous part which prompted the *audiencia* to ask him to resign. Álzaga and the *cabildo* of Buenos Aires were not satisfied with this moderate course. A new General Congress was summoned and by a majority vote the Marquis of Sobremonte was suspended from his office, arrested, and sent back to Spain. The Spanish government likewise suspended him and appointed in his place Ruiz Huidobro who, unknown to them, was already a prisoner of the British. Again the local people acted and invested Liniers with the powers of Viceroy *ad interim.*

The second British assault on Buenos Aires was an unqualified disaster. Although they had a heavy superiority of forces and equipment the whole enterprise was rotten in the heart of the British commander, Major-General Whitelocke. He had only one course of action: to land heavy guns and blow the city flat, house by house and street by street until the Spaniards could be brought out into the open to meet the superior British infantry and artillery. This course Whitelocke refused to adopt on the grounds of political realism and humanity. Instead he deliberately undertook to fight in the adverse circumstances which Beresford encountered because he could not do otherwise. The British troops advanced down the straight narrow streets raked with artillery fire and assaulted by musket fire from above. The casualties were heavy. By the second day of the assault 3,000 of the British force were dead, wounded, or prisoners. Whitelocke took the advice of his senior officers and decided to quit. Liniers came to a quick agreement. If the British would get out lock, stock, and barrel and evacuate every place in their possession, all prisoners would be released to return to Europe. It was a more than generous end to a stupid and greedy enterprise.

While the Argentine community were thus demonstrating their capacity to play in the rough game of international politics and hold their own against a major world power, events were simultaneously developing otherwise for the Spanish monarchy. While the British forces were assembling to assault Buenos Aires the first resistance to the disastrous pro-French policies of Godoy began to manifest itself. The heir to the throne, Ferdinand, was at the head of the opposition in the Court, and this resistance to Godoy found support among the classes excluded from politics. In March there was a popular uprising against Godoy at Aranjuez which persuaded Charles IV to abdicate. The French Emperor then began to intervene seriously in Spanish affairs, and by June 1807 Napoleon had installed his brother Joseph as King of Spain. Then commenced the dissolution of authority and the long agony of the Spanish people.

This dissolution projected itself overseas as the fundamental revolutionary question: who is to govern? Liniers was the Viceroy *ad interim* endowed with the popular esteem and respect born of heroic labours successfully performed. But he was a Frenchman. When the emissary of the new French King of Spain appeared in Buenos Aires, Liniers played a cautious game. He knew the temper of his people and so he refused to see the Marquis de Sassinay in private. He insisted that the communications from Madrid be opened and discussed in the *audiencia*. Liniers himself seems to have been of two minds about the changes which had taken place in Spain, but was sufficiently a realist to recognize that sentiment in the Viceroyalty, like sentiment in Spain, was opposed to the Napoleonic plans. Sassenay was turned away.

Suspicion of Liniers' open mind and 'Frenchness' precipitated a fundamental division in the community. Those committed wholeheartedly to the Spanish connection and wholeheartedly opposed to the Bonapartist domination initiated a movement to remove Liniers. Up to this point the determination to defeat the British had united the community, thus concealing the fact that an absolutely new political situation had been created by mass action undirected by the legitimate Spanish authorities. Now some of the forces which had raised Liniers to power and had helped to legitimize his authority, began to doubt what Liniers' political intentions were, and by the accidents of circumstances the legitimacy of the ultimate power in Spain itself was in doubt. Two leading men in particular were sufficiently doubtful about him to consider his removal. These were Álzaga, one of the brains behind the resistance to Britain, and Elío, the governor of Montevideo. Both these men could in any showdown call on armed forces: Álzaga on the military formations of peninsular Spaniards which had been created in the fight against the British, and Elío upon the troops under his command in Montevideo. Liniers commanded general popularity and prestige, but he controlled no particular force of his own, and the elements in the community favourable to Napoleon were few in number and unorganized. There was, however, a third force in the political equation: the armed formations of creoles, the hussars commanded by Pueyrredón and Martín Rodríguez, and the Regiment of the Patricios commanded by Cornelio Saavedra. The break between Liniers on the one hand and Elío and Álzaga on the other led to a confrontation of forces: formations predominantly Spanish opposed to formations predominantly creole. That blood-letting did not ensue can be attributed to Liniers' political skill and firm creole support. When confronted with the demand that he should hand over his powers to a *Junta* he declared that he would hand over his powers to anyone who could legally take them but not to an illegal committee. The man who could legally take office, Ruiz Huidobro, an ex-governor of Montevideo and a man senior in rank to Liniers in the Spanish service, was present. Álzaga and his supporters were disconcerted by this turn of events and Liniers surrounded by the officers of the creole regiments walked out of the gathering still Spanish Viceroy with the consent and support of creole soldiers. At once the military formations of peninsular Spaniards were dissolved, and the café where the partisans of Álzaga met prudently closed its doors.

Events in Spain made it possible to avoid for the time being a further crisis of legitimacy. The *Junta Central* set up to govern in the name of Ferdinand VII established itself in Seville, and pro-claimed a plan to establish a Spanish Parliament representative not only of the Spanish community but the communities overseas. In theory the Spanish empire was dissolved, and a new and bigger Spain conceived. In Buenos Aires the new authority was accepted, and the Viceroy appointed by the *Junta Central*, Admiral Don Baltasar Hidalgo de Cisneros y Torre Ceijasy Jofré, took the place of Liniers, who retired gracefully to Córdoba. Although a crisis of legitimacy is one of the most fundamental in political life, such crises are seldom encountered in isolation. This was particularly the case in the Río de la Plata. Problems of economic and commercial policy had been obscured by the excitement of invasion, victory, and the upsets in Spain, but they were real and persistent. Fundamentally, the pro-blem concerned the matter of markets and the sale of pastoral products. Unless trade with neutrals was allowed to continue and a further expansion permitted in the direction of trading with Britain (no longer an enemy, but now an ally of that government in Spain which the Viceroyalty acknowledged as legitimate) an economic crisis would develop at the moment when the revenues of the Viceroyalty were needed to pay the heavy costs of defence and the repair of damage done during the invasion. Liniers had inclined to a liberal commercial policy not on principle but, like his pre-decessors, as a response to an emergency situation. This relaxation of the Spanish system of trade restriction had been a factor in the opposition of Álzaga and the Spanish mercantile interest, and this interest had a considerable local support from those who were more interested in protecting local industry than they were in maximizing sales of pastoral products in the world market. Thus a split emerged over economic policy which reinforced the political division between creoles and *peninsulares*.

It is possible to discern in these critical years between the British invasion in 1806 and the extinction of the authority of the anti-French *Junta Central* in November 1809, the definition of the character and polarities of Argentine politics. During these years, as it were, the pack of political cards used by the Argentine people was designed, the value of the suits established and the rules of the game laid down. Since then some cards have been dropped and some others added, but the essentials of the game remain the same.

In the first place the game is Argentine. Foreigners can be dealt hands and sometimes they can win, but the game is always Argentine and so are the rules and the referees. The British early learned this. So did the Portuguese and the Brazilians and a little later the French. For a long time the North Americans stayed out of the game, and they have sometimes failed to grasp the situation and recognize its implications. The Spaniards were knocked out of the game early, but the style of play and the language of the game have sometimes caused the Argentines to deal the Spaniards in for a few hands.

Like canasta the game is always played with two decks, but the decks are not the same. One is a military deck and the other is civil, and no interest can win on one deck alone. The great masters of Argentine politics like Rosas, Urquiza, Mitre, Sarmiento, Roca, and Carlos Pellegrini were skilful with both decks. Hipólito Yrigoyen was a famous player but essentially a one-deck man: so was Arturo Frondizi, and so were other great players of the more distant past, notably San Martín and Rivadavia.

The military factor in the Argentine political process has been present from the moment of Argentina's conception, for it was in response to a military situation and by the development of military organizations that the first independent political action of the Argentine community was expressed. But an historical fact alone does not explain the persistence of the military element in Argentine politics. In 1806–07 the armed forces expressed operationally the unity of the community in action for a strongly felt and dominant purpose. None the less that community was divided economically, socially, intellectually, and hence politically. These differences became more open and more manifest with every blow struck at the legitimate authority of the Spanish Crown. But simultaneously the community created an institution about which there was no question: the armed forces, a body which saved the people and united them. For people imbued strongly with the symbols of religion it has been easy to invest the soldiers as a body with a supra-political character so that like the monarchy in some communities or the Church or a revolutionary party in others they are a moral force regardless of what they actually do in any particular situation. And this fact is the basic element in their capacity for political initiative.

As to the community itself it divided like other communities along the lines of interest and social groupings. The most powerful revolutionary group was the cattle interest. This interest existed in most of the provinces of the Viceroyalty, but it was a dynamic interest particularly in Buenos Aires and its hinterland, in Uruguay and in Corrientes and Santa Fé, collectively known as the *Litoral*. This interest was narrowly economic in that it was the producer interest most geared to the world market and most indifferent to or opposed both to Spanish trade restrictions and to other local producer interests. But it was, too, something more than a narrow economic interest, for it ramified through society as a way of life: rustic, virile, anti-intellectual, free, and rough. At the same time it was expansive, and the welfare of shopkeepers, merchants, moneylenders, transport and port-workers, shipowners, and foreign buyers depended on the cattle industry. Unlike the mining interests of the interior the cattle industry did not depend on forced labour. Its workers were free men even though efforts were increasingly made to convert the gaucho into a *peón* tied to a particular *estancia*. The cattle worker had all the prestige of a mounted man, and he could only survive through courage, strength, and skill with the knife and the *bolas*. He could be led and he could be used, but he could not be driven. And always he could be enlisted as a soldier: not a disciplined soldier but a fighter at home in the deserts, capable of quick movement, used to living off the country, and subtle in his capacity both to evade and harass better organized troops.

The other interests and groupings of the Argentine community constituted in terms of numbers and often in terms of human quality a larger and superior force compared with the cattle interest, but they were divided, dependent, and some of them failing in their capacity for survival. The mining interest in what is today Bolivia was historically the most important and productive, and remained so until the revolution. Bullion production nourished the state, and provided a market for the agricultural, pastoral, and handicraft producers of the interim provinces. It provided, too, the most easily saleable and transportable product of the Viceroyalty. In spite of these advantages the mining industry proved itself incapable of survival once the struggle of interests was unleashed by the shattering of the Viceregal authority. Technologically the industry was backward and manpower intensive. Manpower, on the other hand, was scarce and its recruitment was always a politically difficult and dangerous business, which political rivalries among the top élite accentuated to the point that production declined catastrophically once the revolution started. The collapse of the mining interest had important secondary effects because it impaired the markets on which the interior provinces depended for their prosperity.

The *vignerons*, handicraftsmen in leather, textiles, and iron wares, and the mule breeders and cattlemen of the interior were themselves important, and, compared with those in the *Litoral*, a numerous interest. Free trade with Spain had exposed them to competitive forces, but to a considerable degree they were protected by the fact that Spanish enterprise was not as dangerous a competitor as English, American, and European industry. Once the Spanish interest was knocked out by events in Spain and the interplay of forces in Buenos Aires, the interior industrial interests had no allies.

In Buenos Aires itself there was a town interest which identified itself with civilization and urban refinement of a European kind. Basically it was commercial, professional, and bureaucratic and therefore not self-sufficient in the way that the rural cattle interest was. Enlightened, prosperous, and energetic, the townsmen of Buenos Aires – the *porteños* – thought of themselves – as they still do – as the élite, the leaders and the administrators of the community, but they had no solid base in the community and economy as a whole. Abstract ideas and sentiments meant much to them because they lacked the self-sufficiency which came from a way of life united to a clearly defined economic interest. In fact the townsmen of Buenos Aires were dependent upon whatever interest was predominant at any one time. They were buffeted by the winds and tides of political life, and they were never able to master the community. Predominantly liberal in thought, they could serve any revolutionary interest, but their liberalism was not a means of ordering the community.

An illustration of the *porteño* problem is provided by almost any of the great *porteños* of the revolutionary period. We need only look at two examples: Mariano Moreno and Bernardino Rivadavia. Both men emerged on the scene scarcely more than youths as supporters, thinkers, and publicists in the service of Spanish interests. Moreno was a partisan of Martín de Álzaga and Rivadavia was a protégé of Liniers. Yet very quickly these men identified themselves with other interests. Moreno wrote the *Representación de los Hacendados*, an able and persuasive statement of the case for complete free trade and the maximization of the market opportunities of the cattle interests. It was an outright and uncompromising attack on the system of which his first patron had been the main support. Rivadavia, on the other hand, became the brains behind the most revolutionary regime – the Triumvirate of 1811–12, which aimed at democratizing society. After a long and mixed career he was driven from the scene by a combination of provincial and cattle interests which he was able neither to placate nor control. Moreno and Rivadavia were both liberals. Moreno occupied an office of influence for only a very short space of time. Rivadavia held many offices of the highest order and his political life lasted for a quarter of a century. And yet the permanent impact on policy of Moreno was greater than that of Rivadavia, and an important factor in the difference can be attributed to Moreno prescribing a policy for a strong, developing interest while Rivadavia attempted to dominate that interest and to bring it under administrative and political control.

Moreno's influence grew directly out of an interest rooted in the country. Rivadavia, on the other hand, attempted to use and was forced to depend on a powerful but less permanently reliable interest, i.e. foreign commercial interests. Of these the most capable of influencing the course of events were the British. They were neither the only nor the majority interest in seeking to open the markets of the Río de la Plata, but they possessed more political leverage than others on account of their naval power. Once the British government abandoned the notion that conquest was a practical means of opening the River Plate to commerce and recognized the wisdom of seeking to assist either in the reform of the Spanish empire or in its dissolution into independent states as a means of advancing their commercial interests, their position in the area underwent a noticeable and quick change for the better. As the unchallenged naval power in the Atlantic (and in the war of 1812–14 they destroyed any local advantages the Americans may have had) the British were able, by a judicious use of blockade or its opposite, the freedom of navigation, to bargain with the interests in the area. Bargaining, of course, was not a unilateral activity and the British weapon would have been completely ineffective had there not been in Buenos Aires the powerful cattle interest whose own objectives were in varying degrees parallel to those of British enterprise. From the Napoleonic Wars to World War II this relationship between the cattle interests and British commercial and financial interests was a fixed element in Argentine politics, and one of the most formative. As time passed the naval element in the bargaining diminished and disappeared, but the essentials of the relationship remained, and its recognition is indispensable to any understanding of Argentina both in its internal evolution and in its relationship with the rest of the world until World War II.

The pushing and hauling of interests and the existence of a locally based armed force determined the course of events from the first moment when Cisneros was installed as the Viceroy appointed by the authorities in Spain and accepted as legitimate in the Viceroyalty. Where social tension was greatest revolution first flared up: in the mining areas in the Andes. The commotion was initiated in 1809 by a scholastic debate in the University of San Francisco Xavier in Chuquisaca. The syllogism of Chuquisaca set forth the dilemma about legitimacy created by the news that no Spanish monarch ruled in Spain. The major premise was: the Indies are the personal dominion of the King and not of Spain. The minor premise: the King is prevented from ruling. The conclusion: therefore the Indies ought to govern themselves paying no attention to Spain. An uproar followed this exercise in logic. The bishops, canons, *oidores*, doctors of law, civil servants, and students were completely at a loss what to do, and committees formed themselves shouting abuse at one another. Meanwhile a slave revolt broke out in Santa Cruz de la Sierra, and the long process of disorganizing the work-force began with slaughter and flight. From the Viceroyalty of Peru came the force under Goyeneche to restore order, and from Cisneros in Buenos Aires the authority to do so. Order was restored in Charcas, Chuquisaca, and La Paz. The leaders were hanged. The last words of Murillo, the leader, call to mind those of Latimer in similar circumstances: 'The torch which I leave burning will never be put out.'

And it was burning. Whether order was restored or not, a basic part of the Viceroyalty of the Río de la Plata, the mining sector, was beginning to die. In Buenos Aires itself Cisneros was able to arrest the progress of revolutionary unrest. The armed forces were reduced in number and reorganized. A special officer was appointed to watch disaffected persons and apprehend spies. In spite of the savagery of the repression practised by Goyeneche in upper Peru and the imperialist arrogance of the governor of Montevideo, Cisneros sought to soften differences with the creole 'patriots' and to maintain their confidence. The local interest groups he tried to conciliate by reversing Liniers' policy of permitting the easy entry of foreign merchants and foreign goods.

This last move, however, provoked the opposition of the cattle interest and the British merchants who had established themselves in Buenos Aires as a result of Liniers' emergency opening of the port. Thus in the critical winter of 1809 Cisneros found himself exposed to internal and external opposition. Discussion in the *cabildo* and the *consulado* revealed an inclination towards compromise in the matter of admitting some foreign goods but not those directly competitive with local products. The Spanish merchants, of course, raised the alarm against foreign goods in the name of local industry. The riposte to this policy was the *Representación de los Hacendados y Labradores* – the plea of the landowners and workers – of Mariano Moreno. This was a document which made no compromise. Absolute and complete freedom was demanded as a demonstrably scientific means of maximizing the welfare of all.

It is unlikely that the policy advocated by Moreno and his friends would ever have commanded sufficient support had the Viceroyalty endured as a political institution. The Viceroy's power rested on a balance of forces as well as on tradition and communal habits of mind. One of these forces was the support of the Spanish mercantile interest. When this force was weakened and then knocked out the whole pattern changed, and tradition and habits of mind were insufficient to sustain the government. Already materially weakened by the prolonged effects of the war, the Spanish mercantile interests were further weakened by the fact that the Napoleonic occupation of Spain was even more serious for them than the British naval power had been. They had long been obliged to acquiesce in trade with neutral states simply because Spain could not buy or sell on a sufficient scale to maintain the economy and government of the Río de la

Plata. The neutrals and the British had gradually come to occupy their place in the economy so that there was a serious incongruence between what they were able to do as merchants and what they claimed as factors in the equation of politics.

So long as the Viceregal government was Spanish the position of the Spanish mercantile interest was not irremediable, and the bold, harsh attack of Moreno and his supporters could have been contained. Then came the news that no Spanish government existed in Spain and that Napoleon's puppet and his forces had military control of the peninsula. The spirit which had inspired the resistance to the British awakened, and determination not to stand still and pass under French domination bubbled up. But on this occasion the leaders were creoles – not Liniers and Álzaga with the creole Pueyrredón as a junior partner – but Saavedra, Castelli, Belgrano, Passo, Larrea, and Moreno. There was little or no response in the community even among the governing class, to the argument of the bishop of Buenos Aires that Spanish authority should be obeyed unless or until not a single Spaniard remained alive in the peninsula. Crowds began to congregate in the plaza and under the arches of the *cabildo*, and they cried out for a *Junta* to resist and to rule.

The political élite responded to this cry in which was mingled fear, uncertainty, and humiliation transmuted into pride, determination, and virile hardness. The important fact of the moment consisted in the changed composition of the political élite brought about by the British invasion, the elevation of Liniers to the Viceregal office, and the experience of political action outside the framework of established institutions. Their response to popular demand was quicker and more radical than anything the Viceroy by himself could devise. Cisneros agreed to summon a *Cabildo Abierto*, i.e. a meeting of the town council enlarged by the addition of citizens, priests, and government officers not normally concerned in the affairs of the city. Four hundred and fifty invitations were issued. Some could not attend and some would not. Two hundred and fifty-one turned up. On the central question of whether or not the Viceroy should be retained with or without collaborators the vote went as shown on the next page.

An attempt to leave military power in the hands of Cisneros and to include him in the new government was defeated. On 25 May 1810, the Viceroy ceased to govern, and in his place there was a *Junta* authorized by the *cabildo* of Buenos Aires to rule in the name

	For	Against
Civil Servants	18	6
Merchants	22	25
Military officers	12	51
Ecclesiastics	6	18
Citizens	3	26
Lawyers	1	17
Scribes (solicitors)	1	3
Ward mayors	1	10
Members of the *Hermandad* (religious tribunal)	0	2

21 present abstained

of Ferdinand VII. The *Junta* had as its president Lt.-Colonel Cornelio Saavedra, commander of the Regiment of the Patricios. Its members were Juan José Castelli, a lawyer; Manuel Belgrano, lawyer, economist, and soldier; Lt.-Colonel Miguel de Azcuénega, a retired officer; Prebendary Manuel Alberti, a priest; Domingo Matheu, a merchant; and Juan Larrea, a merchant. The secretaries were Juan José Passo, a lawyer, and Manuel Moreno, a lawyer and economist.

It is outside the scope of this book to present a narrative of the revolution. The establishment of the *Junta* was only the first, if the most important, step in the direction of independence. A formal declaration of independence which denied the sovereignty of Ferdinand VII was not made until 9 July 1816, and Spanish power in South America was not at an end until December 1824. During these years the Viceroyalty of the Río de la Plata was broken apart as a political entity. Part of its economy was destroyed or enfeebled. The unity of society both regionally and socially was weakened. Long accepted ideas concerning the political, social, and economic order came under question and many were wiped out or forgotten. The hierarchical order was overthrown.

The revolution which ended the Spanish empire in South America was one of three great politico-social upheavals which brought to birth modern society. Whether these three upheavals were inevitable and necessary for the growth of industry based on machine technology, of competitive commerce, of capitalist investment processes, and of an open democratic system of politics is not a question we can properly examine, but in considering what happened in South

America one is bound to ask why the revolution in Latin America was so much more of an unmitigated catastrophe than it was in North America; why it fragmented society politically and socially, weakened all authority, and produced long periods of economic stagnation which has in some areas endured to the present day. The revolution in North America opened the way to the strengthening of the state, the creation of a large political unit, a large integrated economic community, an expansive economy, and a growing population. In South America the consequences of revolution were otherwise.

The short answer to the question posed is this. The revolution against Spain, unlike the North American revolution or the French Revolution or the cessation of Portuguese authority in Brazil, was a thorough-going revolution which was social and economic as well as political. For example, the revolution in the Viceroyalty of the Río de la Plata and elsewhere in Spanish America ended slavery, something which did not happen either in the United States or in Brazil. Revolution in Spanish America did not increase the power and improve the administrative apparatus of the state as it did in France and in Europe generally. In Spanish America the rhetoric of liberty became a social reality, and society was dissolved into its elements, so that those who aspired to a European pattern of civilization were confronted with problems of order and organization of a very intractable nature. The alternative to a European pattern of civilization, pre-Columbian civilization, was not a possibility because 300 years of Spanish conquest, colonization, missionary work, and authority had destroyed the powerful central core of Indian civilization so that what remained were the scattered, weak substructures of Indian life. The notion of some that the Inca should be restored was a non-starter. In many respects the revolution against Spain produced a Hobbesian state of nature out of which man in Spanish Latin America was obliged to fashion something new, a labour not yet at an end and one which only the Latin Americans can themselves perform. Their revolution was a profound and terrible experience, a true and agonizing crucifixion from which only the forces within themselves – the part of God within themselves – if one likes to describe it so – can procure a resurrection. Certainly no one else can, and those who believe otherwise do not know the Latin Americans or their history.

In the case of the Viceroyalty of the Río de la Plata the features of the revolution deserving of notice for an understanding of Argentine life are *three* in number. The first was the shattering of the Viceroyalty as a politico-economic unit. When Goyeneche, the *intendente* of Cuzco, employing force supplied by the Viceroy of Peru, put down the *Junta* in upper Peru (modern Bolivia) he effectively began the cutting off of the mining centre of the Viceroyalty from Buenos Aires, and thus struck the first blow at the integrity of the Viceroyalty. When Cisneros was deposed in 1810 one of the first efforts of the new government was directed at recovering upper Peru, and bringing it under the authority of the *Junta* in Buenos Aires. An army was despatched northwards under the command of Belgrano. At Suipacha it overthrew the Spanish forces and occupied the main centres of upper Peru. Revolutionary zealots taking their cue from the young militants like Moreno and Monteagudo began attacking the Church and preaching liberty for all, an explosive proceeding in a society organized as it was in the mining regions. As a result, the Spanish authorities in the Viceroyalty of Peru counter-attacked, rallying the people with religious slogans. At Huaqui the revolutionaries were overthrown, and their forces obliged to retreat. In effect the mining regions ceased to be part of the Viceroyalty, and when revolution came again to upper Peru ten years later, it was part of the baggage of the army of Sucre from Colombia.

Paraguay separated from the Viceroyalty. There was no enthusiasm for a government centred in Buenos Aires, nor for the prospect of an invasion by foreign and *porteño* commercial enterprise. Delegations sent to negotiate a confederal relationship got nowhere. Paraguay sealed its doors and turned in upon itself for half a century.

The pampas beyond the Río Uruguay – the *Banda Oriental* – were part of the *Litoral* region. In economic structure as well as geographically the hinterland of Montevideo was closely similar to that of Buenos Aires. But Buenos Aires and Montevideo were rival metropolises – too much alike to be close friends. Montevideo, being more a military town than Buenos Aires, remained loyal longer than the capital city, and when Cisneros was deposed the governor of Montevideo, Xavier de Elío, became in theory his successor. From Montevideo the only Spanish effort to attack Buenos Aires directly was made by a naval force. This Spanish bastion was, however, beset by two perils – one from Brazil, the other from the countryside where the gauchos and landed interest were responsive to the revolutionary call. A revolutionary junior officer in the Spanish service, José

Gervasio Artigas, armed the gauchos against the royal government, and with a little help from Buenos Aires, brought the royalists to battle and defeated them. But he could not take Montevideo, and this fact shaped the course of events on the east bank. The royalists turned to the Portuguese, and eventually the east bank was incorporated into the Brazilian empire as the Cisplatine Province, but only nominally. No real control of the countryside was ever re-established once Artigas had put the gauchos in motion: no real control by Buenos Aires either; for the Oriental Republic of Uruguay emerged after years of struggle. In spite of its similarity to the province of Buenos Aires, Uruguay remains still 'outside the Argentine family', as the Argentines like to put it.

The reaction in the interior province to the deposition of Cisneros was mixed. Liniers had retired to Córdoba, upon his replacement by Cisneros. If he had any intention of organizing resistance such as Elío was doing in Montevideo, he was given little chance. The force he attempted to raise was weakened by desertions, and the *Junta* in Buenos Aires simply ordered that Liniers be eliminated. He was seized and executed without appeal together with his companions. Only the bishop of Córdoba who supported him was spared. Savage and uncompromising though the *Junta* were in this matter, it is quite clear that the support for the *Junta* and for creole political power was widespread and real in Mendoza, Córdoba, Tucumán, Salta, and Jujuy, and it is possible to see why the course of events resembled the developments in the *Litoral* and differed from that in upper Peru. Here the Spanish colonization and conversion had been a milder process than in the mining regions. The *estancias*, workshops, and plantations were not the grim establishments which mines were. No ceremonial masses and mourning attended the rounding up of Indians for forced labour such as happened among the Indians conscripted to work in the mines. The Spanish governors and intendants in sub-Andean provinces were never divided morally on the meaning of their relations with the Indians. The integrity of society and the preservation of its structure did not require the assistance of power reinforced from the outside. The creoles in the top levels of the social structure did not consider Spanish power indispensable to their existence. They were willing to accept the *Junta* and its successors and only turned against the authority developed in Buenos Aires when it became apparent that authority was prejudicial to their rights and interests.

It may be wondered why they threw in their lot with Buenos
Aires when some at least of their economic interests lay with the
mining regions of upper Peru. But several factors entered into this
relationship. In the first place they could not know, when the decision for local power was taken, that the revolution would weaken
and destroy the mining economy, any more than they could know
that the triumph of free trade in Buenos Aires would weaken their
economic position *vis-à-vis* the *Litoral*. In the second place their
economy was rudely self-sufficient, particularly in the case of the
landed interest. It must be remembered that the potentially strongest
elements in the society of the interior were cattle men, just as they
were in Buenos Aires, Corrientes, Entre Rios, or Santa Fé, or beyond
the Río Uruguay, even though they had less to gain from policies of
international free trade.

The second consequence of the revolution flowed naturally from
the shattering of the politico-economic structures of the Viceroyalty,
i.e. the dismantlement of all the economic and commercial controls
which the Spanish authorities had employed. Argentina became a
laissez faire, free-trading community long before Britain did. The
Spanish controls were designed to create a Spanish trading area, and
as such served to protect from competition some of the agricultural
and industrial activities of the Viceroyalty. The Triumvirate, the
revolutionary government in Buenos Aires which succeeded the
Junta in 1812, threw open the port of Buenos Aires and permitted
foreigners to own property and trade on equal terms with natives.
Protective tariffs were replaced by low revenue tariffs, and the control of exports was eliminated. Thus the area acknowledging the
authority of the government in Buenos Aires was integrated into
the world market very thoroughly at an early stage of the industrial
revolution, and experienced the effects of expansive industrial capitalism as soon or sooner than the United States or western Europe.
The principal effect was derived from the operation of the law of
comparative advantage which, other things being equal, prompts
producers and investors to concentrate their activities on those products which they can sell to the greatest advantage in the widest
market. A simplification and specialization of the economy set in.
Cheap imports of flour, textiles, sugar, wine, and ironmongery hit
local industry hard, while the producers of hides, salted meat, bones,
and grease flourished. Flourished is, however, only a comparative
word in this context, because the disorders in society, the high mili-

tary costs and the diminution of the labour force by military service, the end of slavery, and the general indiscipline and relaxation of social control adversely affected all branches of the economy. None the less, there emerged as a result of the revolution the factor of specialization in pastoral and/or agricultural production and free international trading which characterized the Argentine economy without any serious interruption until World War II. The revolution transformed Argentina into an export-import economy. It had been an export-import economy under Spanish rule, but after the revolution this characteristic was rigorously intensified, so that one sector of the economy had an unrivalled position as policy-maker, accumulator of capital, and beneficiary of enterprise. This development has been and still is a central element in Argentine life, and much of the politics, the culture, and the values of the community ramify from this core.

The third feature of the revolution which determined, and still determines, the character of Argentina was the loosening and simplification of the relations among the groups, classes, and sub-organizations which made up the community. As we have already noticed the geographical character of the great plains of the *Litoral* presented to the Spaniards problems of working, organizing, and living which were radically different from those encountered in the interior and the main centres of productivity and power in their empire. On the pampas the men who lived there were mounted mobile creatures who survived in proportion to their capacity to ride horses and to control, protect, and kill cattle. This was true of the Indians, the Indo-Europeans, and the pure Spaniards. A horse, like a motor-car, is an extension of the individual's powers, and this is one of the powerful reasons why they are so loved in a way which many other objects in life are not. In this case of the mounted inhabitants of the pampas the political implications of individual power and mobility are deserving of notice, and these implications were fundamental for social organization and for all who sought, for whatever reason, power and authority – whether as an Indian *cacique* or an *estanciero* or a military leader. It is interesting to observe that *all* the men who emerged from the revolution as leaders with long survival capacity – Quiroga, Güemes, Aráoz de la Madrid, Urquiza, Artigas, Paz, and above all Rosas – either were themselves gaucho-horsemen or had adapted themselves to the ethos, the skills, and the image of the gaucho: the mounted cattle-killer, the man possessed of qualities of virility, courage, and stoicism, which are associated with the word *machismo*. It is worth noting, too, that even the short list of leaders contains the names of men with diverse political objectives, and in the instance of Rosas, provides an example of a man in whom the diversity of objectives was contained within the man himself. What was common to all of them was an adaptation to a way of life, a willingness to immerse themselves in the social milieu and work from within it.

The Spaniards had endeavoured to control their environment by the devices they had perfected in their long history – and they did this with some success. They built cities; they founded churches; they set up administrative apparatus and they made laws and devised policies of control. They worked with and within the concepts of hierarchy. When the British attempted to conquer the Viceroyalty they aimed at replacing the top of the hierarchy and altering the commercial policy of the community, but, no matter what Popham may have thought about liberation, they did not seek to change anything in the social order. As we have already argued, the response to this blow did change the social order, and open the way for the revolution. The revolution further activated the elementary particles and aggregations of the community, and the stresses of this activation destroyed the Spanish control mechanisms. The revolutionary intellectuals like Moreno, Belgrano, Monteagudo, Chiclana, Castelli, and Rivadavia found it easy to destroy the Spanish apparatus of government; to weaken profoundly the bonds between the Church and the state; to create revolutionary armies; to liberate commerce; to end slavery; to free the press; and to call into being elected assemblies. But they found it extremely difficult – in fact they found it impossible – to reconstitute and strengthen hierarchical controls. The Convention, the Directory, and finally Napoleon had taken hold of the French Revolution, and employed the energy of that event to strengthen the structure of the state so that France was endowed with an administration, an army, and an economic system which was stronger, more rational, and more powerful than any Colbert and Louis XIV had ever achieved. In spite of the defects inflicted by the follies and abuses of Napoleon, the consequences in terms of administration and the integration of the state were never undone in France. Not so in the Río de la Plata. The efforts of Rivadavia to build a strong state based on a modern administration, a modern army, and a modern system of finance failed, and it failed because the weight and power of the horsemen of the pampas was greater than the skill, intelligence, and planning capacity of the townsmen and their allies both inside and outside Argentina.

Chapter 3

From Revolution to Rosas:
the Entrenchment of the Landed Élite

WHEN ONE ATTEMPTS to draw up a balance sheet of the revolution which produced political independence one is faced with the problem of definition. Very few modern Argentines would suggest that the revolution was a disaster and the origin of their present troubles. It is a basic article of public faith that the revolution was 'a good thing', and that it is proper and indeed necessary to have an unquestioned respect for at least one revolutionary hero: General San Martín. But in what way was the revolution a 'good thing'? No one can seriously doubt that it was good to alter or abolish some of the institutions of the Spanish empire, e.g. slavery and forced labour. It is not difficult to say the same of the Inquisition. There is a strong case for the end of primogeniture and the entailment of estates. The establishment of equality before the law as respects not only citizens but foreigners resident or travelling in the country seems defensible on almost any grounds. The loosening of the bonds between Church and state was probably an advantage, but here one enters an area of controversy which has been resolved but not necessarily in the most advantageous way.

When one comes to consider the changes in the structure of the state, the alteration of the system of authority, and the attempts to achieve a new basis for order and social co-operation, the good which came out of the revolution is much more difficult to discern. When, as a result of the social and political commotion which we have described, the questions arose: what do we do now? how are we to order our affairs?, answers had to be found, and this was no easy matter. Some wanted to maintain the institution of monarchy, which implied the preservation of a hierarchical political order. Unfortunately there was no agreement about who should be monarch: the Inca, Ferdinand VII, his sister Carlota Joaquína, the wife of the prince regent of Portugal and resident in Rio de Janeiro, or, perhaps, some member of a European royal family? The principal recommendation of monarchy as a system of government derives from its solution of the problem of selecting a final authority in the state. Once there is doubt about who is the 'legitimate' monarch, monarchy as an institution loses one of its main advantages. Thus, the possibility of monarchy as a means of preserving and reforming the political order was out.

In any case monarchy as an institution was under severe attack in this epoch of revolution. The enlightenment of the early eighteenth century and the romantic movement associated with the name of Rousseau exercised a powerful and confusing influence among the intellectual élite in the Río de la Plata. The notion that the public authority should be an expression of the general will of society was very congenial, particularly in the circumstances in Buenos Aires, where for the first time the creoles had gained the initiative by saving themselves from conquest and by standing alone when their mother country fell under foreign domination. If the romantic postulate of a general will was acceptable, so was the rather different notion of the utilitarians that each man is an entity engaged in seeking his own pleasure and advantage. While these disparate ideas could with some colour of justification be maintained in the light of experience, they unfortunately offered little practical guidance about government and how it can be organized.

So long as the existing organs of the state, such as for instance the *cabildos*, could be used as agencies of decision-making the problem of government was not insuperable, but once the contention of interests and personalities prompted the protagonists to seek to change the decision-making bodies and to call in question their legitimacy, the doors were opened to something approaching anarchy. This point was reached in the year 1820 when the constitution of a unitary state was destroyed in battle, and when at least twenty-four governments rose and fell in the province of Buenos Aires – three in one day.

So far modern man, and this is true of man in South America as elsewhere, has not discovered anything better than the state for ordering society and ensuring at least the minimum degree of social co-operation necessary for life, work, and the perpetuation of the species. And yet this agency was all but destroyed in Argentina during the revolution. How, then, was this dissolution overcome? An answer cannot be found in an exploration of the ideas which Argentines had on this subject. Instead we have to enquire about what secondary organizations in society survived, what was their strength, and how did they serve as a means of reconstituting the state and restoring public order.

Leaving aside the family as a basic secondary social organization and paying attention to those organizations which ramified through the public entity which we can call Argentina, it is possible to identify four secondary institutions of varying degrees of consequence.

In the first place there were the armed forces. These were stronger and more numerous than they had been in the old Spanish Viceroyalty. They had been created first as a response to the need to defend the community from invasion, and then as an instrument of revolution and protection from counter-revolution. An élite capable of organizing armed forces and directing their use had grown up, and had become a semi-autonomous factor in society. The most sophisticated part of the armed forces – the regular regiments of artillery, cavalry, and infantry – required supplies and pay, and their needs therefore required the existence in society of the means of mobilizing resources for their use: in short they required a state apparatus capable of taxing, purchasing supplies, and enlisting men. When, for example, San Martín undertook the task of organizing a professionally trained army capable of driving the Spaniards out of South America and securing the independence of Argentina, he was made governor of the interior province of Cuyo with its centre in the city of Mendoza. As a political leader he mobilized the resources of the community for the creation of the army which he commanded.

The army of San Martín was, however, not the only type of effective armed force which the invasion and the revolution produced. Another was the lightly armed, irregular militia recruited from the gauchos: an army which did not have the problems of supply and pay of the regular army, which lived off the country and relied for its effectiveness on mobility and dispersion. This type of army could and did survive the dissolution of the state, whereas the other type of sophisticated army depended ultimately upon the strength and capacity of the state apparatus which supported it and used it.

Both types of army were, however, political communication systems, systems of holding men together socially and giving them a way of life together. As such they were a political system, and, as the state which used them weakened, they, and particularly the second type of army, became nearly autonomous political entities.

But not quite. Even a purely predatory army of the Mongol type is obliged to have some kind of orderly relationship with the working community upon which it feeds and from which it steals. The gaucho armies of the *caudillos* were not predatory hordes. They were connected with and were a part of another secondary institution which survived, and in fact grew stronger during the revolution: the *estancia*. This was both a social and an economic institution: social in that it brought together different kinds of people – for example, the owner, who could generally read and write and had connection with the world beyond the pampas and its herds, and the gaucho, generally illiterate, who herded cattle, branded them, killed them, skinned them, and salted their meat and hides; and economic in that it constituted a unit for the protection of resources, for their processing, their renewal, and their sale in the markets of the world. As an economic institution the Argentine *estancia* of the early nineteenth century was as much a large-scale unit of production for a competitive world market as a cotton mill in Lancashire or a coal mine in Belgium, or a cotton plantation in Alabama. This may not have been entirely so of an *estancia* in Córdoba or Salta, but it was certainly the case in the provinces of Buenos Aires, Santa Fé, Entre Rios, and southern Corrientes. If the *estancia* was a large-scale enterprise and part of the world economy, it was neither an enterprise staffed with free wage-workers nor worked by slaves. As we have already emphasized the gaucho was a free, mounted man, and the circumstances of the pampas ensured the possibility of independence. This fact determined the social relationships on the *estancia*. The *estanciero* was not the gaucho's employer but his patron. They were equals, and yet they were different. Each served the other. The *estanciero* was a chief not by virtue of owning the land, nor was he sustained in his position by a web of political and administrative power. He was an authority by reason of his identification with, and capacity for playing a leading part in, rural life. General Rosas was a great politician, a rich *estanciero*, an owner of slaughtering establishments, and a soldier, but his first strength derived from his skill as a gaucho, as a breaker of horses, as a performer of dangerous equestrian sports, and as a man who could deal equally well on his own terms with a cowboy and a foreign ambassador. The state of society in the Río de la Plata after the revolution was such that *estancieros* who aspired to live remote from their properties and remote from their work-people had little hope of survival politically or economically.

This description of the social relations characteristic of the *estancia* in the time of the *caudillos* is consistent with the fact that the *estancieros* were determined to use the violence of the state to preserve order on their estates and in the countryside. They were as zealous against the *gauchos vagabundos* – the man who lived entirely free – as they were hostile to the Indians. In General Rosas' old home at the Rincón de López on the Río Salado in the eastern part of Buenos Aires province, there are preserved today many of the objects used in the time of the *caudillos*. Among the swords, guns, and *boleadoras* of those days are the police passes which every man had to carry identifying him as an employed person. There are, too, the heavy wooden head-stocks which were locked on obstreperous cowboys. But it must be remembered that the discipline and order which the *estanciero* maintained, was kept by himself in close relationship with men who shared a way of life, crude, brutal, and free. Even after the passage of a century and a half, erosion by civilization and the separation of the *estancieros* and their *peóns* by wealth, one can still discern in the cattle areas something of the old relationship of brotherhood across barriers of class which comes from the loneliness of the vast prairies, the closeness to land and animals, and the delight in an equestrian way of life.

As the state weakened under the impact of revolution and the incapacity of the élite to create an effective substitute for the authority of the Spanish Crown, the *estancia* grew stronger so that the great *estancieros* did not just control the state; they became the state. In the age of the *caudillos* which first took shape during the anarchy of 1820 and lasted until the overthrow of Rosas in 1852, the political structure of Argentina bore some resemblance to that which existed in England in the fifteenth century. Great families whose strength lay in their estates and their retainers preserved a precarious peace on the basis of a balance of power among them. This balance frequently broke down, and when it did the spoils of victory were lands and cattle and the control of commerce. To foreigners and Argentines alike, who cherished a notion of a more settled, liberal, and rational political order, this condition of affairs was deplorable, but what must be noticed is the growth in a shattered society of an institution which held men together in a rudimentary but powerful social bond, thus enabling them to participate in a wider world of economic and political co-operation.

Another institution which survived the revolutionary solvent was the Church. In the Spanish empire the Church had played a fundamental role as an agency of government and of social and cultural transformation. The fact that Spanish is spoken and the Roman Catholic creed acknowledged by millions from the Río Grande to Tierra del Fuego, who are racially in no sense Spaniards, is witness to the success of the Church as a hand-maiden of the Spanish state. In no way did the Spanish Bourbons of the eighteenth century more open the way to radical change than they did by their assault upon the Church. The dissolution of the Society of Jesus in 1768 and the seizure and distribution of its property deprived the Church of its brains and its property, and left it seriously enfeebled but still living. The revolutionaries were either indifferent to the Church or actively hostile. Without believing God was dead, many ecclesiastics themselves believed that He favoured revolution and served the revolutionary cause. The Church was partially separated from the state, and was reduced to the role of an institution concerned with its own affairs rather than those of the whole society. The Inquisition was dissolved. The legal powers of the Church except in matters of its internal government were taken from it. Freedom of religion was proclaimed as an aspect of equality before the law.

Nevertheless the Church survived both as an organization capable of perpetuating itself and as a faith capable of moving men and women. How much allegiance it could command among the gauchos is uncertain. Even today the Church is conspicuous by its absence on the pampas. It is clear, however, that the *caudillos* like Rosas and Quiroga thought it worth their while to proclaim the protection of the Church as one of the first of their political principles. Rosas both depended on the Church and used it for political purposes. This suggests that the Church was an important factor in the life of the people at large, and a communication and control system which a politician could not afford to neglect. To what people the Church was important is not entirely clear. The gauchos were not distinguished by their devotion to religion, and their moral codes and cosmology were much more related to their immediate experience than to Christianity. On the other hand, the people in the oldest settled parts in Cuyo, Córdoba, and the north-west provinces were much affected by religious zeal. There religion had a popular character, as it still has today, and churches existed in the countryside as well as in the towns. The shopkeepers of Córdoba may have used the books of the great Jesuit library as wrapping paper for over thirty years, but they were religious none the less. The annual *Semana Santa* was a great popular festival in the cities of the interior. What there was of education, charity, and nursing was associated with the Church, and nothing more alienated the people of the interior than the elaborate plans for secular education projected by the revolutionaries in Buenos Aires.

The fourth class of secondary institutions which survived the revolution was commercial and economic. Survival is hardly the right word, for in no part of the community did the revolution have greater impact than in the sphere of commerce and industry. None the less the revolution did not destroy commerce, although it changed the character of industry and destroyed part of it. In colonial times merchants were a group of great account. Contemporary comment suggests that a merchant or a miller was much more esteemed than *estancieros* and cattle men. They held the community together as much as the Church or the state. Blockade, invasion, and revolution weakened and then destroyed the Spanish merchants. Revolution, however, greatly enlarged the foreign mercantile community. Although North American ships were almost as numerous as British in the River Plate, once commerce was open to all, it was the British who came to occupy a foremost place in the commerce of the area. Both as buyers of produce and as sellers of textiles, haberdashery, and iron and steel wares they had great advantages, for they were part of a world-wide complex of industrial production and credit. Once the barriers to foreign traders came down, as they did in 1812, British mercantile enterprise spread with extraordinary speed over the whole country, buying and selling with great success and to the detriment of existing industry and trade. This was, however, a temporary phenomenon. In the interior and even in the *Litoral* a reaction quickly set in, which made deep penetration hazardous and nearly impossible. Paraguay, for example, completely closed its doors to foreign traders, and in Corrientes and Entre Rios local traders and *estancieros* made direct buying and selling by British merchants and their agents very difficult. In short, local interests relying on local political power forced their way into the commercial system even though they did not deflect it from its international orientation, and did not re-establish the old internal economy based to a considerable extent on local products. By the time the revolution had run its course, British commercial enterprise was largely confined to wholesale trade in Buenos Aires.

The effect which the revolution had on commerce and industry has provoked some Argentine historians to argue that Argentina, ceasing to be a part of the Spanish empire, became a British colony. The Argentines who advocated and fought for freedom of commerce are described as traitors, and it has been suggested that men like Mariano Moreno were British agents. Quite apart from the fact that there is no evidence of this, the argument is absurd. The decisions made during the revolution, like all the subsequent decisions of Argentine history, were based on a calculation of advantages made by Argentine interests – by the interests which in the process of political struggle manoeuvred themselves into a position to make their conceptions of right policy prevail.

For a brief moment in history from 1822 to 1827, British commercial interests and the British government believed that by establishing close commercial and peaceful and equal political relations with the United Provinces of the Río de la Plata they were opening up a new frontier of expansion and development. The kind of optimism about the wealth of Spanish America which had blown up the South Sea Bubble at the beginning of the eighteenth century once more blazed in the city of London during these years, and resulted in the flotation by Baring Brothers of a loan of £1 million nominal value for the government in Buenos Aires, and the launching of a number of joint-stock companies whose purposes included mining, colonization, and industrial production. If this was British imperialism, then it was imperialism – a tautology; but in fact it was a response to the plans of the government in Buenos Aires which came to power in 1821.

It is worthwhile pausing to consider what this government attempted to do and how it failed, for the political and economic problems involved are not entirely irrelevant in Argentina today. The principal architect of this government's policy was Bernardino Rivadavia. In economic understanding, capacity for translating ideas into policy, and largeness of ambition both for his country and for himself, Rivadavia was, perhaps, the greatest man to emerge from the revolution. He possessed the mental agility and powers of invention in the sphere of policy-making which are best exemplified today in Arturo Frondizi, who was President of Argentina from 1958 to 1962. But Rivadavia, like Frondizi, lacked good political judgement and luck.

In terms of policy, however, it will assist understanding to compare Rivadavia with Alexander Hamilton, the great architect of economic policy in the United States after the American Revolution. Like Hamilton it was Rivadavia's belief that strong government was a necessity, and that such government could be created by rallying the support of all those who had lent money to the state or who were in possession of its promises to pay. He believed that the secret of political stability, the expansion of production, and the growth of civilization depend upon the mobilization of wealth by means of a system of investment and reinvestment of money resources. In his view three institutions were necessary: (1) the state which taxes not only to meet current expenditure, but which uses the public revenues to pay interest on loans and to amortize these loans; (2) banks which pool money resources to finance commercial transactions; and (3) joint-stock companies which pool resources to finance productive work. In short, Rivadavia sought to endow Argentina with what we have learned to call capitalist institutions of economic organization, which allow the possessors of resources to co-operate in a free and flexible system of maintaining and adding to wealth by buying and selling goods and services in a great market: a system which in Rivadavia's day was best developed in Great Britain, the United States, and the Netherlands.

Between 1821 and 1825 Rivadavia, as Minister of Government, enjoyed considerable success in his plan of modernization. The public debt including the debts of the Viceroyalty was consolidated, and a scheme of repayment of interest and principal worked out. A bank was established. A treaty based on the principle of equality and freedom of intercourse with Great Britain was negotiated. Joint-stock companies for mining and colonization were established. The system of taxation was reformed with a view to removing export and import duties and substituting income and land taxes. Plans were made for schools, a university, the construction of a canal between the Bermejo and Paraná rivers, and so on. With the victory over Spain in 1824, armament expenditure ceased to grow. By 1825 the United Provinces of the Río de la Plata were, on paper, the most advanced liberal and capitalist community in the world.

And not only on paper. Trade and production began to grow,

immigrants began to arrive. Peace and order appeared to be returning. Then misfortune and misjudgement afflicted the government. It
would be difficult to judge how much of the breakdown in the
policies of Rivadavia can be attributed to the nature of society and
how much to failures in the estimation of possibilities. If we can
imagine what the United States would have been like if the North
Americans had attempted to organize their constitution, organize the
Bank of the United States, fight the war of 1812–14, and work out
the effect of Jacksonian democracy all before the year 1793, we can
gain some idea of what happened in Argentina between 1821 and
1828. What the North Americans succeeded in doing in half a century, the Argentines were obliged to undertake in less than a decade,
and they failed.

It can be argued that Rivadavia and his supporters tried to do
too much too quickly, and that being men of ideas they allowed
their ideas to govern their actions to the neglect of certain stubborn
realities of the Argentine situation. These stubborn realities were the
immense size of the territories the people in Buenos Aires aspired to
govern, the smallness of the population, and the existence of regional
centres of power representative of interests which did not fit exactly
into or were opposed to the system which Rivadavia was endeavouring to establish. Rivadavia's system depended for its success upon an
expansion of production in the countryside, the increase in trade,
and a broadening of the spectrum of productive activities; in short
to repair the damage caused by the revolution within a new and
thoroughly capitalist, *laissez faire* framework. Most fundamental
was the first of these factors: the increase of rural production. This
was impaired by the fact that part of the most productive cattle
country beyond the Uruguay had fallen into the hands of the
Emperor of Brazil, and it was not impossible that another great productive area in Entre Rios and Corrientes might become a part of a
complex centred on Montevideo and Puerto Alegre in Rio Grande
do Sul, and all of it in control of the Brazilians. At this stage of
Argentine history the province of Buenos Aires, except along the route
to Córdoba, was not the best cattle area. Save for a strip along the
south shore of the River Plate as far as the Río Salado, the rest of
Buenos Aires province was more or less under the control of the
Indians. Thus it was that the rural foundations of Rivadavia's policy
were restricted, and that expansion involved alternatives: either
securing the traditional hinterland of Buenos Aires along the banks

of the great rivers and beyond the Río Uruguay or expanding the frontier of Buenos Aires province southward.

At the outset there was no serious division among the big interests, the cattle men, and the mercantile groups, about what Rivadavia and his friends were attempting. Such opposition which existed was in-choate and largely centred in the north-west where foreign com-petition and the decline of mining had created economic difficulties among local industries. With Spain defeated and having obtained recognition as an independent government from Portugal, the United States, and Great Britain, the regime in Buenos Aires was in a strong position by the beginning of 1825. And yet by the end of January 1829 a profound blood feud had developed in the Argentine com-munity the echoes of which can still be heard today. Why?

There are no easy answers. Perhaps the most obvious answer is the best, viz. that the war with Brazil over the possession of Montevideo and the *Banda Oriental* of Uruguay so exhausted the resources of the state and so disrupted commerce that Rivadavia's plans and policies came to naught, and that alternatives had to be found. The war against Brazil started as a revolution by guerrillas who crossed from Buenos Aires and raised the gauchos against the authority of the Brazilian Emperor in May 1825. Brazil was at this time militarily a much stronger power than Argentina, for Brazil had not ex-perienced the wasting effects of revolution and had achieved its independence without making any serious changes in its economy and social relations. On the other hand the snatching of the *Banda Oriental* of Uruguay had seriously over-extended the Emperor's commitments, and the foundations of his authority in what he called the Cisplatine Province were extremely shaky.

This was quickly demonstrated by the guerrillas. The gauchos flocked to the revolutionary standard raised by General Lavalleja and he imposed upon them sufficient organization to bring the im-perial troops to battle. At the same time the native Uruguayan com-mander of the Brazilian forces, General Fructuoso Rivera, deserted and joined the revolution. In October 1825 at Sarandí deep in the heart of the Uruguayan pampas, the imperial forces were overcome and General Lavalleja sent to Buenos Aires an enthusiastic order of the day which raised to a fever pitch the demand in the Congress that Uruguay be incorporated in the United Provinces of the Río de la Plata.

If the Brazilians could not control the Uruguayan countryside they still had cards to play. They held the strong-points of Montevideo and Colonia, and they possessed a large and well-equipped navy, which they sent into the River Plate to lay down a blockade designed to ruin the commerce of Buenos Aires. The Argentines had only a rudimentary navy, but in Admiral Guillermo Brown, an Irish sailor, they had an intrepid and skilful commander. With comparatively poor arms he battered the Brazilians about, but he won battles without winning the war, for he was never able completely to lift the blockade, nor were the Argentine forces ever able by a combined operation from land and sea to take Montevideo. In fact they never tried in spite of utterly destroying the Brazilian forces in the open country a second time at Ituzaíngo in February 1827.

Whether the Argentine government could have avoided the war with Brazil and whether they could limit themselves simply to helping the revolutionary forces in the Uruguayan countryside are not questions one can answer. What is evident, however, is that the Argentine government did not have the resources of manpower, money, or organization to bring the war to a successful conclusion and to incorporate Uruguay into the Argentine community. Brazil lost the war, but so did Argentina, and in so doing the edifice which Rivadavia had planned and partly built was destroyed. When Rivadavia sent to the Congress his resignation in July 1827, it was accepted. The National Congress representative of all the provinces dissolved itself. A committee appointed a man who had helped Rivadavia come to power in 1821, Manuel Dorrego, as governor and Captain-General of the province of Buenos Aires. Dorrego then made peace with Brazil through the intermediary of the Colombian government, and recognized the independence of Uruguay as a sovereign state.

When the war was over there was no money in the treasury, the country had been drained of bullion, the public debt was in default, and the administrative apparatus unequal to collecting taxes based on income and land rents. The consequences of blockade were not altogether disastrous economically even though the interruption of international trade had destroyed the confidence necessary for free investment from abroad. The physical barriers to imports had helped native industry and internal trade to revive. Merchants had switched capital from trade to investment in *estancias*, and the incapacity of the government to collect the land rents, which Rivadavia had envisaged as an important source of revenue and as the security for the public debt, made land an even better investment. The slackening of cattle slaughter caused the herds to increase. What seems to have happened simultaneously was the debilitation of the commercial system based on Buenos Aires and the international market and the strengthening of local economic forces.

The only remnant of the state apparatus which remained comparatively intact was the regular armed forces: both the army and the navy. These began to return from Uruguay early in 1829. Rivadavia and his supporters used them to seize power. The Fort in Buenos Aires was surrounded, and the seat of authority occupied. Colonel Dorrego managed to slip away and fled to the country hoping to assert his authority by the use of the militia. He managed to assemble a force of 2,000 militiamen, but either by calculation or circumstance did not seek the aid of the principal commander of the militia, General Juan Manuel Rosas. With the force he had, Dorrego met the regular forces of General Lavalle. There was a bloody slaughter, and Dorrego escaped to a frontier post. Hearing of the victory by Lavalle, the officer of the post arrested Dorrego and handed him over to Lavalle. Lavalle promptly shot Dorrego.

This seemed to indicate to General Rosas that compromise between the militia forces and the new provisional government was not possible. He began to move, while in Buenos Aires the workers in the corrals and slaughterhouses threatened violence against Rivadavia and his supporters. Even well-to-do persons deplored the crime committed, in spite of their support for the provisional regime. Meanwhile, Rosas and his troops moved on Buenos Aires slowly, avoiding a pitched battle he knew they could not win. The longer he delayed while the regular forces were harassed by small parties of gauchos, the more the debility of the state told against Lavalle. His troops began to desert for want of pay. In Buenos Aires the sailors commanded by Admiral Brown, who garrisoned the town, began looting to make good the arrears in their pay.

The civil war lasted some six months. Rosas warily waited, and only confronted Lavalle when he knew he could win. Late in April 1829 at the Río Conchas, 15 miles from Buenos Aires, he fell upon Lavalle's force weakened by desertions, weary from prolonged harassment, and cut off from their supplies of fresh horses. Rivadavia fled to France. Even then Rosas did not enter Buenos Aires where there was a great fear of gauchos and Indian savagery. Rosas had the town in his grasp, but he was a shrewd politician. He wanted to keep control of his forces and at the same time win over as many people to his side as he possibly could. In fact he secretly agreed with Lavalle that a party of compromise should win the elections they proposed to hold.

Meanwhile a remnant of the regular army, under the able leadership of General Paz, penetrated into Córdoba and defeated the local *caudillo*, General Bustos. This put heart into the supporters of Lavalle in Buenos Aires, and they proceeded to win the election which they had promised only half to win. This treachery was repaired by Rosas and Lavalle putting up a joint compromise candidate for governor of Buenos Aires to hold office for six months, and prepare fresh elections.

Rosas made sure that compromise was only a stage on the road to victory. Dorrego's remains were dug up and brought to Buenos Aires for reburial in the Cathedral. A great popular demonstration in support of Rosas was organized. Instead of elections he reconvened the Provincial Assembly which Lavalle had dispersed when he seized power. Without a dissenting voice, on 5 December 1829, General Juan Manuel Rosas was elected governor and Captain-General of Buenos Aires. Lavalle fled to Uruguay and Admiral Brown followed him. The regular army was broken up. The navy was put on a peace footing. The *estado Rivadaviano* was completely destroyed.

It is easier to set down a narrative of these events than to say what they meant. It is part of the conventional wisdom of Argentina to describe this split in society as a difference of principles between the federalists on the one hand and the unitarians on the other; between Rosas who advocated provincial self-government by gaucho *caudillos* and Rivadavia – Lavalle who advocated a centralized, unitary state; between a dictatorial system of government and a liberal, representative system of government. Superficially this describes something of the difference but it throws no light upon what interest differed from what interest and why. The notion entertained by some Argentine political writers and historians is too simple, that the federalists under Rosas were popular democrats, the real working people of Argentina aligned against a capitalist-imperialist oligarchy whose liberalism was a mask for privilege and tyranny. In fact the federalists in the province of Buenos Aires numbered in their ranks many great landlords who were foundation members of the class described as the oligarchy. When General Lavalle endeavoured to immobilize the opposition to himself and Rivadavia, he arrested and sent into exile the Anchorena brothers, then as now a by-word for landed wealth, and men of high position like Balcarce, Iriarte, Aguirre, and Martínez. On the other hand, the landed interest was by no means unanimously on the federalist side. In the course of the political struggles Rosas, for example, seized the estates of his friend and neighbour Miguens, who was a unitarian, but mitigated the punishment for what he regarded as a political crime by suspending the expropriation so long as the head of the family lived, and this because old Señor Miguens had given Rosas shelter when he was a runaway boy.

Nor was it the case that foreigners were opposed to Rosas and the federalists. The British community in Argentina was well treated by Rosas, and he respected their treaty rights scrupulously. When in 1845–46 the British government clashed with him and blockaded Buenos Aires, it was the pressure of the British mercantile interest on Lord Aberdeen that changed British policy and restored good relations with Rosas. When Rosas fell, it was the British Chargé d'Affaires who saved his life by conducting him secretly on board a British ship which took him away to a secure exile in Hampshire.

Nor was it the case that Rosas and the federalists were democrats serving the interests of the common working people, and devoted to the principle of popular participation in decision-making. Rosas identified himself with the common people, he organized them, and he used them. Only in the sense that he taught them to follow him did he serve them. He knew the working people of the countryside and of the slaughterhouses and corrals. His capacity to appeal to them and to organize them was based on practical knowledge as an *estanciero*, a militia officer, and an Indian fighter. When he came to power he paid close attention to them and gave them a place in the community as defenders of himself against the host of enemies real and imaginary which he pointed out to them. Rivadavia and his friends had sought to build up a mechanism of authority consisting of any army, an administration, an educational system, and a supporting financial structure. Rosas, instead, built a political party – the *Mazorca* – a machine for generating public enthusiasm, for expressing fear and hatred, and for searching out anyone who doubted the wisdom of Rosas' policies.

Rosas himself had a very clear view of what he was doing and why. In 1834 he wrote to his fellow *caudillo*, Quiroga:

'No one is more persuaded than you and I of the necessity to organize a general government as being the only means of giving responsible existence to our republic...who organizes a disciplined army from groups of men without leaders, without officers, without obedience, without rank...? Please observe how costly and painful experience has made us see in a practical way that the federal system is absolutely necessary for us because, among other powerful reasons, we totally lack the elements required for a unified government. Furthermore, because our country was dominated by a party that was deaf to this need, the means and resources available to sustain the state were destroyed and annulled. That party incited the people, perverted their beliefs, set private interests against each other, propagated immorality and intrigue, and split society into so many factions that they have not left even the remnants of its common bonds. They extended their fury to the point of breaking the most sacred of those bonds, the only one that could serve to re-establish the others – religion. With the country in this pitiful condition, it is necessary to create everything anew, first labouring on a small scale and piecemeal, and thereby prepare a general system that may embrace everything.'[1]

In a community which delights to remember its political past with statues of its heroes and leaders, there are no memorials in stone or bronze to General Rosas. And yet he more than any politician in Argentine history fixed the socio-political structure of the country and determined the outcome of the revolution. He knitted the past and the present together and hence determined the future. He called himself the Restorer of the Laws, but he did not restore; he consolidated what the revolution had changed. He was the captain of the winners and firmly established their place in the community, and hence determined its character.

In the first place he strengthened and liberated the landlords. Under the Crown of Spain and under the unitary state projected by Rivadavia the landed class had a place in the community, but far from a dominant position. Rivadavia had in fact nationalized land so that under his system of emphyteusis the land belonged to the state, and the working estanciero was a tenant whose rent could be

---

[1] Quoted in J. L. Romero, *A History of Argentine Political Thought* translated by T. F. McGann (Stanford, 1963), pp. 119–20.

revised and part of whose income it was intended would be taken by the state to support its activities and to finance public investment. Rivadavia did not have time to make the system work, and very little rent was ever collected, but had the system been put into operation, the *estancieros* would inevitably have been a dependent group in the same way that the mining concessionaires of the old Spanish empire were under the control of the Crown and the Spanish mercantile interests. Rosas did not destroy Rivadavia's system of emphyteusis with a single blow. He made it a system for transferring large blocs of land to his supporters – unoccupied lands and land seized from political opponents in the province of Buenos Aires. Periodically he gave to the tenants of those vast domains the option of buying their holdings outright or surrendering them. No limits had ever been set to the size of grants under the law of emphyteusis in the province of Buenos Aires. Rosas simply provided a mechanism by which tenancies became freehold and the state ceased to have any control over or share in land sales or land revenues. What happened in Buenos Aires happened elsewhere except in the province of Santa Fé where a limit of 18,300 acres was fixed for land grants.

In this way the basic resource of Argentina was distributed and thus was the economic foundation laid of the class structure and the structure of political power.

Landed estates without people to work them are, of course, meaningless. Rosas brought the native people under control by identifying himself with them, and making them an instrument of the public power and for the defeat of all interests which sought to challenge him. He did not give to the workers of that time independence or bargaining power. Quite the contrary. But he gave them self-esteem and as much dignity as dependence allows. Something of their way of life was honoured, and all of it was not despised. Under Rosas, Argentina was a democracy of what is; not of what ought to be. It derived its doctrines from the prejudices and practices of the community at large and not from books nor from prophets of progress and enlightenment. In this way he was able to establish a disciplined order of work so that the *estancias* and the slaughterhouses were able to function. Not that there was any problem of strikes or disorders. The problem of labour supply was rather different. Essentially it was a matter of keeping men together as a work force and preventing social dissolution through vagabondage, which was so easy and so natural, and the reversion to a pure state of nature and of association with the Indians as a rival body of hunters and suppliers of export markets.

Rosas also reserved and strengthened the Church. It must not be supposed in this connection that Rosas was a restorer of the old Spanish system of close identity of Church and state. The last thing Rosas was prepared to countenance was his submission to clerical control. On the contrary he selected the bishops and controlled the hierarchy. One of his last political quarrels was with the Papal Nuncio who objected to the conduct and policies of one of Rosas' appointees. Rosas went to the extraordinary length of having his portrait displayed on the altars of the churches so that the faithful could gain a better understanding of how God manifested Himself in the province of Buenos Aires. This was not vainglory on Rosas' part. It was a conscious employment of religion for political and social purposes with the object of holding together in bonds of emotion the better to serve his conceptions of the public good.

With respect to trade Rosas never seriously undertook to undo the work of the revolution, nor did he wish to do so. He did not restore the complete integration in the international system of capital flows which Rivadavia had endeavoured to establish, but on the other hand he never repudiated the English loan of 1824, nor did he willingly default on public credit. Rosas wanted to pay, tried to pay, and did pay what he could, but generally his treasury was so depleted of hard currency and exhausted by war and the business of keeping himself in power that he could not participate fully in the investment and reinvestment process. In order to improve his credit rating he was willing to exchange the Argentine claim to the Falkland Islands for a cancellation of the Baring loan, but inasmuch as the British government had effective possession of the islands they refused to exchange the claims of a group of bondholders for a real asset.

Commercially Rosas maintained a system of free trade over most of his period of power. In 1835 he introduced a system of protective tariffs with the object of conciliating the interior provinces and fostering handicrafts and grain-growing in Buenos Aires, but when the French blockade cut off supplies of foreign manufactures during the years 1838–41 it was plain that domestic industry could not supply the markets except at very high cost. When international trade resumed Rosas quietly abandoned protection as a system, retaining tariffs for revenue purposes only. This step lost him support in the provinces, but in his own province of Buenos Aires and among his own class of *estancieros* it won support. After the protectionist experiment of 1835, Argentina never attempted to industrialize behind a tariff barrier until World War II. Rosas' brief flirtation with protection must not be viewed except for what it was: a political concession to conservative interests in decline and not a boldly conceived programme of industrialization. Nothing in Argentine circumstances in Rosas' time made industrialization conceivably possible: no coal or waterpower, little capital, scantily skilled manpower, and little entrepreneurial talent. In terms of obeying the dictates of economic interest of the *estancieros* and meat processors Rosas did not seriously differ from Mariano Moreno and Rivadavia before him or Mitre and Sarmiento after him.

In another important respect Rosas was a basic and average Argentine political leader like those who went before him and came after, namely in his dedicated determination to maintain national independence and to reject foreign interference in policy-making. The principal powers with which he had to deal were Britain, France, the United States, and Brazil. With the United States, Rosas had no diplomatic relations until 1842 on account of the action of American warships in destroying Argentine installations in the Falkland Islands, but thereafter he accepted American moral support in the pushing and hauling of international politics, and the Americans came to regard General Rosas as a sort of Argentine equivalent of Andrew Jackson, which in some respects he was. The North Americans had a trading interest in the River Plate, but they never became seriously involved in its politics. In Rosas' time the Monroe doctrine was a theoretical proposition which Latin Americans could admire, and Rosas no less than others.

Rosas' first international difficulties were with the French. The restored Bourbons had tended to support the Spanish Crown in its effort to stifle the revolution. When the revolution came to an end, their efforts to establish relations with Argentina were characterized by arrogance and stupidity, which ended in French warships burning a number of Argentine war vessels in the harbour of Buenos Aires during the civil war that brought Rosas to power. The Orleanist monarchy managed matters somewhat differently, but they, like the British before them, were obliged to learn that force was of little use in advancing their interests in the River Plate. What worked in Algeria failed in Argentina. Because there was no Franco-Argentine treaty defining the rights of Frenchmen in Argentina, the French government seized on the supposed injustices practised on Frenchmen to embark on a policy of pressure which took the form of blockading Buenos Aires and giving arms and aid to the enemies of General Rosas operating from the safety of Uruguay. Just what the French had in mind is not clear, but whatever it was, their attempts to upset Rosas, like their simultaneous attempts to back the internal enemies of the Sultan of Turkey, encountered the opposition of the British. Rosas was able to look after himself. He defeated and exterminated the opposition, and the French decided that, being over-committed around the world, they had to abandon whatever it was they were attempting in the River Plate. Once they lifted their blockade Rosas quickly reached an agreement with them according the French the same rights as the British in Argentina, which were in fact nothing more than a statement in treaty form of equality before the law and freedom of residence and movement, established by the revolution.

The end of the French intervention did not conclude Rosas' difficulties with the Great Powers. He was determined to root his enemies out of Uruguay, and install there a regime favourable to himself, perhaps as a step to incorporating Uruguay in the Argentine Confederation. At this time Montevideo was becoming a more important centre of trade than it had been during the long anarchy which had followed the expulsion of the Brazilians. Furthermore, being free of the French blockade, Montevideo had benefited from the interference with international trade through Buenos Aires during the trouble with France. As a consequence a British trade interest had developed in Montevideo so that the troubles between Rosas and the government in Montevideo were bound to inflict some damage on British commerce.

When, in 1841, Lord Aberdeen became Foreign Secretary in the government of Sir Robert Peel, he hearkened to the complaints of British merchants about their troubles in the River Plate. His representative in Buenos Aires was invited by the Uruguayans to take over Uruguay as a protectorate. This was refused. This was a sensible decision, but Aberdeen conceived of a stupid alternative, viz. to organize a joint Anglo-French mediation involving the use of pressure for the purpose of compelling Rosas to make peace with his enemies in Montevideo. Rosas flatly refused to yield to this kind of interference. He smashed his enemies, even though his friends in Uruguay were unable to capture Montevideo. In this endeavour they were obstructed by the British and French. British troops were actually redirected from South Africa to Montevideo, and an Anglo-French fleet blockaded Buenos Aires and interfered with Argentine naval operations at Montevideo. A British fleet forced its way up the River Paraná to Entre Rios, Corrientes, and Paraguay with the object of 'opening up trade'.

Rosas out-manoeuvred Aberdeen. The absurdity of the notion that trade is improved by the use of force was soon exposed. British trade suffered terribly during the years 1845 and 1846 with the result that commercial interests in Liverpool, London, and Buenos Aires began to bring pressure on the Peel government to abandon its policy, and to reveal that much of the agitation against Rosas was the work of commercial interests in Montevideo and southern Brazil who were benefiting from the disasters being suffered by their fellow British merchants trading with Argentina. Rosas stimulated this pressure and held out the prospect to the British that their position would improve once their government abandoned its interference. Aberdeen himself admitted that his policy had been wrong and unjust, and blamed it all on his representative in Buenos Aires. When Palmerston replaced Aberdeen he rapidly wound up the fiasco and negotiated a new treaty of peace and navigation which acknowledged the wrongs done to Argentina by returning all Argentine warships captured during the troubles and by having British warships salute the Argentine flag in recognition of Argentine sovereignty in the River Plate.

Rosas thus solved a number of major problems of the post-revolutionary phase, but he did not solve them all. He may have out-manoeuvred and defeated France and Britain, but he was less successful in dealing with his immediate neighbours – Uruguay, Paraguay, Bolivia, and Brazil. Part of Rosas' difficulty stemmed from the fact that he had never clearly established in his own mind whether the first three countries were independent nations or errant Argentine provinces which it was his business to incorporate into the Confederation as part of the federal structure controlled by Buenos Aires. As a result he was constantly bogged down in troubles with his neighbours so that on the eve of his overthrow it looked as if a new war involving Brazil as well as Uruguay and, perhaps, Paraguay was about to break out.

In a sense Rosas' confusion about his relations with neighbouring states was part of a more general dilemma which he never overcame, viz. the contradiction between the interests of the city and province

of Buenos Aires and the interests of the other provinces. As a federalist he had proclaimed himself a protector of provincial rights, interests, and initiative. As governor and Captain-General of the
province of Buenos Aires he governed that province; on behalf of the
Confederation he conducted the foreign affairs of all the provinces
and collected the customs revenue levied on international trade. But
what was good for the provinces of the Confederation was not necessarily good for Buenos Aires and vice versa. Rosas' policy of protective tariffs inaugurated in 1835 was represented as an endeavour to
create an internal market for Argentine industry and to revive internal trade based on local production. Inevitably this raised costs for
the export sector which was strongest in the province of Buenos Aires
and in the *Litoral* provinces of Santa Fé, Entre Rios, and Corrientes.
Rosas was willing to pay this price, but his supporters in his own
province were not. The French blockade provided an excuse for
abandoning the prohibition of certain imports, and for revising tariffs
downward. This process of downward revision continued from 1838
onwards so that in the end provincial governments began erecting
their own protective tariffs. From an economic and commercial point
of view, Rosas, once he abandoned the protective policies of 1835,
differed not at all from Rivadavia in his preference for a *laissez faire*,
internationally oriented economy.

Thus, Rosas failed to find a way out of the conflict over economic
policy, and this in its turn rendered the provinces increasingly restless
and dissatisfied with Rosista federalism, which, it was increasingly
agreed in the late 1840s, was only a cloak for the selfish sectionalism of
the *porteños* and the *estancieros* of Buenos Aires. And this cloak wore
very thin when once Rosas had no formidable foreign enemies to fight.

There was another problem Rosas never solved. His was a popular
regime which aimed at securing the support of the working class in
town and countryside. This he succeeded in doing politically, but in
the end economic discontent eroded popular support. Rosas' financial
problems were largely created by his war expenditure, and this he
chose to solve in the simplest way by the issue of paper currency with
its consequent inflation of prices. In this he yielded to the opposition
to taxation by the wealthiest class, and the consequence was a steady
shift of the burdens of public expenditure on to the shoulders of the
middle and working classes through increases in the price of the
necessities of life. By the time of his overthrow Rosas' regime was
more popular in its style than in its real mass support.

Chapter 4

The Economics of a *Laissez Faire* Community

O N 3 FEBRUARY 1852, General Rosas was overthrown in a battle at Monte Caseros outside Buenos Aires. The nature of the battle and its participants suggest something of the profound change which was taking place in the Argentine community. Rosas was defeated because he had been deserted by all but the division of Palermo, his personal formation of guards. They stood and fought. The rest of the troops fled. In this they but followed the example of their officers, for the Commander-in-Chief, General Mansilla, Rosas' own brother-in-law, had retired on the ground of ill-health as the enemies of the regime gathered their forces. It was discovered too that Bernardo de Irigoyen, his private secretary and intimate adviser, had, before the battle, made an arrangement with his enemies. Rosas, when he was brought down, was in fact isolated and without support, and he saved his life only by throwing himself on the protection of the British Chargé d'Affaires, who at great risk to himself conducted the fallen idol of the people in disguise and in darkness past the revolutionary guards and put him on board a British steamship. This took him to safety in Hampshire where he lived until his death in 1877 and where he still lies beneath a modest memorial stone in an ill-kept burial ground in a suburb of Southampton.

The conjunction of forces which brought about this overthrow deserves description. The victor at Caseros was General Justo José de Urquiza. And who was he? He was a man very like Rosas as a social type: a great *estanciero* in the province of Entre Rios, a patriarch who fathered many children and owned great herds of cattle; who commanded an army which had overthrown the enemies of General Rosas at Pago Largo and India Muerta; and who controlled and governed his province. In style of life and political methods few people except Rosas himself could have less resembled the liberal and enlightened critics of General Rosas who lived in exile or underground during his dictatorship. None the less this man and what he represented joined forces with the liberal intellectuals to create a new Argentina. Under the protection of General Urquiza and with his full support the exiles came home to work out a constitution and a policy designed to solve the problems of the nation: the establishment of a viable relationship among the provinces; the modernization of society; and the invention of a political process that did not involve the periodic slaughter or exile of dissident elements.

The cattle interests could agree that General Rosas had firmly secured their position. They owned large estates. The Indian frontier had been pushed back. The gauchos had been brought under control. Their costs had been reduced or were kept down by free trade and inflation. But they could ask, and they did ask, legitimate questions. 'Was life under Rosas worth living?' and 'Did his strict control permit the kind of development which was taking place in the United States or in Brazil?' 'Was boredom relieved only by terror, isolation from humane understanding, and narrow piety and fanaticism enough?'

Rosas had been overthrown once a sufficient number of the established interests answered 'No' to the questions to which the young liberal intellectuals of the 'Generation of 1837' had always returned a negative. Thus was born the liberal aristocratic Argentina, which after much glory and many recent vicissitudes is not yet dead. Rosas had been a sovereign such as Hobbes had imagined as the answer to an anarchic state of nature. Urquiza and Mitre became the sort of rulers Locke had imagined as necessary to permit the men in possession to enjoy their natural rights under a system of constitutional liberty.

The new élite which succeeded to the order established by Rosas were seriously divided on only one issue: the place of the city and province of Buenos Aires *vis-à-vis* the rest of the nation. This issue plagued them for a decade, and was only finally settled in 1880 when the city of Buenos Aires was separated administratively and politically from its province, converted into a national capital, and so became the metropolis of the Argentine community as a whole. Underlying the issue was the relative position and power of the mercantile and financial interests in respect to the landed interest. Briefly, it may be said that in this matter the landed interest under the leadership of the provincial politicians prevailed. In the fifty years which elapsed between the overthrow of General Rosas and the Baring crisis, Argentina had six Presidents. Of these only Mitre was a man of Buenos Aires. Urquiza, Sarmienta, Avellaneda, Roca, and Juárez Celman were all provincials.

If these Presidents can be distinguished by their origins and for regional political affiliations, they can all be classified together – Mitre and the others – as modernizers, landlord-liberals, and believers in strong, concentrated presidential power centred in Buenos Aires. There was a consistency in what they did with their power. They were all devoted to the rapid economic development of the pastoral and agricultural industries, to the widest expansion of market opportunities for ranching, sheep-breeding, and for grain-farming, to the import of capital to develop the infrastructure of railways, docks, and commercial facilities, to the increased supply of labour through immigration, and to expansion of the frontier by building railways and destroying the Indians. In these policies, the Presidents had the unanimous support of the dominant interests, and no other interests challenged them. Even the first cries of the urban working class, which were just beginning to be heard in the late 1880s, were not a challenge to what was being done but a well justified complaint about how it was being done by inflation at the expense of their standards of living. As for the gauchos, they were all but voiceless. When in April 1870 the gaucho *caudillo* López Jordán broke into Urquiza's home and murdered him, the desperate end of the gauchos was in sight. It remained only for José Hernández to celebrate their passing in his rude epic, *Martín Fierro*.

The landlord class were rich in land and poor in capital. Their problem as a class and as individuals was to find the means of making more productive their principal asset. They could do this either by reinvesting surpluses available after providing for their wants and those of the community at large, or they could sell off part of their assets to get the means of more effectively working what they retained, or they could borrow from outside their enterprises and outside their community. As individuals and as a class they resorted to all these possibilities, but mainly to the third. Both the Argentine public authorities and the individual landowners became debtors: the public authorities to build the infrastructure of railways and ports and the landlords to fence their land, dig wells, install windmills and Australian tanks, to buy farm machinery, and to acquire high-grade breeding stock. In the first stages the state played a very important part in procuring foreign capital. The British capitalists were from the beginning the largest foreign investment interest, and in the first stage, which ended with the depression of 1875, nearly 60 per cent of all British money invested in Argentina – apart from that invested in land itself – took the form of interest-bearing Argentine government bonds. Even major investments in private enterprises such as railways had their profits guaranteed by the state, and they were helped in some instances with land subsidies and government purchases of shares. As the economy expanded more and more private-risk capital without state guarantee entered the country, and the proportion of government bonds fell, but until the possibilities of foreign investment began to exhaust themselves in the late 1920s Argentine government borrowing continued to be an important feature of foreign investment.

The position of the creditors in Argentina was unique or nearly so. In nations like Britain, France, and Germany and in communities more nearly analogous to Argentina such as the United States, Canada, and Australia, the creditor class had considerable political power. Individuals in such communities could repudiate their debts through a process of bankruptcy, but the general repudiation of debts was impossible directly or even indirectly through manipulation of money, credit, and prices. Nations like Egypt, or Turkey or China, had imposed upon them by force, or threats of force, financial regimes which protected creditors and guaranteed the functioning of a system which ensured that they be paid and that private capital had a good chance of earning profits. Not so in Argentina. There the debtor class and a debtor government had the political power to assert its interest and ensure its well-being. Rosas had demonstrated that sea-borne military force was useless against Argentina even when allied with dissident local forces. Nothing happened to alter this circumstance. The creditors could not or would not exercise political power. The only sanction they could apply was to cut off capital. Hence only a business relationship between debtor and creditor could exist: a calculation of advantage on both sides which led to solutions in the presence of difficulties productive of 'give and take' and of compromise.

Given the need of the dominant Argentine interests to compromise with their creditors and of their creditors to compromise with them, it is not surprising that a mechanism developed for shifting the burden of compromise on to other elements in the community: wage-workers, professional people, and the non-owning classes generally. Until the end of the nineteenth century the Argentine economy operated under a system of paper currency and loose banking policies. Price inflation was a constant feature. None of the non-owning classes had any political power, and little means of directly resisting the effects of prices rising faster than incomes. But even in the case of the non-owning classes economic factors operated to prevent their total subjection. Labour, particularly skilled labour, was scarce, and market factors ensured high wages and equitable share-cropping contracts in the countryside. If the inflationary weapon was used too drastically it had the same effect on labour supplies as repudiation had on capital flows. Immigrants ceased to come to Argentina, and those there started going home. A certain number might be trapped in Argentina and many more became tied to their new homes, but any drastic persistence in policies diminishing popular well-being had the effect of stopping the whole process of development. Thus, compromise and business solutions had to be reached in dealing with the non-owning classes as well as foreign creditors.

The basic freedom of Argentina created by the landlord-liberal successors of General Rosas was economic and so were the dynamics of the system. The essential difference between the leadership from Urquiza to Juárez Celman and the leadership of Rosas consisted in the willingness of the landlord-liberals to permit the social developments necessary for the full functioning of an internationally oriented *laissez faire* economy. The differences were not narrowly political nor did they depend on doctrine. Rosas always governed with the assistance of an elected Assembly in the province of Buenos Aires just as his liberal successors did. He interfered with provincial regimes and so did they. He guaranteed freedom of worship to non-Catholics just as they did. He worked an export-import economy just as they did. He wanted to co-operate with international banking interests just as they did. What they did new and different was to preserve power and order at the point of contact between Argentina and the outside world, i.e. in the River Plate; to permit a variety of opinions which made it possible for a variety of people to come to and work in Argentina; to develop a system of secular education which opened opportunities of development for humble people of many faiths and of none. Rosas' society was an internationally oriented capitalist order dominated by large landlords. So was

Mitre's and Sarmiento's. But Rosas ruled a closed society and Mitre and Sarmiento an open one.

This free, open society lasted from 1852 to 1930. It depended on a conjunction of world circumstances. When these circumstances changed fundamentally, as they did with the catastrophic economic depression of 1929, Argentina was forced to change. The conjunction of circumstances was at first centred around the Atlantic Ocean and in Europe. In 1846 Britain abolished the Corn Laws and opened the way to a completely free system of international and domestic trading. The revolutions of 1848 broke the shell of the past, particularly in the economic sphere. In France, Holland, Belgium, and the German states trade became either free or at least freer of controls than it had ever been. The American Civil War greatly stimulated the expansion of industry, trade, and immigration in North America. The serfs were emancipated in Russia. Methods of making cheap steel vastly extended the potentiality of steam as a motive force, and opened the way for the invention of new sources of power and economical forms of transport. New institutional devices for mobilizing surplus spending power for the finance of new enterprises were developed. The mobility of both wealth and manpower was improved, and the notion took hold that man's principal business is the mastery not of himself but of his environment. For a brief moment it was even believed that economic action was more important than political action, and that bankers, railway contractors, industrial entrepreneurs, and merchants had more to contribute to the progress of civilization than soldiers, priests, politicians, and public administrators. Religion and art were relegated increasingly to the private sphere of life, and the public philosophy was increasingly influenced by scientists, technologists, and economists.

In this conjunction, Argentina had certain natural advantages: rich land, a good location on a great ocean, and people few in number and all but subdued to the control of a class capable of embracing to their advantage the new circumstances. The foremost Argentine thinkers – Juan Bautista Alberdi, Bartolomé Mitre, and Domingo Faustino Sarmiento – were agreed that the world of Europe and of North America was the one to which Argentina must belong and to which it must unite itself. The constitution of 1853, devised in the main by Alberdi, and presented to the nation by Urquiza, proclaimed this purpose precisely: 'Congress shall have the power to provide for all that conduces to the prosperity of the

country, to the advancement and welfare of all the provinces, and
to the advancement of the people by prescribing plans for general
and university education and by promoting industrial enterprise,
immigration, the construction of railways and navigable canals, the
colonization of public land, the introduction and establishment of
more industries, and the importation of foreign capital' (Article 67).

We can discern four stages in the development of the free, open
society of the landlord-liberals: the initial stage of integration into
the international capital-manpower flow system which was completed
in the first decade following the overthrow of General Rosas; the
critical stage connected with the Baring crisis of 1890–96; the golden
age of high prosperity from the Boer War to World War I; and the
stage of maturity which ended with the collapse of prices and the
cessation of capital-manpower flows in 1929.

In the first stage three critical issues were resolved. The first was
the establishment of peace in the basin of the River Plate. Urquiza
terminated the possibility of war with Brazil by recognizing the independence of Paraguay and Uruguay, and by signing a series of
international treaties of free navigation of the Plata-Paraná river
system, first with Britain and France and then with the United
States, Chile, Paraguay, Bolivia, Belgium, Brazil, Prussia, and
Sardinia. The second was the preservation of peace between the
province of Buenos Aires and the rest of the nation. Urquiza succeeded in isolating Buenos Aires from the international community
so that the politicians there were never able to secure recognition as
an independent state even though they managed to deny the constitution of 1853, and subvert Urquiza's authority for seven years.
Finally he thrashed the *porteño* forces in 1859, and when they again
rebelled he decided to retire from politics, and handed over authority
to the *porteño* leader Mitre, who continued his policies.

The third issue involved the repayment of the defaulted British
loan of 1824. The province of Buenos Aires owed the British bondholders approximately £1 million plus unpaid interest plus interest
on the unpaid interest. For any programme which looked to importation of foreign capital this problem of unpaid debt was fundamental.
Was Argentina to attempt the autonomous accumulation of capital
needed for development, or was the nation to tap the pools of capital
overseas? Some *porteños* appeared to have considered the possibility
of autonomous accumulation. They started a railway on their own,
and this was possible in the relatively well-populated areas near

Buenos Aires. The provincial interests thought otherwise. Development elsewhere required large sums of capital, and this meant turning to international supplies. Even the government in the province of Buenos Aires came around to the view that there were advantages in establishing their credit in London and Paris. In 1857 the government in Buenos Aires agreed to repay these debts. The payment of a sum as large as one million pounds with accumulated interest meant in a community with extremely limited resources a drastic reorganization of public finance so that income distribution between capital and current expenditure was affected fundamentally. Argentina thus became connected with the international capital flow system so that Argentine surpluses flowed into the pools of capital overseas and capital flowed back to Argentina in an ever-increasing volume.

Once this was effected and a national government was set up embracing all the provinces, the stage was set for comprehensive national development. In a matter of months national and foreign banks were established, railway companies formed, and colonization enterprises organized. The importance for the development of the interior and the frontier regions of the compromise reached by Mitre and sealed by Urquiza's definitive retirement from politics was soon revealed. In a sense Urquiza won the battle for the interior and poorer provinces by leaving to Mitre, the man of Buenos Aires, the task of mobilizing the wealth of Buenos Aires to support development outside Buenos Aires province. Urquiza, for example, had realized the importance of railways to the up-river provinces such as Santa Fé, Entre Rios, and Corrientes and the interior provinces like Córdoba, Tucumán, and Mendoza, but his plan for a railway from the deep-water port of Rosario on the Paraná to Córdoba across the almost desert pampas of Santa Fé failed because all he could offer the railway capitalists was land grants. These had not sufficient attraction for entrepreneurs or investors because no one could be sure that land in an undeveloped area could yield the profits necessary to attract the investment required to build the railway. Once, however, the national government possessing the power to tax the only serious sources of accessible wealth, namely the trade through Buenos Aires, was able to underwrite railways by guaranteeing profits and/or by supporting provincial government credit the capital for railway construction was forthcoming. As a result, railways were projected and built, some by private companies like the Central Argentine Railway

Co. Ltd., and some by the provincial authorities connecting old centres like Córdoba, Tucumán, Santiago del Estero, and Mendoza with the sea and the markets of Buenos Aires and the world overseas. At the same time alternative trading centres were created such as Rosario, which became a port of call for deep-sea ships in the same way that Buenos Aires and Montevideo had long been.

The support of the state was indispensable for this type of development. Nothing in the circumstances of the nation outside the immediate region of the city of Buenos Aires itself could have induced the investment of the large sums necessary to build railways hundreds and even thousands of miles long through territory where there was little or no demand for railway services and where the building of a railway was a preliminary to development and hence to railway traffic. In order to find the means of buying the equipment and paying the engineers and construction workers the Argentine government was obliged directly or indirectly to guarantee the possessors of capital that they would be rewarded with at least 7 per cent on this money if they invested in undertakings which no one could possibly imagine could yield profits out of receipts. In this process the main source of investment funds was outside Argentina, but the means of guaranteeing the annual payments necessary to induce investment was inside Argentina, viz. the economically most advanced and active community mainly in the province of Buenos Aires.

All this seems so elementary that it need hardly be spelled out, but it is necessary to do so because for fifty years the Argentine people have been bemused and confused by misunderstanding on this subject. The argument was that Mitre and the liberals sold Argentina to foreign capitalists, who have since then exploited Argentina and either prevented or distorted its economic development. In fact Argentina was, after the United States and Canada, among the first beneficiaries of a set of circumstances almost unique in human history, i.e. the existence of surpluses of wealth in a tiny part of the world, western Europe, whose possessors and whose political authorities preferred to use it, or allow it to be used, outside their own community for some purpose other than war, luxury, or religion. The Spaniards came to South America and took one hundred per cent of what they found lying around surplus to the requirements of the community. Indeed, the decline of population in Peru and Mexico which set in after their coming suggests that they took more than this figure. The foreigners who came to Argentina in the mid-nineteenth century brought wealth to the country and they brought skill and the power to work. That they received something in return – and many received nothing – has been depicted as a spoliation, and for this misrepresentation Argentina has paid dearly during the last twenty-five years.

While the state played a major role in initiating and sustaining development, there were areas of enterprise and regions of the country where private investment served to expand production. The expansion of ranching and farming, which better communications and better banking and commercial facilities made possible, was entirely the result of private investment both local and international. Where development was already sufficient to provide a market for services, even railways could be built by private capital. The government of the province of Buenos Aires offered to guarantee profits on a line across the pampas south-west in the direction of Bahía Blanca. A British company was formed to build this road, but the directors soon discovered that they needed no guarantee because they were earning profits almost as fast as they built the railway, and this for the very simple reason that the country through which they were building was already inhabited and productive. Similarly private capital without state support provided gas supplies in Buenos Aires, tramways, banking services throughout the Republic, shipping services, and industrial production in lines where there were comparative advantages in local activity.

There is great difficulty in ascertaining how much of this development was financed from abroad and how much by Argentines. As we have remarked, one indispensable element in the whole process was the existence in Argentina of a sufficiently productive nucleus to provide for the interest and amortization charges on loans and to pay the short-fall of profits on guaranteed enterprises. Further than this, Argentine investable funds tended to go into improvements in rural production, but even in this area borrowing either from banks or from the sale of land mortgage bonds was important. Argentines were not investors in railways or generally in joint-stock enterprises. Their wealth was largely land, and with the prospect of expansion their resources were directed to the acquisition of more land and its development.

The advantages to the dominant interest of an open over a closed society were demonstrated to be enormous. The influx of manpower

and capital from abroad during the decade following Mitre's inauguration as President enabled Argentina to survive a number of
disasters: some of them like the war with Paraguay a hangover from
the past, and others like the terrible yellow fever epidemic of 1876
the result of rapid urban growth without the modernization of water
supplies and waste disposal systems. In previous epochs wars, plagues,
and droughts had simply been disasters from which the community
only slowly recovered. Under the new order they were overcome and
growth sustained. Indeed the sum of the disasters contributed to
transformation. The war in Paraguay did not interrupt international
trade as all previous wars had done. On the contrary it stimulated
trade and at the same time was the means of absorbing the energies
of the restless gauchos in battle and hardships which reduced their
numbers and weakened their influence, while a new type of worker
was coming in from Italy and Spain and to a lesser degree from other
parts of Europe.

The flow of capital and manpower to Argentina which began as a
sustained process in 1862 continued, with only a short period of
interruption in the mid 1870s, until 1890. During the late 1880s, it
reached a high intensity so that in 1888–89 between a quarter and
a half of the new issues in the London capital market were made on
behalf of enterprises in Argentina and nearly a quarter of a million
immigrants from Europe entered the country. During all this time
more goods were flowing into Argentina than were being exported.
This could not last for ever, and in 1890 a crisis developed, the
resolution of which determined the future of Argentina and its
relations with the rest of the world for another forty years.

This crisis took its name from the banking firm of Baring Brothers
because Barings were threatened with bankruptcy on account of their
Argentine accounts. The name Baring was rightly used for another
reason. Barings were the first international banking firm to raise
money for Argentina in Europe – in 1824; they had re-established
the flow of capital to Argentina by inducing the government of
Buenos Aires to repay its defaulted debts in 1857; and they were the
leading bankers concerned in marketing Argentine securities during
the 1880s. In 1890 they faced bankruptcy for a simple and fundamental reason. They had undertaken to pay the contractors who had
built the large port-works in Buenos Aires, in return for which they
had received bonds of the Argentine government with a face value
of approximately 25 million dollars. These they found they could

not sell to the investing public. Confidence in the capacity of the Argentine government to pay had departed.

This confidence had lasted up to this moment for a variety of reasons. In the first place the national and provincial governments of Argentina had always up to this point paid in gold or gold-backed currencies the interest and amortization charges required by their creditors. In the second place the contractors who had built railways, docks, and public utilities had always done well out of their work. In the third place the landed interest in Argentina had benefited from the increased value of land and the increased returns from increasing production. In the fourth place workers had been sufficiently well paid to induce them to migrate to Argentina and work there. By 1890 confidence became increasingly undermined for one general reason: the Argentine economy was not producing enough to satisfy all the demands on it. Prices in Argentina began to rise faster than wages and the real incomes of the wage-workers fell more and more rapidly as the crisis approached. The revenue of the national and provincial governments failed to increase fast enough to buy the gold or gold-backed currency necessary to pay their creditors. Finally it was beginning to look as if some of the contractors were not going to be paid.

This was a fairly familiar crisis of development in the international economy of the world before 1914. It had occurred several times in the history of the United States, in European countries, in Turkey, in Egypt, in China, in Australia, and in Canada and had occurred and was to occur again in other Latin American countries. How these crises were resolved had varied. In some instances, particularly in the Middle and Far East, such crises led directly or indirectly to politico-economic solutions of an imperialist kind involving taking over all or part of the state apparatus by European powers in order to organize and administer the community so that the foreign capitalists could be paid. In the Americas the solution of such crises by political domination followed by economic and administrative reform had not been possible. The United States solved its crises, such as that of 1837, in its own way, partly by the repudiation of debts and partly by the expansion of production. Intervention in Mexico by the European powers was a fiasco. After the United States had emerged from its civil war, which as a military exercise matched anything Europe could show, prudence suggested that political intervention in the Americas – at least anywhere near the United States – was hardly

feasible. Britain recognized the power of the United States in settlement of the Alabama claims and the Treaty of Washington, and
henceforth tactfully and consistently phased out its power in North
America. Canada was left to stand on its own feet, and the British
forces, never a threat to the United States, were bit by bit withdrawn
so that from a military point of view the British empire in North
America meant nothing.

General Rosas had already demonstrated that the European military and naval presence in the south Atlantic was an ineffective
factor in the equation of politics. Nothing subsequent to his overthrow had altered this circumstance. During an armed domestic
outbreak at the end of President Avellaneda's Presidency in 1880 the
British minister in Buenos Aires had observed from his position
sitting on the fence that the Argentine naval forces in the River Plate
were for the first time superior to the European naval forces there.
Without any consideration of the Monroe doctrine and what it might
mean in the south Atlantic, there were good reasons why a political
solution of an economic crisis could not be attempted by the European creditor nations, even if they had ventured to think in such
terms.

Well before Barings found themselves in difficulties the Argentine
community was afflicted with tension: bankruptcies, agitation, and
bitterness among the wage-workers, a decline in immigration, difficulties in obtaining credit, and political discontent directed against
the government both by young people and by some of the well-
established and respectable propertied class. The President, Juárez
Celman, had the enthusiastic support of the beneficiaries of the
development process: contractors, company promoters, and land
speculators. Their operations depended upon easy credit and optimism
about the future. Although the ultimate sources of the investments
being made depended upon production and sales at remunerative
prices, few of the immediate beneficiaries of the forces making paper
profits as landlords and company promoters, were much concerned
with the real problems of the productive capacity of the land and the
enterprises they were launching.

And yet there were in the community elements who recognized the
perils of the situation. As early as 1885 the European bankers and the
Argentine government had recognized the possibility that the rate of
capital investment might exceed the capacity to produce. A former
Minister of Finance, Dr Carlos Pellegrini, reached an agreement on

behalf of the Argentine government with a group of international bankers including Barings, Morgan & Co., and Banque de Paris et des Pays-Bas which put a limit on borrowing without consent of the banks and which gave to the bankers a first mortgage on the revenues of the Argentine customs. In fact no mechanism or control system existed which could check investment. As the tide of optimism mounted, energized by the rise in paper profits, both the Argentine government and the bankers themselves broke their agreement to limit investments. As a consequence the volume of investment and the volume of claims on the Argentine productive system mounted, particularly because so much investment was made in bonds and debentures on which interest payments were an obligation, and comparatively little in common stocks floated on hope and bearing no contractual obligation to pay anything if there were no surpluses earmarked out of productive operations.

Although the crisis in the Argentine economy was well developed by October 1889, a year elapsed before the leading figures in the City of London, such as the Governor of the Bank of England, grasped the significance of what was happening. The description and analysis of the situation provided by the British minister in Buenos Aires appears to have had no effect whatsoever either to alert the Chancellor of the Exchequer or to warn the Bank of England. In fact when the crisis broke in the City of London and the Chancellor of the Exchequer, Lord Goschen, and the Governor of the Bank of England were forced to co-operate in an emergency rescue operation and began talking about 'working on the Argentine Government', the political process in Argentina had already generated the basic elements of a solution. This is an important fact which must be underlined and emphasized, because it explains why the demand for foreign intervention in Argentine affairs was absurd and unnecessary and why Argentine myths on the same subject have no substance.

Let us look at what happened. The denunciation of the scandals of the *nouveaux riches* by members of the entrenched old aristocracy of Buenos Aires, the discontent and bitterness of the wage-workers, the idealism of youth, and the normal thirst for public office on the part of aspiring politicians combined in 1889 to bring together a great variety of critics of the President, Juárez Celman, and his supporters in a new political organization, the *Unión Cívica Radical*. The *Unión Cívica* began to rally the people against the government in demonstrations and outbreaks of violence. At the same time banking experts, both foreign and Argentine, were urging the government to alter its economic policies in the direction of tightening up credit, increasing taxation of imports – particularly of luxuries – and cutting public expenditure. In March 1890, Juárez Celman sent to the Congress a number of decrees for approval which constituted a full programme of reform to check inflation and deflate the boom: to levy customs duties in gold; to end the system of guaranteeing railway profits; to investigate joint-stock flotations; and to cut public expenditure. Unfortunately, Juárez's programme involved discarding and destroying the major part of his supporters, and this he was unwilling or unable to do. Congress did not act. No one could expect this, because the majority were beneficiaries of the existing system. Things went from bad to worse during March 1890. The financial resources of the province of Buenos Aires were so exhausted that the provincial authorities put up for sale their last asset – the Western Railway, which they owned. An unnamed group of capitalists bought the railway through the agency of the Bank of London and the River Plate for £8,200,000. Even this sum could not render solvent the government of the richest province of Argentina.

On 10, 11, and 12 April the *Unión Cívica Radical* led a series of large popular demonstrations in the streets of Buenos Aires. This achieved what the constitutional political processes had failed to do: a change in the personnel of the government. The President appointed a young, upper-class radical, Roque Sáenz Peña, as Foreign Minister, and an old, conservative aristocrat, José Uriburu, as Minister of Finance. Uriburu had only to look at the reports of the *Comisión Inspectora de Bancos* to find officially stated what everyone on the *Bolsa*[1] already knew, viz. that the law of Guaranteed Banks was being systematically violated by illegal emissions of currency and by granting credits on inadequate security or on no security at all. Uriburu was unwilling to break the banks. Instead he lent money to the National Bank and the Provincial Bank of Buenos Aires, but he demanded the resignation of the president of the National Bank. At the same time he raised import duties by 15 per cent and decreed the collection of 50 per cent of them in gold.

Faced with Uriburu's demand that he sack the president of the National Bank and thus start a house-cleaning of the administration, Juárez Celman chose his supporters and refused to take action. Uriburu resigned and the gold premium jumped from 118 to 165 in

[1] Stock Exchange.

one day. A new flood of paper currency was released and the Congress authorized the National Hypothecary Bank to issue new mortgage notes to the amount of 100 million pesos. Early in the morning of 26 July, militants of the leadership of the *Unión Cívica Radical* appeared in the streets with arms in their hands. The government troops began firing. Four naval vessels anchored in the river commenced shelling the government troops on behalf of the insurgents. Fighting continued all day, through the night and the next day. The President left Buenos Aires, but the Vice-President remained. Towards the evening of the second day of fighting the revolution came to an end. An armistice was arranged and an amnesty proclaimed.

Although the *Unión Cívica Radical* had initiated the movement of opposition to the government, it was the defection of the navy and its capacity to shell the government troops which obliged the President to reconsider his position. He tried to cling to office, which meant perseverance in a policy of inflation and debt repudiation, but the Vice-President, Carlos Pellegrini, and the Minister of the Interior, the prestigious former President and conqueror of the Indians General Julio Roca decided that Juárez Celman must go. Such was their control of the political process that some of the members of Congress who had previously sustained the President now joined with the opposition in demanding his resignation. This he gave, and Carlos Pellegrini was sworn in as President.

Carlos Pellegrini was in many respects a representative figure of the ruling élite which had emerged as the result of rapid economic expansion initiated by Urquiza, Alberdi, and Mitre and sustained by Sarmiento and Avellaneda. He was a tall, handsome, elegant man, famous for feats of gallantry and gambling; the son of an Italian engineer and, on his mother's side, a kinsman of the Rt. Hon. John Bright, the Victorian radical reformer. As a youth he ran through a fortune and made another. He helped to found the Jockey Club, which the Perónistas burned down in 1953 as a symbol of the social exclusiveness and power of the oligarchy. But Carlos Pellegrini was something more than a sybaritic and cosmopolitan inspiration of the rich. He had a shrewd understanding of the economy, a thorough knowledge of political possibilities, and a capacity for firm and carefully measured action in the long-term interest of his country and his class.

Once in the presidential office he extended the base of his government's power by taking into his Cabinet men from the opposition like Vicente López, who became Minister of Finance. These he balanced with representatives of the old-established landed aristocracy and so laid the political foundation for a solution of the economic crisis.

One course of action Pellegrini completely rejected: a policy of debt repudiation and going it alone. The Argentine economy, tied as it increasingly was to world markets, and the position of the dominant groups, dependent as they were upon the international market for commodities and capital, excluded the possibility of autarky. Assuming that Argentina was obliged to keep open its international connections, there were alternatives, and these Pellegrini began to explore. He could either reach some kind of arrangement with the present moneylenders or he could find a new lot. Juárez Celman had explored the possibility of reliance on German and French financial resources in place of the heavy reliance on the existing combination which was predominantly English and French with a marginal German participation. The exploration had yielded the information that the Germans were both cautious and strict, and that dependence on them would require control of credit, land taxes levied in gold, exactly those policies which Juárez was incapable of imposing on the country. Pellegrini now turned to the Americans as a possible alternative.

At this time there had developed in the United States a considerable interest in Latin America as a new frontier of American enterprise and expansion. This interest had culminated in a law passed by Congress in 1888 authorizing the President to invite to Washington representatives of all the Latin Americas for the purpose of considering a customs union, uniform weights and measures, a common silver coinage, the development of an inter-American transport system, and other measures looking in the direction of big and better United States of the Americas or Pan-American Union. The meeting authorized by the U.S. Congress was held, but instead of becoming a step along the road to the political and economic integration of the Americas, it turned into competition between Argentina and the United States about the preservation of the political sovereignty of the Latin American states. It was soon revealed that the Americans wanted everyone to speak English and do business on American terms. Specifically, the Americans wanted to expand their share of Argentine markets but were unwilling to open up their own markets to Argentine produce. The Argentine delegates, Roque Sáenz Peña and Manuel Quintana, ran rings around the American delegates in the conference debating, and succeeded in defeating or emasculating every American proposal of substance: customs union, reciprocal trade agreements, silver coinage, uniform port dues, common weights and measures, and a permanent arbitration tribunal.

The Argentines had just finished bloodying the American nose when economic crisis descended upon them. Unembarrassed, Pellegrini turned now to the Americans, not to beg but to see what they had to offer. A policy of harassing the British was set in train. A run on the banks was organized, but this back-fired because the British banks were able to pay all claims, whereas a number of Argentine banks could not. Then a tax was levied on deposits in foreign banks, and a 7 per cent profits tax on foreign joint-stock companies. While this anti-foreign and particularly anti-British manoeuvre was in progress, Pellegrini was feeling the Americans out. Not too much is known about the details of this negotiation. The British minister in Argentina only heard about it in March 1892 and was so alarmed that he sent home the longest cipher cable which had ever been despatched from Buenos Aires up to that date. It appears that by this time Pellegrini had discovered that the Americans demanded special legislation to protect their banks, and it was rumoured, possibly on the strength of an opinion expressed by an American admiral, that they also wanted a naval base. For a people as sensitive as the Argentines to the implications and value of political independence and for a government as shrewd as that of Pellegrini, the demand for special legislation was enough to end the possibility of doing business with the Americans. European banks and enterprises operated under Argentine law, and the treaties with Britain and France bound the Argentine government to nothing more than equal treatment under the law. The British law officers did not even regard taxes specifically levied on foreign-owned companies as illegal or the occasion of protest so long as the taxes were applied equally to all foreign-owned enterprises and not specifically to British enterprises.

Meanwhile the British were dealing with the crisis at their end. This was too serious and too immediate to consider gunboat diplomacy and intervention. The Chancellor of the Exchequer talked vaguely of 'working on the Argentine Government' as he anticipated the possible and terrible consequences of the bankruptcy of Baring

Brothers, but what he actually did was to abandon the central rule of *laissez faire* which forbade government interference in the processes of a free economy and government assistance to private institutions. Lord Goschen agreed to put the resources of the British Treasury behind the Bank of England in the form of joint guarantee of the bank and the government for a fund to be raised by the private and joint-stock banks to be used in turn to meet the claims of the creditors of Baring Brothers. It was believed, and so it turned out, that guaranteed payment of the claims against Barings would prevent a panic capable of wrecking the entire British financial system. As a result of the initiative of the Chancellor and the Governor of the Bank a fund amounting to £17 million was raised to assist in the orderly liquidation of Barings.

This, of course, was no solution to the problem of restoring the flow of capital resources back and forth between Argentina and Europe. For the time being at least the Argentine economy could not produce enough to pay its bills: to pay for what it consumed on current account together with the claims of its creditors. Pellegrini sent Victorino de la Plaza to London to discuss the matter with European financial interests. They appointed an international committee of English, French, German, and Belgian bankers under the chairmanship of Lord Rothschild. De la Plaza told them frankly that any attempt to extract the last farthing here and now from Argentina would produce misery and revolution. Three views emerged on the subject of how to deal with the interim.

The narrow-minded and dogmatic *laissez faire* school headed by *The Economist* agreed that Argentina ought to put its affairs immediately in order by new heavy taxation, the establishment of a gold-based currency, a severe cut in imports, and an immediate payment of all claims. The German and French members of the Rothschild Committee favoured a slightly more generous arrangement, viz. a small loan of £1,500,000 to be used to meet Argentina's immediate obligation while simultaneously the Argentine government should cut the volume of currency, reform its banking system and restrict credits, levy 100 per cent gold customs duties, and impose a severe land tax. Lord Rothschild and the British members of the committee took a longer and more liberal view. They proposed a loan of £12 – 15 million sufficient to meet Argentina's obligations at the moment and to keep the economy expanding. They based their argument on the fact that capital investment in new projects had ceased, existing projects were coming into production, Argentine exports were increasing, and within a few years Argentina would be able to support its debt structure and the addition made to it of the proposed new loan.

There was something to be said for and against each of these Anglo-European views. The policy advocated by *The Economist* was politically impossible, but *The Economist*'s criticism of Rothschild's policy of a large loan as simply a pyramiding of debt, which put off the day of reckoning, deeply affected the capital market with the result that the flow of capital to Argentina did not revive for another eight to nine years. On the other hand, the English bankers' view expressed by Lord Rothschild was based on a sound analysis of Argentine conditions, and it had the merit of leaving to the Argentines the opportunity of meeting the situation in their own way. The Franco-German view at the same time did involve a sketch of what was required if the flow of capital was to be resumed.

In the end the Argentine government discovered that the Americans or a predominantly Franco-German combination were unwilling to offer better terms than the predominantly British banking groups. For their part the Argentines faced the fact that they had to house-clean their own system and get rid of the fraudulent and parasitic elements feeding on inflation, loose credit, and the system of guaranteeing profits on railways.

This facing-up to the situation came slowly. The politics of the matter were fascinating and complex. *Unión Cívica Radical* had supplied the energy and initiative which had shaken the regime of Juárez Celman. The intervention of the navy had been necessary, however, to neutralize the force at the disposal of the government. The *Unión Cívica* was not able to claim that it had driven Juárez Celman from office. Power still belonged to the landed interest personified by Pellegrini and Juárez's own father-in-law, General Roca. As the elections of 1892 approached a new test of strength between the established interests and the youth and the outsiders of the *Unión Cívica Radical* began to develop. The elections for the Senate and Chamber of Deputies were held in February 1892 in a tense but comparatively peaceful atmosphere – only sixteen killed in Buenos Aires. The government's control was demonstrated, and the *Unión Cívica* were kept out. The new Congress looked just like the old one, but no one supposed this mattered. The real centre of power was the Presidency, and this became the focus of struggle. Pellegrini and his friends had two problems: to find a candidate and to ensure his election.

At this juncture of affairs they needed a new man. They needed, too, a man of great respectability identified with the landed interest – one of their own. The circumstances called, too, for a man pure in his public and private life and untainted by connections with the *nouveaux riches*. They found in Luis Sáenz Peña a man of honour and character – of an old and respected family and of professional reputation as a lawyer. He had the additional and not inconsiderable merit of being the father of Roque Sáenz Peña, the extremely able and radical young man who had demonstrated both his courage and ability as one of the Argentine delegates at the first Pan-American Congress, where he had baffled and defeated the *Americanos del norte*. It was believed, and rightly so, that the candidature of Luis Sáenz Peña would prevent the Radicals from putting forward the name of Roque Sáenz Peña as their candidate.

For Vice-President they selected Dr José E. Uriburu, the man who had attempted to clean up the Juárez regime from inside and who had unambiguously and publicly demonstrated a determination to purge the banks of crooks and parasites.

Having selected candidates with good images and having excluded the ablest opposition candidate capable of appealing across class lines, Pellegrini then prepared an assault upon the opposition. A few days before the election a conspiracy was discovered in the *Unión Cívica*. Their principal organizers were arrested and their headquarters occupied. Pellegrini moved cavalry into the federal capital and established his election headquarters in the central police station. The *Unión Cívica* attempted to discredit the proceedings by a strategy of abstention from the ballot. Not surprisingly the candidate with the right image won.

During the interim regime of Carlos Pellegrini the Argentine government was in a defensive position *vis-à-vis* its creditors and was probing the alternatives open to it. Once the well-established interests were in a commanding position it was possible to move towards a more comprehensive solution. Two basic problems faced the regime of Luis Sáenz Peña: (1) to secure a settlement with the creditors which obliged them to share some of the burden of reorganization while at the same time preserving freedom of trade and the flow of capital; and (2) to preserve the independence of Argentina in the world community. The problems were linked together so that without the solution of one the other could not be solved.

To achieve a solution, Sáenz Peña chose a strong ministerial team of which the two principal players were Dr J. J. Romero at the Ministry of Finance and Señor Tomás de Anchorena at the Ministry of Foreign Affairs. Romero had been associated with President Roca in his ultimately unsuccessful attempt in the early 1880s to stabilize Argentina's domestic currency. He had a long record of resistance to uncontrolled inflation and loose-credit policies, and he was fully familiar with the formal and informal undertakings given to European capitalists in order to procure development funds. Anchorena was a high, dry landed aristocrat, *muy argentino*, who spoke only Spanish and had never travelled outside the republic. A strange man to appoint to the Foreign Office, perhaps, but the head of the greatest landed family in Argentina, a kinsman of General Rosas, and a man who could be counted upon never to surrender the slightest scrap of Argentine sovereignty and independence.

Romero shared with the purists of *The Economist* doubts about the wisdom of the Rothschild policy of funding loans which postponed the day when the Argentine economy would have to stand on its own feet. On the other hand he was not prepared to achieve solvency by economizing exclusively at the expense of Argentina. He wanted a business deal and a business deal is a two-way proposition; both parties have to give if both hope to get. To achieve this objective of a materially beneficial deal he did two things; he removed Dr Victorino de la Plaza as the Argentine financial representative in London on the grounds that he was too much in the hands of the European bankers; and he published in *La Nación* a letter in which he stated boldly that Argentina was not paying its own way and that a settlement must be reached which enabled her to do so. Both Dr Romero's actions produced a shock effect. The gold premium rose; stock-market values fell; and the speculators cried out as if a word of economic truth resembled an obscenity uttered in church.

The *Arreglo Romero* was signed by the Argentine minister in London and Lord Rothschild on 3 July 1893. Although the agreement was complex, the principles of the deal were simple. The Argentine government conceded to the bankers an abandonment of their claims on the Buenos Aires Water Supply Drainage Co., thus easing the position of Baring Brothers who had underwritten the enterprise. They agreed further that the national government would take over the debts of the Argentine provinces. The bankers on their side agreed to accept reduced interest payments for five years and to suspend amortization payments until 1 January 1901. Altogether interest payments were reduced by 30 per cent. In the case of defaulted provincial securities, the bankers agreed to accept a reduction of claims and of interest in exchanging provincial bonds for national bonds. The system of railway guarantee was abolished and claims under guarantee clauses were paid at a rate of approximately 50 per cent. After 1905 guarantees ceased completely, and no railway companies were ever again given a guarantee of profits.

The whole complex of agreements between Argentina and her creditors was based on the principle that Argentina would pay out of current resources and not out of further borrowing. Romero insisted that Argentina would pay up to her productive capacity but would not mortgage the future. No one liked the agreement; the Argentine critics thought it too favourable to the holders of depreciated Argentine securities; the Europeans thought it too soft on Argentine defaulters. In fact it worked because it gave the Argentine economy time to grow into its capital structure and to bring real investment into production. The production of wheat, linseed, wool, mutton, beef, and live cattle for export expanded enormously and total receipts rose rapidly in spite of adverse terms of trade in 1893, 1894, and 1895. The price of Argentine exports began to rise in 1896. In 1897, Argentina resumed full interest and debt service payments a year sooner than the *Arreglo Romero* called for. Thus the conditions were prepared for a resumption of the investment process. Argentina could now draw once more from the pool of capital because she was once more feeding that pool out of her current production.

A business deal is an agreement based upon the real or presumed economic advantages occurring to the parties from the arrangements which the deal establishes. By this definition, the *Arreglo Romero* was a business deal from which political power was absent as a factor in the decisions made. But there were those who wanted to inject the factor of political power, and many more who feared or hoped that this would happen. This is not surprising in the circumstances of the 1890s. In November 1890, Lord Goschen had proposed to 'work on the Argentine Government', but what he meant by this never became clear, nor is there any present evidence that he ever did anything at all in the matter of applying political pressure to Argentina. At the height of the campaign instigated by Pellegrini against foreign banks in the winter (in Buenos Aires) of 1891, an unofficial delegation of British bankers acting privately and without the backing of their employers waited on the Foreign Office to urge intervention in the affairs of Argentina. Their objective was to create 'good Government' in Argentina, and they wanted 'some Power' to intervene and set up a provisional government, which they assumed would be a 'good Government'. These would-be interventionists thought the United States ought to be involved in this enterprise, but such was their woolly-mindedness that they appeared to believe Britain ought 'to do something', or else £200 million would be lost in 'a terrible collapse'.

The Foreign Secretary, Lord Salisbury, who was also the Prime Minister, did not take these proposals seriously. On the contrary he viewed with alarm the growing tide of sentiment in the City of London and in the press in favour of political intervention in Latin America generally. In August 1891, Salisbury seized the opportunity of a speech at the Mansion House to make it abundantly plain that the British government had no intention of intervening anywhere in South America, and he specifically alluded to the demand that the government undertake 'the regeneration of Argentine finance' when emphasizing that he refused absolutely and completely to take on the role of Divine Providence in South America.

When the Conservatives departed from office a year later, and Rosebery replaced Salisbury at the Foreign Office, there was a re-newed wave of speculation about the possibilities of intervention. There is no evidence that the change of government in any way affected the policy of non-intervention in Latin America, but a curious episode threw a revealing light on the political factors in the relations between Britain and Argentina in particular and between Argentina and the rest of the world.

This curious episode developed out of the use of words and a leak in the Foreign Office's security system. In January 1893, Lord Rothschild went to the Foreign Office to ask Rosebery to help him hurry up the Argentine government in the matter of transferring about £6 million of bonds connected with discharging the contrac-tors' bills of the Buenos Aires Water Supply and Drainage Company. Rosebery agreed to ask the British minister in Buenos Aires to take up the matter, and Rothschild paid for the cable instructing the minister. The important part of the cable read as follows: 'Buenos Aires Water Supply and Drainage Company ask for an intervention to obtain more equitable and considerate treatment from the Argentine Government . . . Do what you can. The matter involves large interests . . .'

Lord Rothschild may have been probing to see how far Rosebery might be swayed from the traditional policy of non-intervention, but there is nothing in the record before or after this cable to suggest that any change in policy was contemplated. Rosebery, however, used the word intervention which no longer meant an act of making solemn representations by one government to another, but had come to suggest the fleet and troop landings. Had the word remained lodged in a cable to Buenos Aires no harm could have been done. As it was, someone in the Foreign Office leaked the news to the City of London, or maybe Lord Rothschild did. In any case the rumour went round that Britain was planning to intervene in Argentina.

When the British minister received his instructions he waited on Señor Anchorena and presented him with a polite and moderate Note about the matter of the bonds. Anchorena was friendly, and the British minister described his attitude as 'most considerate' and, it should be added, co-operative and effective. Then came the leak. The rumour spread through the City of London that 'intervention' was being planned. Rumour echoed in Buenos Aires in the form of a press despatch to *La Prensa*. Anchorena acted at once. He called the British minister to the Foreign Office and presented him with a Note which read:

'I must inform you that both the Ministry for Foreign Affairs and the Ministry of Finance have considered themselves bound not to admit any intervention in matters connected with the Public Debt except that of the bondholders or the firms chosen and recognized by the Government as Intermediaries, as it is thought that no foreign official action can be admitted by the Argentine Government, and still less that of other Agents not the private representatives of the Creditors themselves.'

The British minister was thoroughly worried. He cabled home for instructions. The Foreign Office dug out a copy of Lord Palmerston's Circular Memorandum of 1848 stating the policy of the British government in respect to the collection of debts from foreign states, i.e. that ordinarily this was no British official concern. The British minister in Buenos Aires was by inference blamed for what had happened. He was told to keep his papers better locked up.

Other efforts were made to move the British government to intervention – over whether compulsory militia exercises on Sundays constituted a basic infringement of the human right of Welsh settlers in the Chubut; over an alleged robbery of a British scientist, who turned out to be a pedlar of remedies for venereal disease; and so on – but nothing shook the resolution in London to keep out of Argentine politics and preserve relations of equality and cordiality.

Some years later, in 1902, the British government joined with the German and Italian governments in blockading the ports of Venezuela in an effort to force the Venezuelan dictator Cipriano Castro to honour obligations to British, German, and Italian nationals. The Argentine government at once sprang to the alert. The Foreign Minister, Luis Drago, sent a Note to the heads of states asserting as a principle of international law the illegitimacy of a recourse to force in settling debt problems. For some years the Argentine government worked to gain acceptance for this principle. At the second Hague Peace Conference in 1907 the United States proposed that force be declared illegal in matters of debt collection so long as the defaulters agreed to arbitration and the assessment of claims by arbitration. Argentina seconded this proposal on the principle that it enhanced at least an important feature of what had come to be known as the Drago doctrine. The proposal was accepted by a vote of 36 to 0 with 8 abstentions. One of Dag Hammarskjöld's forbears was the Swedish delegate and he spoke against the proposal on the grounds that it gave an indirect sanction to the use of force. The Drago doctrine, as accepted by the Hague Conference, was, however, a very true expression of Argentine high policy. The Argentine government, while strenuously opposed to unilateral intervention in the affairs of sovereign states, did believe in the sanctity of debt contracts and in business negotiation to deal with revisions which the passage of time and changes in circumstance might reveal as necessary for economic development.

The Argentine concern with political sovereignty was not solely a product of moral passion for independence, nor was it less in the heyday of the landed oligarchy than in the days of General Rosas or Hipólito Yrigoyen or General Perón. The Argentine leaders never lacked a clear understanding that political independence is an absolutely essential foundation for advantageous economic and financial organization, and that this independence is of especial importance to communities which borrow and lend, buy and sell in international markets. The Argentine leaders of this age understood with equal clarity that the condition for a beneficial participation in the international commodity and capital markets was a capacity to fulfil contracts and that this capacity is a two-way or three-way proposition in which political violence, no matter which party uses it, destroys economic co-operation and the fruits thereof.

On the whole, the British government understood and respected the Argentine position. Inasmuch as Britain was Argentina's chief trading and investment partner until World War II this was an enormous advantage to both. For Britain this large-scale commercial and financial relationship involved no political costs such as Britain was increasingly incurring in Africa and Asia and the Middle East. For Argentina the advantages were many: freedom to manage its internal affairs in any way the pushing and hauling of domestic politics dictated; freedom to enjoy the advantages of competition among buyers, sellers, lenders, and investors; and finally, and perhaps most importantly, the consciousness of independence and capacity to express the aspirations of the less well-developed Latin American communities.

If the British government understood and respected the Argentine position, the same cannot always be said of all the members of the British business class. The men who went to the Foreign Office seeking political intervention in the Argentine political processes with the object of setting up a 'good Government' represented a strain of opinion which produced irritation and wariness in Argentina, and with good reason. Business leaders of this type were apt to feel that 'Argentina owed them a living', and that when things went awry only the Argentines were to blame. They were, too, insensitive to Argentine annoyance. For example, in the early years of the twentieth century two British-owned Argentine railways decided to amalgamate and they applied to the *British* Parliament for permission to make the necessary changes in their charters. Fortunately, the British government was not, at least in South American matters, very sensitive to the influence of the 'imperialist' business class, who, long before the working classes and the socialists had any influence on government policy, were very apt to ask for state intervention to solve their problems to their advantage.

If British political inactivity in Argentina contrasted markedly with the high level of British economic activity, the reverse may be said of the Americans during the quarter century between the first Pan-American Conference and the outbreak of World War I. The democratic imperialists of the United States had triumphed over and reduced to impotence the native Indians. They had robbed the Mexicans of their frontier lands: Texas, New Mexico, and upper California. They had bought the Russians out of Alaska. They had confined the British to what was then the fringe of the continent. By the 1890s they were looking for fresh fields of influence to control. The purely defensive doctrine of President Monroe was subtly transformed into a claim to primacy in the two American continents. This the Argentines were disposed to resent and resist, and their government was in a position to make effective a policy expressing their opposition to the United States. At this time the United States had far fewer economic connections with the River Plate than the European states, and they invested very little capital there. Their tariff laws and sanitary regulations in respect to the trade in live cattle and frozen and chilled meat were serious obstacles to the sale of Argentine wool and meat in the American market. Argentina, too, was a long way from the United States. Finally the Argentine governing élite had little sympathy with the puritanical, middle-class culture which predominated north of the Río Grande. For them France was the object of their worship and the place where they preferred to spend their wealth. The horse culture, the haber-dashery, the public schools, and the sporting life of the British upper class likewise attracted their interest, and brother spoke to brother across the barriers of language, religion, and oceans. To put it bluntly the liberal oligarchs who dominated the political life of Argentina much resembled the liberal oligarchs who dominated the political life of Britain, and neither had much in common with the business class which dominated the political life of the United States.

The Baring crisis in all its aspects – political and economic – was resolved before the outbreak of the Spanish-American and the Boer Wars. The golden age of Argentina then dawned. Politically independent and economically prosperous, Argentina seemed destined to become one of the richest communities in the world and the leading nation in Latin America. During the decade before the outbreak of World War I, Argentine productivity increased enormously. Capital and immigrants flowed in so that activities requiring more capital and manpower such as cereal production and

modern meat packing added a new expansive dimension to the
Argentine economy. Wheat and linseed exports grew from 5 per cent
of Argentine exports in 1870 to 20 per cent in 1900 to nearly 50 per
cent in 1914. Simultaneously all exports were expanding: from 1900
onward at the rate of 5 per cent a year. The landed class and the
controllers of the supporting commercial structure grew enormously
rich so that in the pleasure capitals of Europe Argentina became a
synonym for wealth and luxury. The grand palaces of the aristocracy around the Plaza San Martín in Buenos Aires and the *petits
hotels* in the *Barrio Norte* rivalled the town houses of the British
aristocracy. Magnates hired private railway coaches and even trains
to transport their establishments from their winter residences to
their summer homes. One *estanciero* took his own herd of milk cows
to Europe in order to ensure that his children had the right milk to
drink. The Jockey Club in the Calle Florida was a centre not only
of private recreation of the upper class, but a treasure house of books
and works of art.

Wealth of this description filtered down through society, but it
tended to concentrate in Buenos Aires and to a lesser extent in
Rosario. Few Argentines were absolutely poor, for food was abundant, cheap, and good. The educational system at the primary level,
at least in the cities, was as good as that developed in Europe and
the United States. The supply of housing tended to run behind demand but not so far behind that people had to resort to self-help
in the shape of *villas miserias* as they have done during the past
thirty years. Nowhere in Argentina during this time was life so hard
that it discouraged immigration from Europe. No one today who
goes to a mass gathering in, say, the football stadium of Boca Juniors
or Huracán or spends Saturday evenings in the working-class
barrios of Buenos Aires or Rosario can doubt that for at least three
generations Argentines have been well fed, adequately clothed, and
to some extent educated, for the men and women one sees are predominantly big, healthy, good-looking, self-confident people whose
immediate forbears knew little of malnutrition, cold, and persistent ill-health.

*

The liberal Argentina planned in the 1850s by Alberdi and
Urquiza, put into practical working order by Mitre, Sarmiento,
Avellaneda, and Roca, and brought safely through its crisis of de-

velopment by Pellegrini lasted until the great world depression of 1929. Applying a variety of quantitative tests, this liberal regime can be counted successful. Between 1869 and 1929 the population increased from 1,750,000 to 11,600,000 or at a rate of 3·2 per cent a year compared with a growth rate of 1·8 per cent a year from 1930 to 1962. Productivity rose at an average of between 4·5 and 5 per cent from 1850 to 1928. Total capital increased at roughly 5 per cent a year. Income *per capita* rose from 2,308 pesos (at 1950 prices) in 1900–04 to 3,207 pesos in 1925–29. It is not so easy to measure political progress, but if we associate the notion of political progress with the existence of political non-violence, we can discern a growth of stability and a diminution of recourse to arms in the making of political decisions. More people voted and fewer of those elected were turned out of office by force, or shows of force, than was the case before 1860 and after 1929. At the highest level only one President was dismissed by revolution, and only two were obliged to meet revolutionary challenges which they overcame.

Since 1929 the Argentine community has not fared so well as it did in the epoch of liberalism. A number of indicators suggest that before 1929 the Argentine gross national product was far above the world average. Even in 1950 it was better than average. Today it is well below the world average. In political terms Argentina has not been a stable community. Argentina did not obviously weather the Great Depression as well as a number of other comparable communities such as Canada, Australia, or Mexico, or great communities like the United States. Compared with communities which have suffered great political disasters like Germany, France, and Japan, Argentina has done very badly. It is the object of the remaining chapters of this book to enquire into why this has been so; why a golden age has been succeeded by an age of lead; and further whether there is any reason to suppose that the age of lead is drawing to a close and that a more glowing age can be expected.

The age of gold did glow indeed, but no one must be blinded by the dazzle. The old liberal Argentina depended on a great many political and economic relations which were destroyed or profoundly changed by the Great Depression. Furthermore the dynamics and the stability of the liberal order were related to a set of internal circumstances which were bound sooner or later to reach a limit, and inevitably would present the community with a problem of transcending those limits or falling back into stagnation and conflict.

In the first place the Argentine economic order and a large part of its productive mechanism were based on the assumption and on the fact of free, unrestrained, and competitive international marketing. Free trade unimpeded by tariffs, quotas, and controls was not, of course, a universal system, but there was a sufficiently large free market, particularly for foodstuffs, to provide a practical *raison d'être* for the Argentine economy. The market for industrial products was less free, but this was of little immediate consequence for Argentina because it was not a producer of industrial products like steel, chemicals, and heavy and light engineering. On the contrary, the search for markets by industrial producers inhibited by tariff barriers elsewhere created certain advantages for Argentina which bought competitively. This was especially so in the years between 1896 and 1914 when the prices of industrial products tended to fall, or not to rise quickly, while the price of foodstuffs improved markedly. Although this relationship changed during World War I and was never restored to a state so favourable to Argentina as it had been before, it did not change so drastically that Argentina was compelled to reconsider policies which so evidently worked not badly and often to Argentine advantage.

In the second place the stable yet dynamic condition of the Argentine economy internally was based upon two factors: the availability of large supplies of good land and the availability of a large immigrant labour force which was predominantly poor but ambitious for the improvement of its lot.

From revolutionary times onward the land resources of Argentina had been distributed (nominally rented) in large blocks to small numbers of people. Families like the Álzagas, the Anchorenas, the Sáenz Valiente, the Aráoz, and so on possessed estates as large as English counties or more. Estates of these dimensions could be justified because there were few people and the character of cattle-ranching and sheep-farming was extensive. Except in Santa Fé province, and here and there on the frontier where land was given to railways or colonization companies, land continued to be alienated by the state in large blocks until most or all of the usable land was under private control. By the end of the nineteenth century this had come to pass. The landowners, however, lacked workers. The gauchos, whom the *caudillos* had brought into subjection, were neither numerous enough nor socially adapted enough to provide a labour force once the possibilities of cereal production, sheep-breeding, and chilled- and frozen-meat marketing began to be recognized and to develop. The landowners could only realize the potential of their assets by renting land, selling it off, and/or establishing large units of production employing modern capital equipment and wage-labour. So long as the landowners needed people to exploit their resources the advantage tended to rest with the working farmers (but not with the wage-workers), and any policy seriously adverse to them checked development (as it did in 1890–92 when immigrants began to leave Argentina). As the countryside began to fill up (i.e. land began to be utilized to the maximum permitted by the existing technology) the relationship of landowner to renting farmer and wage-worker began to change, and the clear advantages of ownership as distinct from opportunities to use land began to manifest themselves. Up to the Baring crisis, the government practised monetary and credit policies very favourable to owners and entrepreneurs. In respect of foreign creditors the government accepted the gold-backed currencies of Europe – principally the pound sterling – as its money of account and the one in which it paid its debts, but internally it employed a paper currency and permitted loose-credit policies. Inevitably creditors and wage-workers suffered and the landowners and working farmers enjoyed the advantage of prices rising faster than wages and debt collections. After the Baring crisis and the solution of the Argentine balance of payments problem the internal currency was stabilized with a gold backing and the banking laws and banking administration were tightened up so that credit was more closely related to assets than hitherto. This change put a further new burden on the renting farmer, and tended to separate him from the landowner as an economic ally. In 1912 there was an attempted strike among farmers known as *el grito de Alcorta*, and real discontent was a factor in the swing to the *Unión Cívica Radical*.

This represented a maturing of the situation. The system of land rental and share cropping had worked with comparative smoothness while land was freely available and the prices of cereals, meat, and wool were rising faster than the prices of goods consumed by the farmers and ranchers. Once the external market situation changed and good land became less available, tensions began to develop.

The politico-economic changes in the countryside were only a particular instance of the changes which came about as the immigrants began to settle down in the cities. As they grew more numerous and became rooted in Argentina, the way to individual fortune became less easy. So long as economic expansion provided opportunities of employment at wages high in relation to what they could earn in Europe and opportunities, too, to set up in business enterprises there was comparatively little tension in society. This absence of tension was reinforced by the fact that the newcomers were broken up into immigrant groupings and were not Argentine classes. Even so, too much tightening of the screw by inflation produced trouble, as it did in 1889–91 in the form of strikes and migration from Argentina. When inflation ceased after the Baring crisis the ordinary pressure of a capitalist society began to develop in the form of trade unionism, socialist agitation for limitation on hours of work and improved conditions of employment, and anarchist and syndicalist violence against the employers and the state. Fundamentally, however, all these problems and the solution depended upon the relationship of Argentina's agricultural, ranching, and meat-packing industries with world markets and upon the terms on which Argentina sold her products there and purchased what she needed. Since the Great Depression, a large and various literature has grown up directed to proving that the landed oligarchy, in connivance with the imperialist monopolists (principally British), selfishly created this situation by the use of their political power; that they deliberately obstructed industrial development; and that they consciously strove to oppress the masses and preferred foreign dominance to Argentina's national interests. There is some colour of truth in this argument, but it is not the truth itself.

On the subject of industrialization versus the development of agro-pecuarian industry there are several observations which must be made. We need pause very little to clear our minds of the popular cant to the effect that the large landed estates of Argentina constitute a feudal interest and are an obstacle to the growth of free capitalist enterprise. Argentine agro-pecuarian enterprise is free capitalist enterprise and always has been since the revolution and even earlier. No country in the world including Great Britain so long practised liberal and economic and commercial policies directed to leaving to market forces the determination of what was produced, who produced it, what was invested, and where it was invested. Profit maximization without state interference was a dogma of Argentine political life even under General Rosas and was enshrined as a liberal principle of public policy from Urquiza to Castillo. That being so, there is no reason to suppose that the dominance of agro-pecuarian industry owed anything to forces other than the propensity to maximize profits. What reason supposes investigation cannot disprove. None of the architects of liberal Argentina from Alberdi onward argued in favour of anything but economic development in general. They assumed this was a linear process, but one which could not be described because only the forces of enterprise and the calculation of advantages would reveal what actually constituted development. They had no prejudice against industry, and the Argentine constitution of 1853 specifically mentions industrial development as an objective. The leaders of the generation of the 1880s supposed that industrial development was a natural aspect of development. As a young man Pellegrini spoke of Argentine industrialization as a natural development, and in fact industry began to develop in the 1880s. The *Unión Industrial* was founded in 1887, and that was the time when one of the largest Argentine light industrial enterprises, Alpargatas S.A., was founded. There was talk at the time of protective tariffs to foster industrial development, and the Rural Society, speaking for the landed interest, pleaded defensively that nothing be done to prejudice Argentine sales in its best markets. Looking at the evidence of the 1890s and taking account of the profitability of agriculture and ranching compared with industrial activity at that time, there was no reason to suppose that industry would not develop as it did in Canada or Australia or other states producing primary products.

The principal factor which determined Argentina's course of development in the direction of extreme specialization in agriculture and ranching was economic. In 1896 the terms of trade began to alter in a way favourable to producers of food products, and these terms of trade became progressively and even fantastically favourable to Argentina until 1929, except for a period after World War I in 1920–24. The production of foodstuffs, linseed, and wool was very profitable. Capital naturally flowed into these activities, and commercial and industrial activities nourished by the agro-pecuarian sector. It was so patently economically advantageous to do what Argentina in fact did that it seems a waste of time and a profitless exercise to look for any other explanation of what happened. Argentina became a highly specialized producer because it was profitable to do so, and those who profited most had no motive to seek alternative policies.

As a result of the development of the agro-pecuarian interest and its absorption of capital in its infrastructure of commerce, transport, and processing there existed in Argentina very little countervailing power interested in autonomous industrialization. The dominant interests had no political or military motives for stimulating heavy industry and engineering. The middle- and working-class opposition to the economic élite had no economic programme apart from more jobs for themselves, more prestige, or better wages and working conditions. They did not seek to change the character of the economy, but merely to get more out of it for themselves. This was a legitimate objective, but not one which had anything to do with industrialization. Any attempt to develop a large-scale industry for the supply of capital equipment for agriculture, ranching, transport, or processing would have immediately raised the costs of the most powerful interests because, no matter what technology might have been employed, the unit costs of complex equipment produced for small markets are high.[1]

In the years between 1900 and 1930 the proportion of Argentine manpower employed in industry remained fairly constant in the neighbourhood of 25–26 per cent compared with 36 per cent engaged in agriculture and ranching. Some industrial enterprises such as meat-packing were large-scale, capital-intensive industries, employing large bodies of workers organized in assembly line patterns. These industries were not, however, the nucleus of autonomous industrial growth. Their size and prosperity depended, like that of the ranchers, on the export economy. True, there was tension between the ranchers and the meat-packers over prices and terms of sale which prompted the ranching interests to make several attempts to form packing plants owned and controlled by the producers, but this was not the sort of economic tension which characterized the antagonism between industrial interests and agrarian interests in the United States, of which the American Civil War was only one manifestation, or the serious differences between the western agricultural provinces of Canada and the protectionist industrial interests in Ontario and Quebec.

Another feature of the Argentine economic scene was the relative absence of solidarity between industrial workers and employers which

[1] The Canadian farmers, for example, had this experience imposed upon them because they did not have power but only the right to bargain from positions of weakness.

in the United States and Canada and to a certain extent in Britain and Germany transcended the class antagonisms arising out of the wage-bargaining process and the social separation of employees and employers. In the United States and Canada the 'full dinner pail' argument more often united industrial employers and industrial employees in support of tariff protection against foreign industrial competition than class antagonisms separated them. In Britain free trade and cheap food united workers and, even after the formation of the Labour Party and the decline of the Liberal Party, this common ground between the two sides rendered even the Conservative Party wary of policies which might impair the cheap-food programme long dear to the hearts of the industrial interests. In Argentina, on the other hand, this class collaboration on the basis of a growth strategy was not well developed. In the railways, which were big employers of skilled labour, an equilibrium had been reached and institutionalized before World War I, so that the organized, skilled railway-workers and the railway companies got along together reasonably well. The railways were part of the agricultural economy; they were not the focal point of industrialization, and their management had the same interest as meat-packers and ranchers in buying their capital equipment where it was cheapest or where it met their technical requirements. The meat-packers were strongly anti-union, and pursued policies of paternalism which rewarded the obedience of key skilled men and offered frank, open, and often brutal opposition to formation of unions and bargaining on behalf of the unskilled and seasonal workers. The large service and commercial sectors of the Argentine economy bigger in their use of manpower than agriculture and ranching, were characterized by employers' opposition to all bargaining, and on the employees' side on one hand by lower-middle-class notions of obedience and respectability, and on the other by the opposite of anarchist and syndicalist intransigence. In any case the large service sector contained few elements of autonomous growth, for in the main the commercial and service apparatus of society was geared to serving the needs of the dominant agricultural and ranching industry and its beneficiaries.

Just as there is a simple economic explanation of the dominance of the agricultural and ranching interests so there is an equally simple explanation of the close Anglo-Argentine relationship in the epoch of liberalism. The international trading policies of Britain and Argentina were similar and complementary. There is no need of a paranoiac theory of conspiracy to explain the fact that Britain was a big supplier and investor in Argentina and Argentina a big supplier of Britain. The loose use of phrases like 'monopolistic imperialism' by men like Scalabrini Ortiz and Puiggros imply a political relationship of patron and client, of dominance and subordination, which they cannot prove. The Foreign Office archives up to World War I are open for anyone to read, and what can be read there suggests that at the level of international politics the British government knew very little about Argentina and cared less. As far as they were concerned, no news was good news. In the Foreign Office papers four fat volumes are concerned with the extradition of a crooked Liberal M.P. and company swindler named Balfour, whereas not more than a dozen pages concern the great Baring crisis. When one analyses the dozen pages they amount to a decision recorded in one word in red ink written by the Marquis of Salisbury to the effect that the British government intended to do nothing. One British Minister recorded the observation that British businessmen who thought they could do better investing in Buenos Aires than in Bolton or Bradford could not expect the assistance of the British government. One of the most attractive and beneficial aspects of the Anglo-Argentine relationship was the fact that it cost nothing politically. There were no troops, no bases, no administrative officers such as there were in Egypt or China, and there were no antagonisms with other great powers which were the reactive consequences of the evil romanticism of the imperialists of the Great Powers.

If there was no political imperialism in the relations of Argentina with the rest of the world, this does not mean that there were no imbalances of power between Argentina and other nations which, in crises, worked disadvantages for her. Argentine policy was based on the assumption of a competitive international market. Experience suggested that so long as such a market existed Argentina as well as her trading partners derived benefits measurable in terms of economic growth and increasing social well-being. In fact Argentina rose in the international market place from poverty to riches, but not necessarily riches for all Argentines, and she did so through the operation of recognizable economic factors: specialization of work and concentration on the exploitation of resource advantages summed up as comparative cost advantages; consumption of products marketed under competitive conditions; the use of capital at competitive rates of interest. When, however, the basic assumptions and increasingly the practice of the international economy began to change, the advantages of high specialization characteristic of the Argentine economy ceased to be a strength and became a weakness like that of a dinosaur in the presence of a change of climate which reduced its food supplies and/or increased the ferocity of more mobile carnivores.

Chapter 5

The Politics of a Free Society

A LARGE PROPORTION of this book has been devoted to the economic affairs of Argentina for the good reason that economic development has been a central problem of the Argentine community and has been so regarded by Argentine leaders. But economic policy and economic development are but instruments in society. What economic policies are devised and how they are executed are matters of politics; a matter of values generated in the community; and a matter of the capacity for leadership of those who have access to the public power. We must now, therefore, consider the political development of Argentina with a view to discovering, if possible, what has produced the stagnation and confusion which has characterized recent Argentine experience.

The Argentine political system, designed by the great liberal reformers who emerged following the overthrow of General Rosas in 1852, was an open one, in which the role of government was important and central, but none the less limited to the preservation of order and the protection of property necessary for the working of a free, competitive economy. In fact, as we have seen, the government did much more than preserve order and protect property. It induced investment and stimulated immigration, and the government itself was a major agency in mobilizing resources for the building of the infrastructure of transport, port works, urban public works, and institutions necessary for development of the agricultural and ranching industries and for the assimilation of the newcomers into society.

The liberal reformers conceived of government as an institution created by the community, responsible to the community, and in which members of the community might participate through political processes such as election, freedom of speech and publication, and the observation of publicly known laws made by legitimate public legislative bodies. The Argentine constitution of 1853 established a federal representative republic whose legislature and executive were created by election. Over most of Argentine history since 1853 this constitution has been operative, and even when the executive power has been overthrown and seized by force, the military men who have done so have either proclaimed their intention, or have been obliged by the pressure of public opinion, to work this constitution. Even the present revolutionary government of General Juan Carlos Onganía, which has suppressed political parties, closed the Congress, and appointed the government of the provinces, operates according to laws made in the past or made by itself and has promised, and more or less preserved, freedom of speech, freedom of publication, and freedom of access to the government.

The purpose of saying this is to emphasize that for more than a century the predominant sentiment of the Argentine community has been favourable to open political processes. A powerful factor in the overthrow of General Perón was his endeavour to destroy these processes in favour of a closed system dominated by an official party. Totalitarianism and authoritarian concepts of government have commanded neither widespread support nor great enthusiasm. Even in the armed forces which have intervened much in Argentine politics and imparted to the Argentine political image an authoritarian and anti-democratic colour, predominant sentiment and patterns of action during and after the numerous *golpes de estado* have not been persistently anti-democratic or anti-constitutional or authoritarian. Compared with many communities reputed to be free and open, Argentina under the regime of General Onganía is a free society even though it lacks a representative and democratically elected government. This can be asserted in terms of freedom of comment and expression, access to the public authorities, and enforceable legal rights, while acknowledging at the same time that the *intendente* of Buenos Aires has forbidden the performance in the municipally owned *Teatro Colón* of a distinguished opera by a famous Argentine musician, that there are anti-communist laws, and that right-wing propaganda has been suppressed. In short, Argentina today, under a revolutionary regime brought to power by a military *coup*, with no intention so far declared of restoring constitutional democracy, is still no better or no worse in the matter of freedom than many communities which are esteemed free and democratic.

This must be remembered because one of the long-standing central facts of Argentine politics is the contentious variety of public opinion

and of the social, economic, and political organizations in which
these diverse views flourish. For over a century Argentina has been a
developing (often a very rapidly developing) and expanding community. Even during the last thirty years of comparative stagnation in
growth rates, there have been great changes in the economic and
social structure. This being so, Argentine society is not unexpectedly
a mobile society and movement up and down the social structure is
as evident there as in other open communities where free, private
enterprise is a predominant mode of economic activity. Like the
United States or any western European country, Argentina has a
pyramidal socio-economic structure in which income is a major
factor in determining the eventual, if not the immediate, status and
range of possibilities of an individual and his family. Sociological
study indicates that the educational system, the career open to talents
in the armed forces, the changing nature of business enterprises, the
buying and selling of all types of property including land, and the
informal and formal processes of politics provide a variety of channels enabling individuals to move up the social scale. Argentine
society is not rigid, and in some respects is more flexible than other
immigrant societies. Lacking problems of race and colour and having
drawn a high proportion of its European immigrants from the old,
civilized societies of the Mediterranean, Argentina has had fewer
problems of assimilation than the United States and Canada, and
this has rendered social movement somewhat freer and easier.

While social mobility is a characteristic of Argentine society, one
is bound to observe, however, that the Spanish inheritance, reinforced
by migration from the European Mediterranean, has imparted to
the social structure a feeling for social distance between the levels and
segments of the structure, which give it a much more aristocratic or
oligarchic character than the degree of mobility would suggest. In
the United States, the social structure is as pyramidal as in Argentina,
and distance in terms of wealth, opportunities, and social accomplishments between the top and the bottom is probably greater than in
Argentina, but in American society the difference between the top
and the bottom is money and technical and cultural accomplishments, and little else. The Americans have an egalitarian ethos, and
this is the source of the traumas they suffer in the presence of the
realities of the social structure and its hatreds, prejudices, and
antagonisms. This is not the case in Argentina. In Argentine society
the classes and strata of the social structure are separated from each

other not just by money and technical and cultural accomplishment, but by their feelings for their social position. In the United States, George Winthrop III is a joke, but in Argentina Juan Carlos Jiménez de Jiménez y Sánchez is regarded very seriously because a man's family and his connections are part of the prestige which enables him to hold up his head and assert himself. Nobody in the United States cares whether George Winthrop Smith is the third or the thirty-third Mr Smith, but in Argentina a great many people will take seriously the meaning of a patronymic because they respect it and expect similarly to be respected. An Argentine taxi-driver asking the way of a lorry-driver does not shout 'Hi, bud, where's ....?', but 'Señor, por favor, donde ....?' Perón weakened himself greatly by trying to democratize the social relations of Argentina and to break down ceremonial distinctions by getting people to think of themselves as Pepe and Evita. The Argentines are as warm and informal in social intercourse in small groups as any people, but there is widely present a feeling for social distinction, the acquisition of which is a goal and a motive for action.

As a result of this feeling for hierarchy, the social separation, to which money, power, and cultural accomplishments contribute, is easily converted into social distance and into social habits obstructive of easy communication and understanding among individuals and groups. Thus the antagonisms, which differences of interest and understanding naturally and inevitably generate, are not so easily attenuated nor are compromises so easily reached as they are in communities where myths of equality bind people together by blurring reality.

For a variety of practical reasons largely connected with the desire and the need to develop economically, the landed élite, partially created and firmly entrenched by General Rosas, established Argentina as an open, *laissez faire* society with a representative system of government and a democratic mystique. These served the processes of development very well, but they constitute a source of friction and contradiction in the presence of the hierarchical social structure and the high regard for social prestige and honourable status. All Argentines cannot be Álzagas any more than all Americans can be Rockefellers, but in the American community the Rockefellers have been obliged to build their image in accordance with the needs of American social myths, whereas an Álzaga can be nothing but an Álzaga because he is admired and envied for being what he in fact is: rich, prestigious, and the centre of a family connection. A prestige system, however, implies as a condition of its existence that there are many without prestige. This they seek to acquire. The driving force of this quest perverts the political process away from the solution of relatively simple problems like the reconciliation of interests towards much harder questions of prestige and power for its own sake.

So long as Argentina was, in terms of numbers, a predominantly immigrant society, preoccupation with survival and advancement ensured that the great majority were concerned neither with prestige nor politics of a formal sort. Once development had taken place and the pace of development slowed down and people had time and the need to assess their position, the social distance generated by the prestige structure began to bewilder and afflict those who lacked it without provoking any determination to end what they respected and longed to have. Without being alienated the lower ranges of the social structure became discontented with their lot.

The 'generation of 1880' is a term used in Argentina to designate the men who presided over the rapid expansion of the economy, pressed forward the creation of an open society through secularized education, carried Argentina through the Baring crisis, and commenced the beautification of Buenos Aires. These men flourished in a situation in which the abundance of resources and the expansion of the economy provided prizes for all who had the inclination, energy, and cunning to pursue them and grab them. Increasingly after the Baring crisis the situation changed so that the distribution of glittering prizes and the creation of prestige situations for more and more people depended not so much on economic expansion as upon either redistribution of prestige positions or the invention of new ones not dependent entirely upon the possession of land and/or upon the infrastructure of the agricultural, ranching, and processing industries. Hence the desire towards more and more posts in the public service and the creation of more ladders upwards for the large number seeking to upgrade themselves. Sociologists have discovered, and find it hard to conceal their surprise, that the Argentine armed forces, for example, are not the preserve of the landed élite. In fact the cattle barons and landlords have comparatively little family and class connection with the armed forces, having regard for their growing occupation of key positions in the decision-making processes of Argentine politics. The Argentine armed forces are organized as a merit system with an open recruitment from all classes. Hence it is a ladder of upward social mobility which can from time to time be accelerated by participation in politics.

The political parties – or at least some of them – have contributed to the same process of social mobility, particularly the *Unión Cívica Radical* and its successors and the Perónist movement. It is interesting to observe that the *Unión Cívica* came into being just at the time when the easy distribution of prizes in the shape of land and railway concessions was coming to an end during the Baring crisis. It is worth remarking, too, that the most notable real reforms having some bearing on social and economic organization had a direct connection with the ladders of social mobility: the reform of the universities and the foundation of the nationally owned oil industry, *Yacimientos Petrolíferos Fiscales*; the first opening the gate wider to the professions and the other providing new opportunities for prestigious economic activity.

The Church, too, has provided opportunities for rising from humble to exalted positions. The Roman Catholic Church of Argentina has had its ups and downs in its relations with the state, but it has always had a special legal status the merits of which have sometimes been doubted by strong elements in the community and sometimes by the Church itself. Whatever the official or unofficial position of the Church, it is quite evident that socially the hierarchy of the Church is not a replica of the socio-economic hierarchy of wealth and earthly power, nor is the Church by reason of affiliation with the agricultural and ranching interests a bastion and support of the social and economic structure. Almost four out of five Argentine bishops are the sons of first generation immigrants. This by itself does not conclusively prove anything, but it does suggest beyond much doubt that the Church is not staffed with sons of the landed aristocracy, and it no more resembles the Church of pre-revolutionary France or contemporary Spain than does the Roman Catholic Church in countries like the United States. It is possible to believe that the very ambiguous and changeful role of the Church in Argentine politics over the last thirty years owes as much to the social background and ambitions of its officers as it does to the confusions and opportunism of Catholic social doctrine and to the temptations of the visible world.

To the social ladders provided to a mixed and heterogeneous immigrant society by the commercial and business world, the professions, the armed forces, and the Church there has been added the trade unions. The Argentine trade unions grew up with the economy, and were shaped by its development. They flourished long before Colonel Perón appeared on the scene to redeem and liberate the working class. They embraced, it is true, a minority of workers and were strongest among the skilled trades in the railways, printing, and textiles. They were pioneers of welfare and social policies, and the hospitals, pension funds, and building funds which they provided for their members involved the management of large funds and the organization of large and technically sophisticated undertakings. This, together with the influence they could bring to bear in politics, provided opportunities for pursuit of respectability and the acquisition of prestige. Perón simply stepped on the accelerator and made the vehicle run faster and carry more passengers to the point of breakdown. Trade unions in Argentina are big business in more than one sense, for their hierarchies control large funds and large amounts of property. Some are honestly administered and provide good services for their members, and some are not; but all have the common characteristic of providing the means by which energetic and ambitious individuals can rise to prestigious positions, the recognition of which is the constant object of their holders to obtain from the other prestigious hierarchies of the country.

To an inhabitant of swinging Britain the Argentine appears to be a very square community, and one too easily applies to it cliché adjectives like Victorian. A family prestige system requires an emphasis on a restrictive morality capable of preserving the structure of the family. It requires, too, the preservation of respectability and conceptions of honour and pure personal conduct. Argentines of all classes do take the ideal of purity, incorruptibility, and honourable conduct very seriously. The contradiction between ideal and reality does not stem primarily from the inappropriateness of the ideals but from the incapacity of the economic system and the political leadership over the past thirty to forty years to provide the material basis for a dynamic family prestige system. The consequence has been the political confusion connected with clamour for jobs and opportunities for which there is no adequate economic means of providing and with the struggle of one set of aspirants snatching jobs from one kind of possessor or other. All major social groupings in Argentina have a 'prestige-giving' structure and, therefore, none have so far committed themselves to making a clean sweep of all other, or even some of the other, prestige-giving structures. None the less each is impelled by the dynamic force of its own system to attempt to enlarge opportunities for its aspirants. So long, however, as the sum total of the economically viable opportunities is less than the demand for prestige positions, the political process can only be a zero-minus game.

If this general character of the socio-political dynamic is kept in mind, one can begin to understand political events in Argentina and grasp in some degree wherein the various political leaders and parties were successful or unsuccessful in preserving themselves and the public peace, which in any society is the only purpose and justification of power.

The contemporary pattern of Argentine politics began to emerge during the Baring crisis of 1890–95. There then appeared on the political scene at that time the *Unión Cívica*, to which in the course of its early evolution was added the adjective radical. At its foundation the *Unión Cívica* was a movement of marginal native elements; marginal in the sense that they had never been, or had not yet been, absorbed into the evolving social structure. One part of the *Unión* consisted of remainders of the popular movement which General Rosas had inspired and controlled, and which had been driven out of public life when the landed élite turned liberal, overthrew General Rosas, and embarked on a policy of rapid economic expansion through the importation of foreign capital and foreign immigrant workers. Leandro Alem, whose father was one of those executed the day after General Urquiza's victory in 1852, represented the old popular element in the new movement. The other major element in the *Unión* was young people who, partly because they had not yet come into their inheritance, were not yet enmeshed in the social structure and partly because they were seeking a place from outside the social structure, were disposed to view through idealist spectacles the sordid birth pangs of the *nouveaux riches* being generated by economic expansion. Associated with these major elements were individual members of the established aristocracy who viewed with both distaste and alarm the excesses and maladministration of the regime of Juárez Celman and recognized that its shortcomings would wreck the experiment in economic expansion and undermine real national independence.

The heroism, energy, and just indignation of the *Unión Cívica* must not blind the observer to its mixed character, for this mixed character explains to a considerable extent why intelligent leaders of the liberal élite like Carlos Pellegrini were able to use its force to overthrow Juárez Celman while at the same time they were able to exclude the *Unión Cívica* from power, and retain exclusive control of political decision-making during the transition from economic crisis to high prosperity and renewed expansion.

The leaders of the liberal élite differed among themselves, but they were never confused about the instruments of power. In working the liberal constitution of 1853 they relied for the control of the essential offices of the state upon the management of the electoral machinery and upon the control of the police and the armed forces to defend them against attempts to sweep them out of office by mass action or to work the electoral machinery to their disadvantage by getting the right people to the polls and counting the ballots in the right way. When rioting and street fighting broke out under the leadership of the *Unión Cívica* in July 1890, the armed forces came to the rescue not of the government but of the political bosses of the liberal élite, who were thus able to decide who should replace the President and what should be the new policies of the government. Electoral management backed by the police, with the armed forces in reserve, continued to be the pattern of power. As for policy, this became increasingly a conservative liberalism of which the essential objectives were to maintain economic confidence through stable currency, credit control, and the payment of debts. The tide of world economic development was flowing strongly in favour of Argentina, and the policies of the conservative liberals obviously worked in terms of expansion of opportunities.

The *Unión Cívica*, did not, however, disappear from the scene. As the élite grew richer the social distance between the classes grew, and respectability became more oppressive and impenetrable. It even became a civil offence to appear in the parks of Buenos Aires without a jacket, collar, and tie. Fashionable churches, fashionable theatres, fashionable tea-rooms, and fashionable clubs flourished to emphasize the pride of riches and position, and the marble palaces of the dead behind the walls of the Recoleto cemetery served to suggest that even death was not the leveller that some supposed. What Buenos Aires could not provide in the way of prestige, liberty, intellectual cultivation, and sensuous excitement Paris did. The prestige ladder mounted to the sky, but it was not markedly wider at the bottom than it had been before the Baring crisis, and this largely because the economy became increasingly set in one pattern.

The *Unión Cívica* became the *Unión Cívica Radical*. The addition of the adjective denoted a determination of the leaders to separate intransigently from the pyramid of power and to seek by revolutionary overthrow to make the constitution of 1853 work. They concentrated on two central activities: agitation among the masses of the people and endeavours to gain the support of the armed forces or part of them. The political *modus operandi* of the liberal élite ensured that the Radicals must be an extra-parliamentary party or nothing; and the strategy and tactics they adopted made certain that their organization and predominant modes of thought would be ill-suited to parliamentary forms of government and policy-making.

In the early years of the *Unión Cívica*, while it was still a mixture of old Rosistas, idealist youth, and concerned liberals, there was some hope that the *Unión Cívica* might have become an effective parliamentary party something like the Democratic Party in the United States or the Canadian Liberal Party. The liberal élite were no richer, no more corrupt, or no more selfishly devoted to entrenched economic interests than the Republican Party of the United States at the turn of the nineteenth into the twentieth centuries, and President Figueroa Alcorta was no more conservative than President Taft. But considering the similarities of the two immigrant, *laissez faire* big business societies, one must bear in mind the vast differences in the political traditions and styles of an English and a Spanish descended society; of the subconscious and inherited value systems of communities of which one regards money and business activity as a means to power and prestige and the other regards power and prestige as a means of acquiring money and economic benefits.

By the year 1900 Hipólito Yrigoyen had established himself as the sole leader of the Radicals. He was a defiant symbol and a representative of those who had not reached the top and were unlikely to do so. He was a *criollo* who had not got any prizes in the massive distribution of the 1870s and 1880s, and he shared none of the illusions or hopes of the immigrants. He had a blood relationship with the Rosistas for he was a nephew of Leandro Alem. He had been a student, a school-teacher, a lawyer, and a police official, and in none of these occupations had he found satisfaction or success. He was shrewd, intelligent, and uneducated. He lived always in a mean flat on the wrong side of the town from the *Barrio Norte* of the aristocrats. He never married his French mistress. He rejected the clear, rational dogmas of the liberals in favour of an obscure, verbose, misty German philosophy which disposed him to preach a vague and confused mixture of Spanish Catholic racism. All this earned him the contempt and finally the hatred of the élite, but it served to identify him as an intransigent outsider without committing him in any way to make a clean sweep of respectability and the social structure which it generated. Such a defiant rejection of the norms of the élite might have been excusable and even admirable had Yrigoyen grasped constructively the problems of his country, but these he imperfectly understood because he knew Argentina very well and the rest of the world not at all. Cloudy rhetoric and vague ideals are frequently the necessary tools of a politician's trade but in Yrigoyen's case they were too often not only the means of influencing people but the instruments of making policy.

Granted that Yrigoyen had little knowledge of economic problems and was little concerned with the social and economic problems of the immigrant working class, he understood very well the power structure of Argentina and what was needed to break it open on behalf of his own militants. On the one hand he went about Argentina which the élite only knew at second hand, if at all, setting up clubs and groups of believers in free, honest elections, all of them organized in direct relation with himself. On the other he concentrated on seeking to influence the officers of the armed forces to rise against the corruption and arrogance of wealth in order to purify and strengthen the state. To counter the controlled election he developed the tactic of public abstention from voting, thus puncturing the legitimating myth of electoral ritual. To counter the force which backed up the electoral fraud, he sought to suborn the instruments of violence. Given that politics is about power and not about what what is done with power, Yrigoyen was a serious realist.

But he had his limitations, and these are attributable to the origins of the Radical movement and to the confusion of Yrigoyen's ideology. A strong element in Yrigoyen's intransigent radicalism was conservative and traditional. The partisans of General Rosas, as distinct from the beneficiaries of Rosas' policies, had cherished a concept of freedom as much as the doctrinaire liberals: a concept of popular, gaucho freedom belonging to cowboy hunters, *charceros* (or small farmers), and slaughterhouse workers. This traditional concept of freedom worked strongly in the mind of Yrigoyen and his partisans. A vein of xenophobia ran forcibly in the Radical movement, and the search for *autenticidad* was directed to the *criollo* past not to the creation of a new nation out of immigrants.

For this reason the popular party of the outsiders was turned against the outsiders who were new to the country. The Radicals were at best suspicious of the immigrant masses and at worst hostile to them.

The immigrants for their part brought with them the predominant political ideas of their European homelands. Large numbers were non-political because their motives for migration were to improve their economic lot by acquiring money or property, but many discovered that they were wage-workers in Argentina as much as they had been wage-workers in Italy or Germany or Spain, and that they had workers' problems of hours of work, real wages, unemployment, and poverty. As an answer to these problems, European ideas about trade unions, socialism, and anarchism were received and flourished among the railway employees, the workers in the processing and milling enterprises, in the building industry, in the ports, and among the large army of waiters and servants who supplied the services demanded by the wealthy classes. These tendencies frightened the élite as much as or more than anything the Radicals could do. The Law of Residence passed in 1902 and the Law of Social Defence passed in 1910 empowered the government to deal directly with immigrant leaders by deportation. Strikes and anarchist violence were far from extraordinary events. In 1909 there was a general strike in which a clash between demonstrators and troops resulted in four dead and forty-five wounded. Later that year the chief of police of Buenos Aires was blown to bits by a bomb.

The Radicals, however, had no programme or strategy capable of mobilizing the popular political energy and directing it to rational, social objectives. Their demand for free, secret elections was something the socialists and trade unionists could support, but this ideal had little attraction for the syndicalists and anarchists. On the other hand, the willingness of the Radicals to rely upon military conspiracy was not in line with socialist conceptions of political progress, and it was not the kind of conspiring to act violently that commanded syndicalist and anarchist support.

This fragmentation of popular political life was an enormous advantage to the élite. Like the easy prosperity of the Golden Age between the Boer War and World War II it contributed to a false view of reality and left them with no challenge capable of obliging them to think with sufficient seriousness of the responsibilities which distinguish an aristocracy from an oligarchy. Individuals of intelligence, learning, and patriotism such as those who produced the great newspapers *La Prensa* and *La Nación* were aware of the short-comings of the élite and of the probable consequences of not leading the community towards a solution of the contradiction between the proclaimed principles of the constitution of 1853 and the actual practice of oligarchic control. The most profound aspect of this failure of the élite was their non-participation in politics and their unwillingness or incapacity to play a part in public life. In the Senate in 1908 only seven out of thirty members were landlords and only seventeen of 120 deputies in the House of Representatives were members of the landed class. A rich man who relies on a *mayordomo* to run his estate is soon transformed into a parasite, and so is a wealthy class which leaves to a few political bosses the control of the public life and thus fails to learn the arts of community living. When this happens the virtues of the rich become meaningless and their vices crimes.

One man who hoped that this could be prevented and strove to that end was Roque Sáenz Peña, one of the ablest, most farsighted, and courageous men in Argentine history, and one of the most tragic. He came of an old-established and respected family. He first appeared on the stage of public life as one of the Argentine delegates to the first Pan-American Congress. There he displayed extraordinary powers as a policy-maker and advocate, so that a plan, initiated as a device by which the United States proposed to control Latin America, was transformed at least on that occasion into a forum for the assertion of the equality and independence of the states of South America. When the Baring crisis developed, and the grip of the *nouveaux riches* on the state was shaken, Sáenz Peña was looked to as a young leader who might gain the Presidency not as a handpicked candidate but as one supported by the growing opposition. This possibility was short-circuited by the bosses, who nominated his father. Patriarchal values obliged the creative son to yield to the respected figurehead. Twenty years later the son was himself picked to occupy the Presidency, an attractive label for the old bottle.

Roque Sáenz Peña, however, was not his father, although by 1910 he was no longer young and rendered by illness older than his years. None the less he asserted himself. In 1905 Yrigoyen had inspired an unsuccessful revolt in the armed forces. In the succeeding election he had led a demonstration against entrenched interest in the form of a boycott of the elections – a device for registering negatively support for the Radicals. He had boycotted the election of Sáenz Peña. In

1 The principal monument in Buenos Aires to General José San Martín. Although San Martín was much more able and successful as a soldier and organizer than he was as a political leader, he has emerged as the one historical personage whom Argentines almost unanimously respect

2 Bernardino Rivadavia,
President 1826–7

3 Juan Manuel Rosas, Governor
and Captain-General of the
province of Buenos Aires,
1829–33, 1835–52

4 Bartolomé Mitre,
President 1862–8

5 Juan Domingo Perón, President 1946–55, and Eva Duarte de Perón

6 San José, Urquiza's *estancia* in Entre Rios

7 The battle of Curupayty, 22 September 1866, during the bitter
and bloody Paraguayan war in which Argentina, Uruguay, and
Brazil united against the Paraguayan dictator Francisco Solano
López and finally defeated him in 1870. This battle was a victory
for López. After it he slaughtered 1,500 allied prisoners

8 Arturo Frondizi (left), President 1958–62, greeting Senator
   Edward Kennedy in Buenos Aires
9 The Cathedral at Córdoba, in Spanish Colonial style

10 Arturo Umberto Illia,
President 1963–6

11 Juan Carlos Onganía,
President 1966–

12 Mass Society. A meeting at the Palermo racecourse, Buenos Aires. Football is even more popular than horseracing. Argentines play and watch every known sport with the possible exception of ice-hockey

13 Calle Florida, Buenos Aires. This straight, narrow, colonial street, now for pedestrians only, is one of the traditional centres of luxury, fashion, and the arts

14 A *villa miseira*. In Buenos Aires more than a quarter of a million people live in shanties built on waste land. Like multi-occupation in Britain they are a 'people's solution' of the housing problem

15 Boarding a *colectivo*. *Colectivos*, buses owned by their drivers, are an Argentine invention. In Buenos Aires there are thousands of *colectivos* and hundreds of separately owned lines providing cheap, frequent, and uncomfortable service to the public and good incomes to their owners

16   The Camp. Until comparatively recently and still to an important degree, Argentines of all classes depended for their well-being on the land, water, plants, and animals of the vast plains between the Atlantic and the Andes

17   Military ceremony at the Casa Rosada, residence of the President of the Republic on the Plaza de Mayo, Buenos Aires

18   The skyline of Buenos Aires from the River Plate

19   In the port of Buenos Aires. The power-station in the background runs on imported fuel and the loading equipment in the foreground handles cereals for export

20 The interior of a tractor plant. Argentina has the capacity to produce 250,000 cars, lorries, and tractors a year, but plants are numerous and small, overhead costs are high, and unit costs to the public high by European and American standards

21 A state school. The white *guardapolvo* is an attractive uniform prescribed in all state schools to minimize the impression of difference between boys and girls, rich and poor. Private schools tend to imitate English school uniforms

22 The sad *café*. Much of what gives character and movement to Argentine life begins and ends in the thousands of *cafés, confiterías,* and bars, some more squalid and some more elegant and luxurious than this one

23 A Perónista picnic in 1951. A Sunday gathering of the 'shirtless' from rural areas who come into the city to work and be organized to support Perón and his wife

24 Buenos Aires, October 1943. Insurrectionist troops occupy the streets and take over Government House in the revolt against President Castillo

25 The destroyed headquarters of Perón's Nationalist Liberation Alliance in Buenos Aires, bombarded in the revolt against him in 1955

27 Mass Society. A demonstration of railway-workers in December 1961 against plans to close useless railway lines and workshops

26 The 'liberation of the Malvinas'. Two Argentine youths who helped hijack an Argentine passenger aircraft in October 1966, forcing it to land near Port Stanley, where the hijackers proclaimed Argentine sovereignty over the islands

28　General Eduardo Lonardi (left) addresses a great crowd from the balcony of Government House after being sworn in as President

order to answer this defiance, the retiring President Figueroa Alcorta advised Sáenz Peña to arrest Yrigoyen. Instead, Sáenz Peña met Yrigoyen, and out of that meeting developed the determination of Sáenz Peña to transform the political process of Argentina by creating the possibility of genuine elections as a means of selecting the members of the formal power structure.

The Sáenz Peña Law, forced through the reluctant Congress by the President, provided for a compulsory, secret ballot conducted by the armed forces who acted as a neutral agency in the preparation of the voters' list from the registers of all male citizens obliged to enrol under the law of compulsory military service. They were charged with the duty of seeing that all voted secretly and voted only once, and that the votes were counted impartially. In order to ensure that there would always be an opposition one-third of all the seats in the Congress in each province would go to the largest minority irrespective of the number of votes cast.

By this measure Sáenz Peña hoped to introduce some reality into the politics of the Congress so that legislation would be the result of an interchange among representative and *represented* interests and ideas. The immediate consequence of the measure was to bring into the Congress Radicals and socialists. Indeed, the city of Buenos Aires returned a strong socialist bloc. The Sáenz Peña Law thus introduced into the formal game of politics some new cards with new values. This was unmistakable. Whether the rules of the game and the method of scoring had been basically altered was open to some doubt.

In the interior provinces, where the change to cereal-farming and modern cattle-breeding and finishing for the fresh- and frozen-meat trade had had the least impact and where immigrants were fewer, the older traditional *criollo* society was less mobile, more firmly structured, and more truly conservative. In these provinces free, secret elections and a universal franchise would not necessarily produce a different result than corrupt elections had done, nor did they. In the *Litoral* regions of rapid growth the effect was otherwise.

In the old province of Córdoba the balance was slightly in favour of the Radicals. In Entre Rios or Santa Fé they had an advantage. In the province of Buenos Aires and the great city of Buenos Aires the variety of productive activity in this enormous region produced a complex political situation. The traditional political forces controlled the provincial government. Popular support for the aspirants to the national Congress were split in three or four ways: some went to the conservatives, some to the Radicals, some to the socialists, and large numbers were either apathetic or were anarchist drop-outs. Free elections did not necessarily mean an easy victory for the Radicals, who in terms of numbers were the only alternative to the traditional political groupings which the electoral system was likely to produce.

In the presence of these obstacles, Yrigoyen continued to place an emphasis on revolutionary means of gaining political power. It is true that the Radicals enjoyed the spontaneous support of the rural middle class of shopkeepers, independent farmers, and renting far- mers in Santa Fé, southern Córdoba, Entre Rios, and the province of Buenos Aires, and middle-class support in the cities of Buenos Aires, Rosario, and Córdoba, but Yrigoyen thought much more in terms of the means of gaining power than in terms of measures and pro- grammes which would draw more and more people into the Radical Party and thus make it an omnibus party capable of satisfying the demand for status and respectability by creating a material basis for a high rate of upward social mobility such as had obtained during the 1870s and 1880s.

Although Yrigoyen was reluctant to try his luck in the election of 1916, he became a candidate and he was elected by a narrow majority. The Radicals did not, however, control the lower house of the Congress, and they had only one representative in the Senate, whose numbers were selected by the provincial governments. Posses- sion of the Presidency was, however, an enormous advantage, for the President of the Republic was Commander-in-Chief of the armed forces and endowed by the constitution with the power of interven- tion in the government of the provinces. With his strong inclination to revolutionary methods, Yrigoyen yielded to the temptations afforded by his office to use the armed forces for political purposes. He employed them in two ways: as agencies for the seizure of power in the provinces by the device of presidential intervention, and as a spearhead in an attack on private business initiative in opening up the petroleum industry. During his term of office there were twenty- two interventions in the provinces, three in the stubbornly conserva- tive stronghold of Mendoza. In the last year of his regime generals of the army were put in charge of the nationalized oil enterprise *Yacimientos Petrolíferos Fiscales.*

Reliance on the armed forces, particularly the army, not only corrupted the political process but was inadequate as a means of serving the essential goals of providing a broad ladder of social mobility. Officers who undertook duties in connection with interventions in the provinces were given war pay, they were promoted, and they were given medals. This increased their upward social mobility, but was an expensive and inadequate means of dealing with a more general problem. Worse than this it divided the armed forces. Many officers were humiliated by the transformation of the armed forces into a political agency, and the irony of war pay, promotion, and honours for active service against the internal enemies of the government embittered them. Following a familiar pattern a *logia*, or secret society, was formed to counter the activity of the President. Officer turned against officer, and those opposed to the policy of the President organized public demonstrations of their displeasure in the form of dinners at which strong expression was given to their view that the armed forces needed better equipment and attention to their duties as defenders of the nation and as professional soldiers. Behind the scenes they approached the most conspicuous Radical next to Yrigoyen, Marcelo T. de Alvear, and secured from him a promise that in the event of his election he would choose a Minister of War who would re-equip the forces with up-to-date weapons and take the armed forces out of politics.

Yrigoyen came to power in the middle of World War I. In spite of internal and external pressure to join in the conflict he resolved on a policy of strict neutrality, and he stuck to this policy to the very end. As the perspective of history lengthens the wisdom of what Yrigoyen did then glows more and more in his record, but it must be remembered that he was adhering to a traditional Argentine strategy in the international community. The good he did for his country consisted not in the originality of his policy, but in the firmness with which he stuck to it in circumstances of wholly unprecedented difficulty.

The economic opportunities of the war Yrigoyen chose to exploit in the traditional way. High prices for Argentine products were offset by the drying up of capital flows and by the great increase in the price of imports. Yrigoyen's government, however, responded passively to the possibilities of the situation. They used surpluses to reduce their foreign indebtedness, not to increase domestic capital. The advantages which scarcity and high prices gave to Argentine industry were not reinforced by investment and were not consolidated by tariff protection over and above the revenue tariffs which provided the principal income of the state. When peace came in Europe with its aftermath of uncertainty, high prices, and revolutionary unrest, Yrigoyen struck out blindly at the working class and converted a strike in a metal works into an assault by the police and the armed forces on the strikers. Many lives were lost during the Tragic Week of January 1919, and worse than the loss of life was the blow struck at the confidence of the community in industrial development. Bitterness and suspicion supervened, and Argentina returned to the old, tried ways of reliance on the big export industries.

Yrigoyen's failures must not be attributed entirely to his incapacity to understand problems of economic development. If he did not, and this seems to be the truth of the matter, his economic illiteracy owed much to the disposition of the social forces which provided the energy and direction of the political movement. Radicalism was a middle-class movement with some working-class support. Its middle-class support was mainly drawn from farmers, shopkeepers, and white-collar workers in private firms and the public service. This middle class had an economic interest parallel in a fundamental way with the big interests they opposed, viz. the landlords, meat-packers, and big ranchers. All were interested in opportunities to sell agricultural products. Where they divided was on questions of rent of land and social prestige. A curious consequence of the stabilization of the peso following the Baring crisis was the development of a parallelism of interest between the wage-workers and the big exporters. The adoption of the gold exchange standard and the cessation of inflation after 1896 reduced the vulnerability of the wage-workers to consequences of rapid and large increases in domestic prices. Their leaders, and particularly the socialists, became strong advocates of price stability and free trade. As a result no conjunction of forces existed capable of imposing upon any political party a policy of industrial development through tariff protection such as existed in similar countries like Canada, the United States, and Australia.

The political process anywhere fixes patterns of prestige and social mobility in the community. Problems of this kind can be solved by politicians either by freezing the patterns conservatively, or rearranging the patterns or by adopting economic policies which enlarge the opportunities to fit into existing patterns. The Radical leaders chose the second option, which is the one most calculated to engender bitterness and produce sterility. Yrigoyen stimulated upwards mobility in the armed forces in the way we have described. Although not a devout Catholic himself, he encouraged the Church and created a feeling for *Hispanidad* which was favourable to it. He dealt out jobs in the public service with a liberal hand.

His celebrated reform of the universities illustrated very well the limitations of what he was trying to do. The Argentine universities were then, as they are now, objects of great public respect and the means of conferring prestige on individuals. Unfortunately, Yrigoyen and his partisans tended to think only of the prestige and influence of the universities and not about their functions in modern society. They regarded them as agencies of the oligarchy in much the same way as the socially envious regarded Oxford and Cambridge in the late 1940s and 1950s. Yrigoyen's reform was directed to opening up the universities, not to improving them as agencies of higher education and research. Students were given a place in the government of the universities, and all appointments were opened to public competition to the extent that any citizen could intervene in the appointment procedure. This did not produce better appointments; it only ensured a procedure so cumbersome that it often required three years of deliberation, intrigue, and confusion to appoint a man for seven years to a post so badly paid he had either to work part-time as a bank clerk, a lawyer, or a taxi-driver—or he had to have a private income. Only the most determined and heroic men and women could devote themselves wholly to teaching and scholarship. The remainder were either rich amateurs or people who found university prestige useful in professional life outside the university. Even more serious was the fact that those interested in the natural sciences—and especially the pure sciences—had no opportunities at all in the universities. One of the saddest and most debilitating elements in Argentine life is the badness and inadequacy of the institutions of higher education and research in a community with a high level of intellectual interest and ability, and a great popular passion for education and learning. Much of this can be jointly attributed to the errors, envy, and misunderstanding of Hipólito Yrigoyen, who opted for phoney reform at no cost instead of real reform calculated to raise the level of capacity to the level of prestige.

The main policies of Yrigoyen based on the second option open to politicians produced general bitterness and dissatisfaction of the kind which afflicted the armed forces. Those who had been dispossessed or put into positions of competition with the protégés of the Radicals felt downgraded. At the same time the beneficiaries felt insufficient counter-satisfaction because the prestige conferred by a job in the public service or a university post was not matched by any marked improvement in the material basis of the prestige. In fact the inflation in the prestige market devalued everything. There was an atmosphere of corruption generated which provoked a romantic reaction and a search for a new scale of values.

In 1922 Yrigoyen was succeeded in the Presidency by Marcelo T. de Alvear. The new President was a Radical but unlike his predecessor he was a member of the old aristocracy whose forbears had helped to make the revolution. One had served General Rosas as an ambassador abroad. Another had beautified Buenos Aires. Alvear's radicalism consisted in having defied the canons of respectability by marrying an opera singer. It is a commentary on the aristocratic and familial *mores* of the élite that they condemned a man for choosing in his wife beauty and talent in preference to family position, exalted social standing, and an incapacity to earn money. As a politician he moved towards the first option. He took the armed forces out of politics. He stimulated traditional industry by further beautifying Buenos Aires, but about developing new dimensions of the economy he did nothing, for in this matter predominant sentiment among the Radicals was the same as the predominant sentiment of the conservatives: *laissez faire* economic policies and a stable currency had served Argentina well in the past and were good enough for all times and circumstances. It could be attributing too much to the speculative propensity of either the Radicals or the conservative élite to suggest that these sentiments were the product of a deep understanding of economic problems and a considered judgement of possibilities. Instead, they were the product of the same mindless optimism and enthusiasm which afflicted possessors of power and property in North America and western Europe during the Jazz Age of the 1920s.

In the matter of economic policy the Argentine socialists were not so mindless as the Radicals and conservatives, but by a process of thinking arrived at approximately the same conclusions as their political rivals. The great socialist leader Justo came to the conclusion that a regime of free trade, stable currency, massive exports of staple products, and cheap imports was a plain and large advantage to the wage-working class. The Argentine socialist movement had its first beginnings in the 1880s when internal inflation and rapidly rising prices were the scourge laid on the back of the working class and the means by which the main burdens of economic development were shifted from the owning and entrepreneurial classes (including the renting farmers) to the shoulders of the wage-workers. Thus low, stable prices were one of the policy goals of the socialists. The stabilization of the currency at the turn of the century, and the alteration in the terms of trade which kept low the price of manufactured products, both imported and Argentine, were not the work of the socialists but these developments had policy implications which the socialists supported. On this score it is not surprising that the socialists and the élite co-operated, and the spectacle of socialists and communists demonstrating in the company of the reactionary landlord Patron Costas against Perón has historical roots nourished by interest and understanding.

The socialists at the same time sought to improve the bargaining position of the working class, and in this they had some success. Workers in skilled crafts, in the textile industry, and in the railways, organized and achieved the means of bargaining over hours and wages and learned the organizational arts of providing their members with welfare services such as pensions and hospitals. These developments to which the socialists contributed were not universal and tended to be concentrated in three lines of activity where European-born workers were concentrated. They were not extended to industries such as meat-packing nor to farm labourers and the fetching and carrying occupations of the cities, which were more heavily *criollo* and hence susceptible to the memories of Rosista populism and bossism. It is also not surprising that as immigration ceased and as the sons and daughters of the immigrants grew up as Argentines, the *criollo* influences rooted in the unorganized masses of less-skilled and well-paid workers should have communicated themselves to the whole body of the wage-working class, thus laying a firm foundation both for the tactics and strategy of Colonel Juan Domingo Perón.

In 1928 the term of office of Marcelo T. de Alvear came to a close. Envy, vanity, and the discontent of the rank and file of the Radicals with the conservative tendencies of the President, prompted Yrigoyen to run again for the presidential office. This was a serious mistake. By 1928 Yrigoyen was old and tired, an empty symbol and no longer a leader. Yrigoyen's incapacity at this juncture was singularly and catastrophically unfortunate because there had developed in the 1920s a sharp rivalry between the United States and Britain as buyers, sellers, and investors in Argentina. Situations of international rivalry in economic as well as political matters had always been exploited to the full and to Argentine advantage by skilful Argentine leaders. Yrigoyen was no Rosas nor a Pellegrini nor a Sáenz Peña. He received a special mission from Britain headed by Lord D'Abernon, and gave every indication of a disposition to capitulate completely to the British proposals designed to bring to an end the *laissez faire* relationship between Britain and Argentina, and to build the system of restrictive bilateralism which eventually became a reality in the Roca-Runciman Agreement.

Before this could happen, however, the Argentine economy was struck by the world-wide depression of 1929 and the Argentine government was struck down by a *golpe de estado* organized and carried out by officers of the armed forces. An epoch opened of military intervention in the political process which has grown in frequency and comprehensiveness so that today Argentina is governed by a General and the governments of the Argentine provinces are mainly in the hands of officers of the army, navy, or air force. No account of Argentina can be complete, or even intelligible which does not offer some explanation of this phenomenon, sufficiently in line with Argentine reality to dispel the cant and prejudices which affect the impressions and sometimes the thinking of foreigners and Argentines themselves on this subject.

The modern armed forces of Argentina were developed as an instrumental part of the liberal political process which was given a formal structure in the constitution. In 1869 the liberal President Sarmiento founded the *Colegio Militar*, the purpose of which was to create cadres of educated and professionally trained officers. Young men entered the *Colegio Militar* by examination and were graduated by the same method of testing. The same merit system has been established in the naval and air force schools, and in the lycées run by the armed forces for secondary education. The rank and file of the armed forces are recruited by conscription. The obligation to serve is universal and now includes women as well as men.

After the end of the Paraguayan War in 1870 the principal military task of the armed forces was the destruction of the power of the Indians of the pampas and Patagonia. This was completed by 1880. Since then the Argentine armed forces have engaged no external enemies. Relations with Chile, Bolivia, Paraguay, Uruguay, and Brazil have not been tense, but nothing in previous history or in the contemporary conduct of these neighbours of Argentina, however, would lead one to exclude absolutely the possibility of armed conflict with them. Indeed, at the turn of the century war with Chile over boundary lines in the Andes was a real possibility, and only forbearance and diplomatic skill on both sides prevented armed conflict and led to the establishment of a system of arbitration. Looking farther afield there was nothing in the conduct of the European powers and the United States which would have disposed an intelligent Argentine to consider armed forces an unnecessary luxury. There is something both ludicrous and comic in the patronizing attitude of Americans and Europeans towards 'Latin American militarism'. The only way in which the Latin American states differ from the European and North American states consists in the small size of their armed forces, the infrequency with which they are employed in international wars, and the small proportions of the national revenues which are spent on them. Deaths by political violence and war are not major diseases in Latin America as they are in Europe and Asia, and compared with the North American states, Latin American states have contributed very little to military death and destruction either in South America or in other parts of the world.

If this is kept in mind one can grasp more accurately what is involved in 'militarism' in Argentina. The armed forces there were designed to protect the national independence and support the civil authorities. After the close of the Indian Wars they became steadily more professional and less involved in domestic politics. This was due to several factors. The liberal oligarchy believed in the supremacy of the civil power for the good reason that they possessed it and for the additional reason that the authority of civil government was part of their ideal view of a civilized community. This view was reinforced by the educational regime to which officers were subjected, and further emphasis was lent by the European military advisers who were imported to assist in training and the development of military technology. The British refused to send training missions to the army largely for reasons of economy but possibly also on account of a determination to prevent any misunderstanding about their position vis-à-vis the United States. They did offer some assistance in naval training. The Germans stepped in where the British feared, or were too mean, to tread. One must, however, remember that a spirit of rigid professionalism dominated the Kaiser's army and that one of the basic tenets of the German officers' faith was loyalty to the constituted authorities of the state and non-involvement in domestic politics. Thus, the Argentine armed forces were indoctrinated by their own civil authorities and by officers of the German army and Royal Navy with a code of rigid professionalism and loyalty to constituted authority.

The man who did most to undermine the non-involvement of the Argentine armed forces was Hipólito Yrigoyen. The armed forces helped the conservatives to keep control of the political process at the time of the rising against Juárez Celman in 1890. Whether the armed forces knew what they were doing is open to question, for they were the supporters of authority. Yrigoyen attempted to subvert a section of the officers in 1905 with no success. When he became President, however, he began to use the armed forces for internal political purposes in the way already described. The code of professionalism *and* loyalty became ambiguous when the President and Commander-in-Chief began to use them for political purposes. Officers are like other human beings. They respond to opportunities to advance their own interest, and especially if this can be done in obedience to legitimate authority. In this instance the effect of Yrigoyen's policy of using the armed forces to intervene in provincial politics split the armed forces and was the beginning of the fissures in them which have lasted down to the present day. The armed forces became part of the political process and a factor in decision-making whether they liked it or not. Some officers liked it; some did not. Whatever the balance of preference, the damage was done. The armed forces were involved in politics because the President of the Republic and their Commander-in-Chief had willed it so.

During a visit to Argentina in 1966 before the *golpe de estado* of General Juan Carlos Onganía, the author of this book interviewed four men on the subject of military intervention: the President, Dr Arturo Illia; a general of the Argentine army; a leading trade unionist; and a high officer of a financial institution. Paraphrases of their views are as follows:

President Illia: 'You must understand that Hipólito Yrigoyen was the first man ever elected President in free, honest elections. He was the leader of the common people. The wealthy classes –

the oligarchy – hated him for this reason, and a conspiracy was organized which overthrew him.'

When questioned in October 1966 ex-President Illia gave the same explanation of his own overthrow. In his view, it would appear that a *golpe de estado* by officers of the armed forces is a means by which the upper classes destroy democracy, frustrate the will of the majority, and keep the Radicals from power.

General X: 'An explanation of the intervention of the armed forces in politics is simple. General Uriburu and General Justo taught the officers by their example that officers who intervene in politics can achieve the highest office in the republic and those who help them can gain promotion and opportunities in civilian society as businessmen, ambassadors etc. For my part I consider this very bad because it weakens the country and impairs professional capacity to protect the nation. But that is our condition. There are groups of ambitious officers and there are groups of people outside who want jobs, business opportunities, higher wages, and so on. The officers and these others get together. The rumour factories in the press and radio create a climate of opinion. Then there is a *golpe*. That is how it is in our poor country. I am absolutely opposed to the intervention of soldiers in politics except to preserve order. I think we officers should all follow the example of our N.C.O's who always obey no matter what the orders of their higher officers are.'

Dr Y of the Banco Z: 'I believe in orderly, open democratic political methods. Unfortunately there are many men in all classes, some educated some not so well educated, who like short cuts and quick ways of getting what they want. They get ideas about what should be done, and so they begin to talk with officers and the officers listen, and then we have a *golpe*. These men cannot see that what they want to happen can be made to happen if it is sensible and honest, and they have the patience to explain what they want to do and get people to support them. But too many people have no patience or trust in others, and so we are always in a confusion, and have *golpes* instead of decision-making by open argument and give and take.'

Señor A of B Trade Union: 'This government has no plan of economic development. That is our trouble. As trade unionists we assume our wages will increase and conditions will get better if we have economic expansion. How can we get economic expansion? One of these days we are going to get together with the big industrial employers and some intelligent patriotic officers and then we will really go places. No, I do not regard military intervention in politics as a bad thing. It depends on the kind of officers you co-operate with. Some are connected with one sector: some with another. The decisions that are made depend on the combinations.'

Underlying their four views is a common diagnosis. Whether one adds 'of the disease' depends on a point of view. As a political process the *golpe* system, which has now been in operation for nearly four decades, must be considered in terms of its effectiveness as a means of achieving the goals of any modern state, viz. the creation of a social environment in which conflicts are resolved, uncertainty is minimized, and incoherence clarified. It seems pretty evident that the *golpe* system as it operates in Argentina is no more lethal or destructive of society than the democratic processes of the United States or the parliamentary-bureaucratic system of Great Britain or the centralized control system of the U.S.S.R. None the less it is plainly not a political process which scores high in terms of reducing uncertainty and clarifying incoherence. On balance the *golpe* system has reduced the capacity of Argentines to co-operate together in the enterprise of producing the means of life and contributing to the life of the world as a whole, and does not compare favourably with the oligarchic liberal system in terms of capacity for demonstrably intelligent response to internal and external change.

With the benefit of hindsight we can see that the transformation of the oligarchic liberal political process into an open system of complete participation formalized in the Sáenz Peña Law and given effect by the Radical Party under the leadership of Hipólito Yrigoyen was a failure. There were two major factors in this failure, both implicit in the foregoing material of this chapter. Firstly, Yrigoyen and his co-religionists (and this was equally true of the élite Radical, Marcelo T. de Alvear) never devised the means of opening new and economically viable channels of upward social mobility. In this respect they were less dynamic economically than the oligarchs whom they condemned and the socialists with whom they competed for popularity. Secondly, they perverted the system of multi-participant decision-making of which they were beneficiaries by using the armed forces as a political tool in their relations with the provinces and the local political processes. Argentine radicalism was, and is, small-minded and backward looking, a better vehicle for expressing social envy than social innovation. To say this is not to exonerate their enemies nor to divest the oligarchic liberals of their share of responsibility for the Argentine condition, but to identify the factors in the failure of the transformation which Roque Sáenz Peña planned and had the courage to implement.

Chapter 6

The Response to Depression and War

THE GREAT economic depression which engulfed the world in 1929 had as profound and revolutionary an effect on Argentina as it did in those nations where its dramatic and catastrophic consequences were more obviously tragic than in South America. Argentina today is still adjusting to the fracture of its external environment which the Great Depression produced, and has not yet discovered fully how to deal with the changed patterns of international economic and political relations which the great crisis of *laissez faire* capitalism engendered. The financial panic in Europe and the United States, which manifested itself like a coronary thrombosis in the form of the Wall Street crash of October 1929, set in train a succession of revolutionary transformations in the Argentine community. The liberal-representative political process gave way to a process by which the pushing and hauling of interests were periodically and unstably defined and contained by *golpes de estado*. The free movement of capital, goods and services, labour and resources gave way to a controlled system which enlarged greatly the role of the state in the organization and direction of the economy. The tensions of society increased and the prestige system suffered acute shocks. Policies in the community of nations based upon the preservation of the neutrality and independence of Argentina gave way to xenophobic fears concerning national purity and integrity. Old friendships were impaired and new ones tried. The relative position of Argentina among the Latin American nations changed. On the eve of the depression, Argentina was unquestionably first among the Latin American states in terms of wealth, stability, and all-round capacity to command the respect of the world. Today Argentina is no longer first on all counts, and far from first on many.

The depression hit Argentina with peculiar and profound force because the Argentine economy was highly specialized and finely ad-

justed to the international division of labour organized in the form
of a world market for commodities, capital, and labour. More completely geared to this system than any economy save that of Great
Britain, the Argentine economy suffered a succession of severe shocks
as a result of the alteration in the international monetary system,
the severe and differential decline in food and raw material prices,
the impairment of the international competitive markets by the imposition of government controls designed to limit and control access
to national markets, and the drying up of investment funds partly as
a result of uncertainty and fear and partly by their diversion into
armaments and state-controlled investment programmes in nations
like the United States and Germany. While it is true that the profound alteration of Argentina's international environment has been
Argentina's principal problem for nearly forty years, it would be
untrue to say that the depression affected Argentina catastrophically
and dramatically in its first stages in the way that it did Germany and
the United States. This is partly why Argentina, like Britain, has
been slow to understand what has been happening and has been confused in its responses.

When the depression set in it looked very like other depressions
Argentina had experienced and overcome by operating the ordinary
mechanisms of the market and by expanding production and/or
cutting costs to make good the consequences of price falls. As prices
of grain and meat fell, Argentina's gold stocks began to flow abroad
to pay for imports into Argentina. The government sought to protect
its gold holdings by suspending the free conversion of paper pesos
into gold. This step was a quite conventional one, and one which
the farming and ranching interests had for long wanted to see more
freely used as a means of cutting their labour costs. To pay for
labour and materials in paper currency and sell the product of labour
abroad for gold or gold-backed currency was an old tradition of the
Argentine rural interest and one very congenial to them. They believed in the gold standard as they believed in God, but they found
paper currency, like infidelity, an agreeable solution of their natural
desires. Accordingly, on 16 December 1929, Argentina went off the
gold standard so far as their domestic economy was concerned. This
strategy began to work as expected. Although the prices of cereals,
linseed, and meat products were falling drastically, Argentine production of these commodities began to rise. By the end of the crop
year 1931, the volume of exports was 38 per cent greater than in the

year 1930 and export earnings were 4·2 per cent greater in spite of a 24·4 per cent decline in prices during the year.

While this paper currency strategy may have worked in terms of maintaining a high level of economic activity, it could not conceal that the rewards of that activity were diminishing in terms of goods and services available to the mass of the people and even to the wealthy class. The price of imported manufactured goods did not fall as fast as that of Argentine exports, with the result that everyone was more or less worse off. The real beneficiaries of the Argentine strategy were the holders of Argentine fixed-interest securities who were still getting their share of Argentine economic activity in gold-backed currency which was now buying more goods and services than had been the case before the great fall in prices. It is not surprising, therefore, that the depression generated a sense of malaise which soon found political expression.

Ten days after the suspension of gold payments on 16 December 1929, an attempt was made on the life of President Hipólito Yrigoyen. Less than three months later, early in March 1930, the Radical Party suffered a severe electoral defeat in the city of Buenos Aires. Right-wing patriotic organizations, vaguely inspired by fascist and Nazi example, sprang to life demanding the resignation of the President. Yrigoyen was by 1930 a feeble old man, but he had not lost all his political imagination. He declared the First of May a national workers' holiday, but in an atmosphere of depression and growing unemployment, the proclamation of a holiday did not evoke a wave of enthusiasm among the workers. At the great annual Palermo cattle show of the Rural Society, the cattle aristocracy hissed and howled at the Minister of Agriculture. The Minister of War, General Dellepiane, resigned. Street demonstrations against the government boiled up. Yrigoyen attempted to delegate his authority to the Vice-President, but on 6 December 1930, General José Felix Uriburu, at the head of the Buenos Aires garrison, seized power, deposed the President and Vice-President, and proclaimed martial law. For sixty-eight years the liberal, representative political process, often imperilled and frequently abused, had endured and had even appeared to grow more robust. Now it had been struck down.

Whether it could be re-created was an open question, and has been so for forty years. The Argentine social, political, and economic élite were in 1930, and still are, ambivalent on the subject of democracy and open political processes. They do not like and do not want dictatorship and rigid authoritarianism. But they do not like the consequences of democracy either; nor do they appear willing to learn the techniques of compromise and political management which are necessary to render compatible a hierarchical prestige system of socio-economic relations with an open flexible, fully participant political system. What has been achieved is neither an operative democracy nor an effective dictatorship, and this statement can be applied equally to every regime since 1930 including that of General Perón.

The confusion and ambivalence of the élite can be best illustrated by regarding the original product of this condition: General Uriburu. He was a soldier with aristocratic, conservative family connections. One of his kinsmen had figured decisively in the resolution of the Baring crisis forty years previously, and now he seemed selected by Providence for a repeat performance in an even more important role. But, as often happens, history repeated itself as farce. General Uriburu was serious but ignorant; revolutionary but imitative; authoritarian but disputatious. Like many of the conservative oligarchy, he had a contempt for popular democracy, but knew next to nothing about the people. Although he was a high-ranking officer in a conscript army drawn from one of the most literate communities outside western Europe, he believed, for example, that 60 per cent of Argentine voters were illiterate. He completely misunderstood fascism, believing that it was an aristocratic movement, the corporative principles of which translated into action would rid the community of politicians. Although a General and a man expected to command, he had a taste for arguing about his ideas in public and he converted his Cabinet into a debating society and his presidential audiences into public meetings. The solid conservatives of the oligarchy soon tired of him, and began to long for a return to the representative system.

Unfortunately, their Radical opponents refused to disappear from the scene. The election in April 1932 in the province of Buenos Aires produced a victory for the Radicals. Uriburu suspended further elections, but the conservatives in his Cabinet and in the community were resolved to reject a fascist system of corporative organization. They rightly detected its dangers just as the American conservative opponents of President Roosevelt did some three years later when they fought the National Recovery Act. Uriburu was obliged to abandon his *ideas* and, instead, serve his *purpose*. This was to use the presidential power to prepare the ground for an election which the Radicals could not win.

The Radical nominee, ex-President Alvear, was removed from the running by presidential decree. The Radicals declared a boycott of the elections. Inevitably these were won by General Augustín P. Justo as President and Julio A. Roca as Vice-President, the nominees of a political combination called the *Concordancia*. From 1931 to 1943 the *Concordancia* controlled the political process of Argentina. It was in its main essentials a loose alliance of established interests: conservatives and liberals with a sprinkling of socialists having connections with the old-established trade unions. The *Concordancia* had something of the character of a European united front against fascism, but unlike any European united front it was dominated and controlled by the right and not by the left. This circumstance created the opportunity which, when the time came, Colonel Perón was so skilful in exploiting. The aim of the *Concordancia* was to find a central position attractive to conservatives from all movements: conservative liberals, conservative conservatives, conservative Radicals, and conservative socialists. Its nominees for the Presidency and Vice-Presidency illustrated this principle of political strategy. General Augustín P. Justo had been the Minister of War in the conservative Radical government of President Marcelo T. de Alvear, where he had restored professionalism in the armed forces, thus striking from the hands of the Yrigoyenistas one of their tools of intervention in the conservatively oriented provinces. Julio A. Roca, on the other hand, was a genuine oligarch, a son of President Roca, one of the main architects of the era of rapid expansion. Behind the scenes and the intellectual generator of the detailed policies of the government was Federico Pinedo, an upper-class socialist of great ability and power of technical invention.

The problems of the Argentine government at this time became more difficult on account of a fresh and fundamental change in their international economic environment. On 12 September 1931, Britain abandoned the traditional gold standard, and the value of the pound measured in United States dollars fell from $4.86 to around $3.40. Up to this point, Argentine economic policy had been based in part upon the assumption that its largest customer always paid in gold or a currency freely exchangeable for gold. Within a matter of months the British abandoned free trade. British farmers were guaranteed a floor price for wheat well above the prevailing international price. Tariffs were raised against imports into Britain. In July and August 1932, Britain agreed at Ottawa to establish a system of bilateral trading within the Commonwealth which ensured the Commonwealth competitors of Argentina a share of the British market for food products in return for preferential opportunities to sell industrial products in Commonwealth markets overseas. Thus was the Argentine economic universe upset and put in disarray.

The response of the Argentine government was not unexpectedly conservative, i.e. it was designed *sauver qui peut*. But it was not blindly and stupidly conservative. A number of control mechanisms were devised which, used in a variety of ways, had a profound influence on the course of Argentine economic development and came in the end to replace the free market as a means of directing the economy. On 10 October 1931, shortly before the election which brought General Justo to power, the government decreed the establishment of an Exchange Control Commission. This commission acting through the Argentine and foreign banks established in Argentina took possession of all foreign currency earned by the sale of the main Argentine exports such as cereals, wool, meat, and linseed. The exporters were obliged to deliver all their foreign earnings to the Commission on pain of being deprived of loading certificates in Argentine ports. The Commission then paid the exporters in Argentine pesos at a rate slightly below what the operations of the Commission revealed to be the market value rate of the peso. Thus was born a kind of tax on exports, which Colonel Perón was eventually to use as a drastic weapon. In the hands of the political leaders of the *Concordancia*, the weapon was used for purposes which the conservatives regarded as legitimate and necessary.

The foreign currencies which the Commission acquired were then auctioned off to the Argentine public requiring the means of payment of debts abroad. These auctions were conducted in accordance with a list of priorities designed to control the economy and achieve economic objectives which the government considered necessary. The first priority was given to the government's own need for foreign currency. Argentina had a large bonded debt held abroad, and the need for foreign currency to pay interest and capital charges on these bonds was very great. The object of giving this first priority to government requirements was the maintenance of Argentine credit in the capital markets of the world. Since 1857, when the government of the province of Buenos Aires undertook to repay the

Baring loan of 1824, the cornerstone of Argentine foreign economic policy was the prompt and full repayment of foreign loans on the assumption that this would induce a flow of foreign capital for development purposes. This policy had demonstrably worked, and no thought was given to the possibility that a scaling-down of debts or outright repudiation might have been to Argentine advantage. On balance the decision in favour of preserving Argentina's credit rating, even at high cost, was probably a sound one. Buenos Aires itself became something it had never been before and has never been since, i.e. a quite respectable capital market. That this was never turned sufficiently to Argentina's advantage is explicable largely by the political catastrophes connected with World War II.

The second priority was given to purchases of industrial raw materials; then fuel; then indispensable consumer goods; then remissions abroad by immigrants; then remissions to Argentines living abroad; then for travellers' expenses; then for non-essential goods; and finally for the settlement of commercial debts. A few unimportant items of export could be sold on the free market, and currency so earned could be sold similarly. These transactions amounted to very small sums.

Much has been written passing judgement on the failure of the politicians of the *Concordancia* to industrialize Argentina, and much abuse has been heaped on their heads because it is alleged that they were too much devoted to the interests of the cattle-breeders and export interests. In fact the Exchange Control system worked to the advantage of industrial development. Users of industrial raw materials and fuel had a high priority in the competition for the means of paying for their imports whereas the importer of non-essential manufactures had a low priority. Furthermore, the low priority for the payment of commercial arrears had the effect of forcing exporters to Argentina to demand cash, and it had the additional effect of checking the flow of dividends abroad and thus forcing reinvestment in Argentina.

The response of the Argentine government to the end of free trade in Britain was less intelligent, and was in many respects at the root of much subsequent economic difficulty. The Ottawa agreements frightened the Argentine government and the dominant interests. They joined the queue at the Foreign Office along with Belgium, Denmark, the Netherlands, Norway, and Sweden to see what could be negotiated to save their markets in Britain. There Vice-President

Roca and the Argentine team found themselves in a difficult negotiating position. They needed, or felt they needed, the British market and that a strategy of salvaging what they could was worth almost any price they might be forced to pay. Britain, on the other hand, had a number of options open, and was in the advantageous position of being buyers in a buyers' market for food and raw materials. But like the Argentine negotiators Runciman and his team were frightened, short-sighted conservatives with a strong propensity to look at economic questions from the point of view of the owners of existing capital rather than to see economic problems in terms of production and the distribution of the benefits thereof. Given the limitations of view of both parties to the negotiation, the outcome of their labours was a success by their own lights and a disaster in the long run. The Roca-Runciman Agreement marked the beginning of the end of the large and beneficial British equity in Argentina and, for the Argentine ranchers and agricultural interest, it was the beginning of economic and technical sclerosis which has lost them the first place as competitors in the world market for food and raw materials like wool and linseed. Of the major participants in world markets, only Russia has lost more ground than Argentina.

Put briefly, the Roca-Runciman Agreement guaranteed Argentina a fixed but reduced share in the British market for meat and bound the British to limit their encouragement of British agricultural producers to subsidies. Tariff protection for cereal producers was ruled out. In return Argentina agreed to stabilize its tariffs on industrial products, to reduce tariffs on some manufactures, and to preserve free entry for fuel. Argentina undertook also to work its exchange control in such a way that the remission of interest and profits on British-owned investments would become easier. Finally vague undertakings were given to pursue policies which preserved the position of British-owned transport enterprises suffering competition from petrol-driven transport.

The principal feature of the Roca-Runciman Agreement, at the root of the long-term disaster which it achieved, was the entrenchment of the past and the destruction of the dynamic of both economic systems. Up to the signature of the Roca-Runciman Agreement, the Argentine food and raw material industry was the most competitive in the world. It had repeatedly demonstrated its capacity to overcome all major crises by increasing production. It had done this at the time of the Baring crisis; it did so again in the crisis of 1913; and it was in the process of doing so during the depression of the 1930s. In 1932, however, Britain took the wrong turning and Argentina acquiesced in this. It can be argued that Argentina had no choice. Narrowly considered from the point of view of the agro-pecuarian interests in Argentina, this was true, but it is not true that Argentina had no other options. Had the dominant interests of Argentina raised their eyes from the immediate perspective, they might have seen the alternatives to what they actually did: a campaign to find new markets; a determined drive to attract new capital into industry and to improvements in the infrastructure designed to cut their own costs of production and open the way to new markets.

As it was, the Roca-Runciman Agreement served notice that change and development were not to be expected in Argentina. The natural facts of Argentina's situation provided opportunities for in-dustrialization and this did in fact take place, but it was industrial-ization without plan and without any consistent assurances that serious investment of money and serious commitment to the acquisi-tion of technical expertise by individuals had long-term expectation of reward. Small-scale industries using borrowed techniques took root and flourished, but they were too often doomed to be high-cost industries because of the weakness of the infrastructure – for example, the lack of cheap, efficient sources of motive power or cheap, efficient transport adapted to urban industrial production.

An examination of the character of the Argentine economy in the mid-1960s reveals the consequences of the kind of development which took place in the 1930s. During the thirty years between 1935 and 1965, Argentina did become an industrial nation, but it changed without becoming different. By 1944 industrial production con-stituted a larger proportion of total production than ranching, the production of cereals, and agricultural raw materials. And yet then, and still in 1965, these traditional activities still played as important a part in the economy as they did before 1914. In the mid-1960s Argentina was still heavily dependent on foreign suppliers for in-dustrial goods and fuel and was still paying for them almost exclusively with exports produced in the rural sector. In 1962, for example, Argentine exports were 93 per cent agro-pecuarian and only 2 per cent manufactures. In 1912 the dependence on agro-pecuarian production was actually less: only 85 per cent. If the pat-tern of Argentine exports did not change, the pattern of imports did. Until the depression of the 1930s the proportion of capital equipment and fuel constituted roughly 50 per cent of all Argentine imports and the remainder were consumer goods. Since 1929 the proportion of consumer goods has steadily fallen. In 1955 it was only 21.3 per cent and by 1965 the proportion was down to approximately 15 per cent. Meanwhile, the proportion of capital equipment, fuel, steel, and manufactured industrial metals had risen to approximately 80 per cent of all imports.

In themselves these propositions prove little or nothing, but they do suggest weaknesses which further investigation confirms. Argentine industry in the first place is predominantly a consumer goods industry, which has grown up without rendering Argentina less dependent on foreign suppliers. Secondly, it is a high-cost industry which is incapable of meeting international competition, and is hence unable to support its own demand for fuel, raw materials, and capital equipment. Thirdly, being predominantly a consumer goods industry and in the main high-cost industry it is incapable of contributing to cost reduction and to improvements in the main industries – ranching and cereal-farming. In the main, industrialization, as it has taken place in Argentina during the past thirty years, has been of the wrong kind, undertaken in the wrong way and for these reasons productive of self-reinforcing weaknesses. The growth of industry in this way has produced also a host of interest groups whose strength has the effect of making the economy rigid and static rather than forward moving.

Within the limits of their intentions the government of General Justo and the administrative élite conducted the economic affairs of the nation with ability and intelligence. The banking system was reformed and a central bank established with the object of improving the liquidity and credit-granting facilities of the banking system as a whole. Under the leadership of Dr Pinedo a form of New Deal on the American pattern was introduced. Marketing boards were set up to handle the export of cereals with the object of preventing wide fluctuations in price, of supporting prices, and of improving the cereal-storage facilities so that farmers would not be exposed to forced sales of unstored grain. An attempt was made to break the power of the privately owned meat-packing companies, and the Argentine government even succeeded in writing into the second revised Roca-Runciman Agreement a guaranteed place in the British market for meat processed and exported by plants owned by Argentine producer groups. The exchange control was manipulated to give encouragement to new exports such as fresh fruit. The road system was improved. Industrial development proceeded in response to the market opportunities created by changing price structure and the difficulties of obtaining foreign exchange for non-essential imports.

In spite of skilful management the fact of a drastic change in Argentina's international economic environment and the conservative response thereto generated tremendous pressures in Argentine society which manifest themselves politically. Whether the holders of power liked it or not the great growth industries of Argentina had reached the end of the line, or at least the end of the traditional line, and their opportunities began to narrow. On the other hand, real growth was taking place in the industrial sector of the economy. A new kind of middle class and a new kind of working class were coming into being, which were not so directly part of the export economy as the grain-clerks, shopkeepers, and railway-workers. Argentina had long been an urbanized society, but now urbanization began to intensify as the composition of the towns began to change.

In the presence of these pressures, the élite began to lose their nerve. This manifested itself as an increasing disposition to desert their liberal, secular approach to life in favour of vague romanticism about the community, narrow conformism, and religiosity. A puritanical, peeping-Tom atmosphere began to develop so that church-going and outward signs of Catholic morality, such as large families, became increasingly a part of the criteria by which the fitness of people for public office was judged. But puritanism did not purify, and the ruthless closing of brothels and the hounding of pimps and prostitutes did not solve the problems of society. Corruption increased rather than diminished so that the political processes at the local and provincial level began to look more like those of Chicago and New York than they did like those of traditional Argentine society, which, whatever the conceptions of the public good, had cherished ideals of honourable and disinterested public conduct. Loose talk about the danger of mob rule and communist conspiracy was more evidence of loss of nerve than a definition of real political and social problems.

General Justo's term as constitutional President came to an end in 1937. The interests in control of the political process were no more disposed to permit a free election than they had been since the *coup* of General Uriburu in 1930, but they recognized the need to find a centre position capable of attracting support from several quarters.

Again they produced a formula of which the ingredients were a manageable Radical and a right-wing conservative. Roberto Ortiz was nominated for the Presidency and Ramón Castillo for the Vice-Presidency. Like General Justo, Dr Ortiz had served in the conservative Radical Cabinet of Marcelo T. de Alvear. Dr Castillo was a provincial politician from the interior province of Catamarca, and an exemplar of conservative narrowness, fear, and blindness to new necessities. This team, of course, won the election.

In office President Ortiz proved himself a man of independent judgement with his own conception of how to broaden the political basis of the *Concordancia*. He believed that this could be done by leading Argentina back to an open political process based on the Sáenz Peña Law. This would once more bring effectively into the decision-making process the intransigent Radicals overthrown by Uriburu, and since then hamstrung in their activities by the harassment of the government and the management of the electoral process to their disadvantage. Unfortunately, President Ortiz was beset by scandal and disease. A Congressional investigation in 1939 of the purchase of a site for an airport revealed that the President and his friends had received a substantial 'rake-off' from the enormous price the government had paid for the land. Ortiz offered his resignation which was not accepted by a vote in Congress of 410 to one. This vote of confidence was only a short-term victory. Far more serious was the fuel it provided for those extra-parliamentary politicians in the armed forces and the nationalist and fascist fringe movements, who alleged that all party politicians were corrupt and unpatriotic. In July 1940, the President was obliged to delegate his power to the Vice-President on account of the wasting disease which afflicted him with blindness.

The withdrawal and eventual death of President Ortiz in June 1941 altered the balance of forces in the *Concordancia* just at the moment when the shape of the world was drastically altering as a result of the Allied defeats in western Europe and the fall of France. The traditional neutral position of Argentina in international politics was subjected to strain. Economically and politically Argentina was oriented towards Britain and western Europe, whereas politically her relations with the United States were cool but not hostile and economically were not as close as they could have been had the United States been willing to buy more from Argentina. What course should Argentina take if Britain followed France to defeat?

This question was much complicated by political agitation over the respective merits of the Allies and the Axis. Lively as this was, it was secondary to the internal strains of Argentine politics, and never was a decisive factor in the course of events. Any Argentine government would have had to decide a policy, and between 1940 and 1942 no intelligent Argentine leader could say with absolute confidence what was the right one for the nation. This ambiguity deeply affected the *Concordancia*. Dr Pinedo, the Minister of Finance, was strongly inclined to a close relationship with the United States. In October 1941, a trade treaty with the U.S.A. was signed which promised to provide the means of solving the shortages of capital goods which the fall of France and the total conversion of Britain to a war economy caused. Simultaneously, Dr Pinedo developed a plan directed to employment of unused resources of labour and capital in an extensive housing programme and other government-sponsored development projects.

Some doubt was cast on the wisdom of Dr Pinedo's orientation towards the United States by the disaster suffered by the Americans at Pearl Harbor. Dr Castillo's scepticism, which need not be attributed entirely to his narrow, conservative sympathy for authoritarian regimes, found expression in the neutral stand of the Argentine Foreign Minister at the meeting of American Foreign Ministers at Rio de Janeiro in January 1942. Dr Pinedo, on the other hand, sought to gain support on the left. He approached the Radical leaders in the Congress seeking their support for his development Plan. They refused to co-operate in getting Congressional support for his programme, and Dr Pineo thereupon resigned from the government.

What motivated Dr Pinedo is not clear, but it would appear that he hoped to use his influence in the *Concordancia* to strengthen the position of the centre at the expense of Vice-President Castillo. The Vice-President had, however, imposed a state of siege following Pearl Harbor, and this was the means of hampering open political activity of a popular kind. This handicap was not serious for a politician of Dr Pinedo's *modus operandi*. What was serious, however, was the death of ex-President Justo, one of the real architects of the *Concordancia* and the key man in preserving the neutrality of the armed forces in political matters.

The resignation of Dr Pinedo, and the death of President Ortiz, freed Dr Castillo from all inhibitions in the development of a narrowly conservative policy. He decided on a course of action no politician of the *Concordancia* had yet attempted: the imposition of a conservative candidate for the Presidency. He chose as candidate a wealthy sugar baron from the province of Salta, Robustiano Patron Costas, and he excluded from the possibility of power the governor of the province of Buenos Aires, Rodolfo Moreno, by a high-handed intervention in that province and the transformation into a puppet the government of the principal province of the Republic. At this juncture in January 1943 General Justo died.

The major factor in the events which followed was the shattering of the *Concordancia* by President Castillo himself. He revealed that failing which distinguishes the second-rate Argentine politician from the first-rate: the determination to rule alone without compromise and without consideration for at least some of the major interest groups outside his own. He exhibited the same failure as Rivadavia, as General Rosas in his late years, as Hipólito Yrigoyen did, and as General Perón and President Illia were to do in the future. Experience has shown that, Argentina being an expansionist and variegated community, no government can long survive, whether military, oligarchic, or democratic, which narrows its support to one sector no matter how powerful and prestigious. President Castillo defied that experience. He fell, and in falling opened the way for a quarter of a century of trouble, hysteria, and finally stagnation.

There are many theories advanced to explain the action of the officers who overthrew President Castillo. One school has explained the *golpe* as the triumph of Nazi political propaganda and German intelligence agencies. Another has suggested that it was the answer of the industrial bourgeoisie to the prospect of a conservative government headed by a member of the landed interest. The exact opposite has been argued: that the officers represented a desperate last throw of the landed oligarchy to save themselves. Another ingenious explanation suggests that the *coup* was a middle- and lower middle-class revolt against the very rich. Yet another theory sees the rising of the officers as a manoeuvre by the Roman Catholic Church in its long struggle against the secular state. All these theories are crudely sociological, characterized by reasoning backward from the consequences, or presumed consequences, of the event to the event itself. The simplest explanation seems to be that the *golpe* by the officers was an aspect of the political incoherence which followed the break-up of the *Concordancia* and the frustration and defeat which afflicted all the major political and economic interest groups when it appeared that President Castillo was bent on excluding them from the political process and from the rewards and opportunities connected therewith.

The *golpe de estado* of 4 June 1943 had, however, a unique character, which lent some colour to the notion that it was the work of the Germans. It was one of the few truly military *golpes* in Argentine history, and the one in which the soldiers acted most on their own and the least as tools of some political interest or other. The energy and direction behind the rising was provided by a semi-secret lodge, the *Grupo de Oficiales Unidos*, whose members were officers of the rank of colonel, major, and captain, i.e. the main strata of unfulfilled ambitions. This G.O.U. was modelled on Nazi lines. In the first public proclamation they frankly stated that 'as in Germany' their government 'would be an inflexible dictatorship', and that they aimed to 'inculcate the masses with the spirit necessary to travel the heroic path in which they will be led'. The main instruments of the G.O.U. were General Ramírez, the Minister of War in Castillo's government, and General Rawson, the commander of the Buenos Aires garrison. General Ramírez told President Castillo in the presence of his Cabinet that his time was up, and the next day the army marched into Buenos Aires. General Rawson was proclaimed President, but he only lasted two days because he wished to call a Congress, thus turning the *golpe* into a means of finding a new government made up of civilian politicians. The G.O.U. deposed him, and installed Ramírez in his stead. Under Ramírez the new character of the *golpe* emerged. For the first time in Argentine history officers were installed in all the main administrative and political posts. The constitution was suspended *sine die*, and a dictatorship proclaimed.

Political incapacity, isolation from the normal political groupings, professional and puritanical disdain for the rest of the community help to explain the particularly disastrous character of the government of the Generals. Having rejected the principles of all the political parties and of the constitution itself and having condemned equally the lack of principle of all politicians, the officers were themselves without any intellectual or moral guidelines for the development of their own political activities. They fell back on the massive generalities of religion, patriotism, and discipline suitable no doubt for the instruction of children and necessary for the formation of a collective will in an army but wholly inadequate for the solution of problems of great technical complexity in the sphere of economics and diplomacy, and the resolution of the conflicts and the clarification of the uncertainties which are the inevitable and necessary features of a rapidly developing society. The officers were capable only of opportunism and response to events they never made, and their inexperience left them prey to every pedlar of nostrums both within their own ranks and in the community at large.

This was well illustrated in their handling of the basic questions of economic development, labour relations, and foreign policy. Because labour relations were, and are, basically a political problem and in this case the one which most transformed the political character of Argentina, it will be best to consider the way in which General Ramírez and his successor General Farrell handled it, or better, failed to handle it.

Without understanding how Hitler and Mussolini had manipulated the labour movements in Germany and Italy, the government of General Ramírez launched a massive assault on the Argentine unions in accordance with their belief that labour problems are caused by socialists, communists, and Jews and can be solved by the establishment of discipline. A number of labour leaders were rounded up and put in concentration camps. This policy did not seem to work; indeed, by October 1943 it looked as if the officers were going to get what they deserved from an aroused populace encouraged by the spectacle of the increasing failure of the fascists and Nazis in Europe. At this stage an officer in the Ministry of War, Colonel Juan Domingo Perón, asked for and was given the relatively obscure but critical job of running the Labour Department.

This remarkable man was born in 1895 in Lobos in the province of Buenos Aires of a poor family of farmers of *criollo* and immigrant stock. His career denies his own myth that Argentina under the oligarchy was a closed society of privilege, for this country boy of humble social origins found the opportunity in the state schools and the merit system of entry into the military college to establish himself in the military profession and to climb the ladder towards a prestigious position. He managed to exhibit two characteristics which are much admired in Argentine society: physical prowess and intellectual imagination. He was an expert skier and a fencing champion. At the same time he interested himself in intellectual questions, writing on Argentine history, studying sociology, and teaching in the Higher School of War. There are many stories of his personal charm as well as instances of his extraordinary capacity to sway mass audiences. On one occasion during his Presidency a group of idealist young officers conspired to assassinate him. The plot came to the attention of a young kinsman of his in the army who reported the names of the conspirators to the President. Perón invited the young men to tea. After two hours of his charm and intellectual exuberance, eleven of the twelve young men emerged from the tea-party Perónistas. The twelfth was kicked out of the army. His enemies feared his charm more than they feared his police. He was a tyrant, but he was also a master politician of great positive prowess.

In spite of his many talents Perón had serious flaws of character. His physical prowess and his intellectual capacity concealed great physical and moral cowardice. At two critical moments in his life, when he was arrested in 1945 and again when the Casa Rosada was bombed by the air force in 1955, he went completely to pieces and was saved on the first occasion by the energetic action of his mistress and on the second by the loyalty of the non-commissioned officers who were his bodyguard. At no time could he endure unpopularity, and much of the extravagance and irresponsibility of his economic policy owed more to his desire for applause than his misunderstand- ing of economic reality. He wanted always to be loved, and he failed to appreciate that for a political leader there is always a point where the loving has to stop and respect has to start. For this reason Perón created more problems than he solved, and Argentina has not yet recovered from the compounding of his folly.

When he took command of the Labour Department in October 1943, Perón had had more opportunity than his brother officers to study how Hitler and Mussolini had actually dealt with labour prob- lems as distinct from their rhetoric about socialists and Jews. He did not essay to imitate them. Instead, he adopted a strategy which more resembled that of Primo de Rivera in Spain than of the German and Italian fascists or General Franco. Perón ended the assault on the workers' organizations, and proceeded to take them over. He did not do this crudely and all at once. The labour movement under Perón's leadership experienced a phase of liberation and growth before pass- ing under his control.

The first step was to raise the Labour Department to the status of a Ministry of Labour and Welfare. He persuaded his nominal superior in the Ministry of War, General Edelmiro Farrell, his friend Colonel Mercante, who had been appointed the interventor in the large railway-workers' union, the *Unión Ferroviaria*, and another friend, Colonel Velasco, to join with him in meeting some of the trade union leaders like Juan Bramuglia, the legal adviser of the *Unión Ferroviaria*, and Angel Borlenghi, and José Argaña of the Commercial Employees' Federation. In Colonel Perón these men discovered a new kind of politician: one who was prepared to do something more than bribe them personally; who was prepared to bribe the entire labour movement.

Bribe is, perhaps, not the right word for what Colonel Perón did. In order to understand what he accomplished and why he has had such a profound effect for good and evil, it is necessary to know something about the state of the Argentine workers a quarter of a century ago. His own rhetoric and that of his wife, Eva Duarte de Perón, about the shirtless ones can be dismissed as rubbish. The Argentine workers enjoyed the highest standard of living in Latin America and in terms of food consumed, housing, and educational opportunity were comparable with workers in the United States and western Europe. The old skilled trades connected with the railways, printing, textiles, and shoe manufacture and some clerical workers like bank clerks and commercial employees were well organized, and in terms of services rendered their members, like medical care, co-operative retail selling, and pensions, the Argentine unions were in advance of most European and American unions. The fact that the unions were so well organized and so well run made nonsense of the crude attacks on them by Ramírez, and helps to explain why the reasonable approach of Perón was so successful.

But not all Argentine workers were organized, not all were well provided for and many were, as a result of rapid industrial growth during the previous ten years, very recent arrivals in the cities and in the labour market. The packing plants, for example, had long resisted the advent of unions, and workers in that industry were subject to wide differentials in wages between the few skilled trades and the many slaughterhouse workers casually employed and often without work on account of seasonal fluctuations in productive activity. In an economy based on agriculture and ranching, there were many fetching and carrying jobs which tended to be seasonal and ill paid and hard to organize, and these workers were badly off, their lot only mitigated by the cheapness of food and benignity of the climate. In many respects the labour movement and the conditions of the workers in Argentina in the early 1940s resembled that which existed in the United States before the New Deal of Franklin D. Roosevelt.

Perón got the worker leaders out of the concentration camps into a negotiating position. They discovered that Perón was prepared to help with the organization of the unorganized. He walked in a demonstration with his arm around the shoulder of Cipriano Reyes, the leader of the packing-house workers. Not surprisingly the meat-packers discovered the wisdom of recognizing the union and negotiating with leaders whom they had only lately denounced as anarchist and communist scum. The union leaders discovered also that Colonel Perón was very free with other people's money. When his department participated in a wage negotiation (and this became standard practice and finally a legal obligation) the workers got more not less than they expected. Some of them discovered that they too could rise in the governmental structure. Bramuglia and Borlenghi rose eventually to the top.

The more astute trade union leaders could see what was happening, and they resisted. José Domenech, the secretary-general of the *Confederación General de Trabajadores*, stated flatly that the unions were losing their autonomy and were becoming part of a state-controlled apparatus in the hands of Colonel Perón. Bargaining with employers was losing its character as a contract, and wage agreements were becoming *diktats* ordered by the state. Perhaps the *diktat* was more beneficial than the bargain, but would it always be so?

But money talks and bribery works with the masses as well as with individuals. The old trade union leaders were outflanked. Colonel Perón was very free with fringe benefits which he himself ordered and made sure that everyone knew he ordered them. Holidays with pay were freely proclaimed. Finally, he decreed the *aguinaldo*, a bonus of one month's pay given at Christmas. The origin of this *conquista social* demonstrates Colonel Perón's methods. Many Argentine firms had developed as family businesses which preserved a family atmosphere in which the patron's relations with his employees were more like a father's with his children than a contractual relationship created by bargaining and market forces. Fathers, of course, exploit their children and treat them cruelly in many instances, but they also are capable of care, kindness, and responsibility. The great shoe and textile firm of Alpargatas, S.A., was an example of the latter. Every year regardless of what their profits had been, Alpargatas gave their employees one week's pay at Christmas as a bonus or present. In 1944 in a moment of euphoria brought on by large profits and great expansion the directors decided to give a months's pay as an *aguinaldo*. Shortly after this Colonel Perón visited the plants of the firm, and was told of this act of generosity on the part of the owners. Colonel Perón thereupon decreed that everyone in Argentina should have an *aguinaldo*. This was good for Perón; it was good for everyone at the moment, but was it good for the economy? Was it good for employer-employee relations to have voluntary acts of generosity and sharing taken over by the state and made into a mandatory act? The whole atmosphere was soured, and one of the elements of flexibility necessary to capitalist labour relations was lost in the interest of making political capital for Colonel Perón and the military officers in the government.

In addition to the large short-run benefits he brought to the wage-workers, Colonel Perón added a large welfare dimension to state activity. Many organized workers and state employees enjoyed the benefits of pensions and health services provided by their unions, but large numbers of workers and lower middle-class people were self-dependent. Colonel Perón inaugurated a state system of pensions and health benefits. Just as Franklin D. Roosevelt's social security legislation won the affection and support of the poor and the unorganized in the United States, so did Perón's welfare system in Argentina. This went very deep, and transformed Argentine politics. It helps to explain why Colonel Perón was able to win politically in a free election against a solid front of organized interests from big conservative landlords on the right through to the socialist and communist trade unionists on the left. More than ten years after Colonel Perón had been overthrown the traces of the impact of his welfare programme were readily discernible in the most unlikely places. The author met an old, Anglo-Argentine lady living in Belgrano in somewhat reduced circumstances – an evangelical Protestant, rather a snob, and no Perónista. He asked her what it had been like under the government of President Perón. She replied: 'Perón was a bad man. My husband always said that. And he burned all those churches and the Jockey Club. But, you know, Perón gave me my pension. There was some good in him, because he cared for the people. I will always say that for him.'

In spite of this high falutin' intention to establish a permanent dictatorship based on the solid support of the masses, disciplined and educated to become the nucleus of a great world power in South

America, the governments of General Ramírez and General Farrell proved themselves different from the governments of the decadent and despised politicians only in their lesser competence and their opportunism. The gas began to leak out of the balloon blown up in 1943 as the fascists and Nazis headed for defeat. The decline of Nazi prestige, however, explains only a very small part of the trouble of the officers' government. Apart from Colonel Perón's transformation of political forces through his work in the Secretariat of Labour and Welfare, the Generals in command did nothing more than maintain the state of siege which prevented all open manifestation of political life. They were as divided and confused about their objectives and how to achieve them as any body of civilian politicians. In August 1945, they lifted the state of siege. An explosion of repressed feeling followed within weeks. On 19 September a vast demonstration filled the streets of Buenos Aires with 400,000 people demanding freedom and the restoration of the constitution. The state of siege was re-imposed. Perón organized a great wave of arrests. The fissures in the ranks of the officers then revealed themselves. General Eduardo Ávalos, who had participated in the treason of June 1943, put himself at the head of the troops in the Campo de Mayo and marched towards Buenos Aires. The air force officers put themselves in their way. Prudently both military factions decided to parley rather than fight. Perón rushed to the radio to appeal to the workers to rise, but they did not respond. Ávalos then resumed his march into Buenos Aires and was not further obstructed. Perón was removed from office and arrested.

At this juncture the civilian partisans of the constitution made some serious mistakes. Not content with the arrest of Perón they demanded the immediate overthrow of President Farrell and trans-fer of power temporarily to the Supreme Court. Simultaneously the employers' organizations announced their intention not to give their workers a paid holiday on 12 October, the Day of the Race, when all Latin America remembers the landing of Columbus in the New World. Thus, the constitutionalists transformed the struggle for liberty and the constitution, which nearly everyone supported, into an attack on the working class which much less than half of the people supported.

When Perón was arrested in his apartment in the Calle Posadas he was with his mistress Eva Duarte. The story is, and it is consistent with what is otherwise known of Perón, that he fell on his knees and begged for his life. Eva Duarte, on the other hand, flew into a rage, and when her lover was removed, immediately rushed to tell Cipriano Reyes of the packing-house workers what had happened. Reyes was a militant – a real fighter – who was determined to answer his enemies and save the friend who had demonstrated on his behalf and helped him win the battle for the recognition of his union. He at once began to organize a counter-demonstration. Rioting began on 15 October. The next day workers from Avellaneda and other working-class *barrios* began to move into central Buenos Aires, burning motor-cars, smashing the fronts of luxury shops, and clearing the streets of those who looked like enemies of the workers. By the 17th they had taken over the city without opposition from the armed forces. General Humberto Soza Molina, in command of the Third Infantry Regiment in Buenos Aires, kept his men confined to barracks. The leaders of the *Confederación General de Trabajadores* did not know what to do. Nor did the constitutional democrats. Perón was released from prison, and appeared on the balcony of the Casa Rosada with General Farrell. He gestured in victory to the crowds which packed the Plaza de Mayo. Then the C.G.T. declared a general strike in support of Perón. Ávalos and his companion in politics, Admiral Vernengo Lima, resigned, were arrested, were released, and were retired. Perón appeared to be master of the situation.

It is a measure of his political genius that he was not deceived by appearances. He recognized that a wholly new political line was necessary, and that the fascist romanticism, which as a leading member of the *Grupo de Oficiales Unidos* he had helped to concoct, was out of date and quite unsuitable in the circumstances of 1945. Perón now emerged as a great democratic socialist seeking to re-establish the constitution and make it work. He shed his military trappings, retired from the army, and described himself to the people as a civilian. He accepted the fact of an open, free election and he began to prepare for it by hammering together a new party to which he gave the name of Labour Party and with which he endowed a set of principles and objectives very like those of the British Labour Party. Perón, however, was never the man to rely on names and principles as essential elements of the struggle for power. In spite of the support given to him by the workers and the general strike on his behalf declared by the C.G.T. he knew very well that some of the union leaders still preferred independent unionism to the state-sponsored and personally controlled system he had built up while Secretary of Labour and Welfare. To remedy this defect in the control of the trade union movement and to cut the ground from under the feet of the socialists and communists, he had the government issue a decree requiring all unions wishing to make valid collective bargains with employers to have a certificate of *personaría gremial* (union personality) issued by his secretariat. The decree further ordered that only one union could receive such a certificate for any negotiation. Two old and well-established unions still resisted Perón: the National Shoe-Workers' Union and the Textile Union. Certificates of *personaría gremial* were refused these unions. Rival unions were started and were given the necessary certificates. Within six months both the old unions were ruined.

Thus was complete control established over the trade unions. Bramuglia, the able adviser of the *Unión Ferroviaria*, had long since been seduced. So had Angel Borlenghi. Cipriano Reyes of the packing-house workers was deeply indebted to Perón, and the only danger to him was the debt Perón owed him. No one could further corrupt the port-workers. It had been demonstrated that dissidents could be smashed. The rest went along with Perón, and why not? Money, wages, and real wages were rising. The workers had never had it so good. All the socialists and communists had were some principles and some memories. Even memories of past struggles were becoming less meaningful as expanding industry recruited more and more *criollo* labour from the rural areas and the interior. Perón was a reality they could understand, not a vaguely discerned prophet dead and buried in Europe.

Perón was not, however, so foolish as to depend entirely for success on the organized and controlled working class. He had already won over the controlling elements in the armed forces, and his victory in October had a snowball effect among the officers and N.C.O's. There was another secondary organization which cut class lines, and had a growing influence among the lower-middle class, the upper-middle class, and the landed élite: viz. the Roman Catholic Church. Perón's personal position *vis-à-vis* the Church required consideration, and so did the development of a policy with respect to the hierarchy.

The Church in Argentina had always had an official position in the community even though at times a shaky one. The President of the Republic was required by the constitution to be a Roman

Catholic, and the laws of the Republic gave the Church something more than a private status. Religious freedom was, however, guaranteed by law and was also a social fact. Under the liberal oligarchy the Church had been excluded from the educational system supported by the state, and Argentina was for all practical purposes a secular state. But many of the Argentine priests were Spaniards and Italians, and migration to Argentina caused few of them to shed their ultramontane beliefs or to accept the liberal, secular character of Argentine society. As the self-confidence of the liberals waned in the presence of economic depression and disenchantment with the wonders of a free-market economy, the appeal of Catholicism grew. Pretensions to piety became a part of the style of all political movements except the socialists and communists. Scepticism among the upper classes became a private predilection rather than a public attitude. One of the first strokes of policy of the Ramírez government in 1943 was to make compulsory Catholic instruction in all state schools, with the proviso that Protestants, Jews, Muslims, and non-believers could opt out if they were so bold as to declare their religious eccentricities.

Perón could be expected not to reverse this policy, but he was himself in some difficulties. Like Hipólito Yrigoyen before him he lived publicly in sin with his mistress, the actress and working-class and feminist militant, Eva Duarte. This extraordinary woman was beautiful, brave, unscrupulous, and overflowing with sentiment on behalf of the outcasts of which she was herself one. She had repeatedly demonstrated her utility to Perón not just as an object of his affections but as a political adviser and organizer. He could not drop her and there is no evidence that he wished to, but he had to do something about her in an atmosphere so different from that which had permitted Yrigoyen to exhibit as an aspect of his radicalism his indifference to the institution of marriage.

Perón had already run into difficulty about his beloved Eva. On one occasion in 1944 an officer from the Campo de Mayo had waited on him to express the indignation of his brother officers about his irregular life and to order him to put away 'the woman Duarte', a phrase which was publicly employed by the newspaper *La Prensa* only a few weeks before she became the First Lady of Argentina. Perón was able to ignore his brother officers, but it was not so easy to neglect the opinion of an independent institution so influential as the Church. Henri IV had considered Paris to be worth a Mass, and Juan Domingo Perón decided Argentina was worth a wedding. Shortly after his triumphant re-entry into Buenos Aires, he was married to Eva Duarte privately in a civil ceremony, and a few days later in a great, well-publicized religious ceremony.

The reward of Perón for this act of repentance for past sin was not exactly an endorsement by the Church but something very close to it. On 15 November 1945, Cardinal Santiago Luis Copello and the archbishops and bishops of the Church in Argentina signed a letter read out in all the churches of the country declaring that 'No Catholic can vote for a candidate who supports: (1) the separation of Church and state; (2) the suppression of the laws which recognize the rights of the Church and particularly the swearing of religious oaths; (3) lay schools; and (4) legal divorce.' The archbishop of Santa Fé, Zenobio L. Guilland, followed this up by a pastoral letter in which he declared that no Catholic could vote for a party or person that had any relationship with socialists or communists. Inasmuch as the opposition to Perón, the *Unión Democrática*, included socialists and communists this was, by an operation of Thomist logic, a direct endorsement of Perón. Finally, Perón was invited to a special Mass in the Church of the Virgin of Luján, a national shrine, where the bishop of Luján prayed for Perón's victory. A Catholic rump opposed Perón, but they had no backing from the hierarchy and were the object of pious suspicion. Thus, the Argentine Church imitated the mistakes of His Holiness Pius XII in his long and disastrous relations with Mussolini and Hitler: short-term gains and a long-term crucifixion.

The other major secondary organizations to which Perón directed his attention were the political parties. He did not suppose that he could seduce all of them, but he tried his arts on the largest and most popular of them: the *Unión Cívica Radical*. The two wings of radicalism, the anti-Personalistas and the Personalistas, were, taken together, the largest and most persistent political groupings in Argentina. Uriburu may have overthrown Yrigoyen, but he could not destroy the Radical Party. The *Concordancia* always contained within it a strong anti-Personalista Radical element. Even the military regime of Ramírez and Farrell had given important offices to Radicals. Perón improved upon this tactic. Although he had been part of the conspiracy which overthrew Yrigoyen in 1930, he now declared that Hipólito Yrigoyen was a great Argentine, whose principal merit consisted in his recognition that the poor existed and were deserving of the beneficent attention of the state. He secured a Radical, Dr Hortencio Guijano, as his vice-presidential running mate. A *Junta Renovadora de la Unión Cívica Radical* was formed to organize the Radicals-for-Perón movement and get out the vote.

All these preparations for the election were very necessary. The political array against Perón was formidable. All the major interest groups were opposed to him: the Conservative Party, which numbered among its members many of the old élite, the *Sociedad Rural* which, from its elegant marble palace in the Calle Florida, spoke for the big *estancieros* of the province of Buenos Aires, the *Sociedad Rural de Rosario*, which spoke for the big cattlemen of the northern pampas, the *Confederación Rural Argentina*, which spoke for the grain-farmers, the *Unión Industrial*, which spoke for big industrial capital; some 300 other employers' organizations; the old parties such as the Democratic Progressives, the official *Unión Cívica Radical*, the Socialist Party, and the Communist Party. The conservatives refused to enter any alliance of interests, but the main political groups formed the *Unión Democrática*, which put up for President Vice-President José P. Tamborini, like Justo and Ortiz a former Minister in the anti-Personalista Radical Cabinet of President Marcelo T. de Alvear, and for Vice-President Enrique Mosca.

The election which followed was one of the few free and honest elections in Argentine history. The government, and probably Perón himself, was anxious to prevent the inevitable post-election charges of a *fraude*, and, indeed, the persistence of blatant frauds at election times was one of the most general causes of bitterness and disillusionment among Radicals. The police were put aside as superintendents of the election because they had in the past been one of the main agents of election frauds. In this instance, this danger was very real because the Chief of Police in Buenos Aires, Colonel Velasco, was a notorious partisan of Colonel Perón. In place of the police, the armed forces took over the voting process, and the general testimony is that, as near as was administratively possible, all those entitled to vote voted and their votes were honestly counted. As far as the presidential contest was concerned the victory for Perón was clear but not overwhelming: 1,479,517 for Perón and Guijano and 1,220,822 for Tamborini and Mosca. In the elections for the Congress the result was more favourable for Perón. In the Chamber of Deputies his Labour Party won 109 seats, the Radicals 44, the conservatives 2, and the anti-Personalista Radicals 2. In the Senate the followers of Perón won 26 seats and independents 2. All the provincial governorships were won by the Perónistas. For the first time since the passage of the Sáenz Peña Law in 1912, no socialists won any seats in the Congress.

The election was hard fought. The supporters of Perón resorted to bullying by armed gangs and encouraged anti-semitic violence, but their opponents were not above similar methods. How much influence this had on the result cannot be determined: probably none. What did operate against the opposition was the initiative in the hands of the government, for its powers were used to hound the extreme left and to smear the *Unión Democrática* with the communist label. But the significant elements in the victory were the careful way in which Perón aligned behind himself the secondary organizations of society equipped with an apparatus for influencing the political behaviour of the masses: the trade unions, the Church, and a part of the Radical Party. Perón's own Labour Party was a scratch affair, rapidly put together and having little life of its own, but it was the means of directing the vote where the trade unions, the Church, and the *Junta Renovadora de la Unión Cívica Radical* instructed it to go.

The opposition to Perón had certain obvious handicaps. Love of the constitution was an insufficient bond to unite together convincingly diverse and antagonistic groups who were lined up against a man who was obviously operating the constitution. This was as much one of his gimmicks as theirs, and consequently could not serve to underline the differences between the *Unión Democrática* and the Perónistas. The artificiality of the *Unión Democrática* was apparent to everyone including its most fervent advocates. There are many amusing stories of the ironies of the situation. One communist leader tells the tale of how he was walking in a demonstration arm in arm with a stranger in the common cause. This stranger turned out to be Robustiano Patron Costas, the great sugar magnate whose candidature for the Presidency provoked the *golpe* of June 1943. When they made themselves known to each other, Patron Costas gripped the communist more firmly, declaring fervently how he loved the workers and intended to see that every Argentine worker had a cottage with roses growing by the door. But even in this field of imaginative projection, Perón had already improved on Patron Costas.

The outcome owed something to chance, and chance went against the *Unión Democrática*. Any politician, for example, could hardly be expected to allow for the intervention of the United States in the election, nor could he be counted on to survive ham-handed support from this quarter. Well before the outbreak of World War II, President Roosevelt had taken over the foreign policy of the United States, leaving to the State Department and its Secretary, Cordell Hull, the business of managing American policy in marginal areas like Latin America. Cordell Hull was a doctrinaire liberal who believed it his duty to act according to the Wilsonian principle that Latin American communities should be taught to elect good governments and should, additionally, be conscripted into the American crusade against fascism. Argentina was an obvious eyesore to Cordell Hull, and his constant harassment of Ramírez and Farrell was one of their great political advantages in the internal politics of Argentina. As far as its effect on the Allied war effort was concerned it added up to zero. When Argentina entered the war, largely for the purpose of laying hands on German assets and patent rights, she was cautiously readmitted to the American presence, and an ambassador, Mr Spruille Braden, was sent to Argentina. This man knew a good deal about Latin America, and this was a disadvantage. He threw himself into the election as if he were campaigning for President Truman in Texas or California. In his enthusiasm he had produced a Blue Book setting forth all the sins of Perón and his friends in respect to their connections with the fascists and the Nazis. This Blue Book he circulated on a massive scale in Argentina. Perón's riposte was too easy. He circulated a Blue and White (the Argentine national colours) Book telling the Americans to mind their own business, decorating this message with some fancy variations on the anti-imperialist theme. With sorrow and indignation Tamborini saw Spruille Braden thus throw a trump on his only ace. No man could be expected to win against such friends.

Chapter 7

The Revolution that Failed:
the Regime of Perón

WHEN JUAN DOMINGO PERÓN was elected President of the Republic on 24 February 1946, he came to power with everything in his favour. He had been elected by a majority in a free election about which there could be no complaint. This majority was drawn predominantly from the working and lower-middle classes, but by no means exclusively so, nor was it a majority concentrated in one region of the country. In spite of the serious controversy surrounding him there was a widespread disposition to welcome him and support him as a man capable of breaking with the past and leading the nation to a new and better future. The means to do so were there. Industrial development had already made great strides so that it was no longer possible, nor was there a strong disposition, to think of Argentina as a vast cow pasture and grain farm. Argentina had plenty of money in the bank; purchasing power in international markets worth 1,500 million U.S. dollars in the form of sterling and dollar balances earned from the sale of supplies to the Allies during the war. Argentina having declared war against the Axis, the Germans, Italians, and Japanese had no claims against her, and the Argentine government had seized all enemy assets in Argentina. The prices of food and agricultural raw materials were rising relative to industrial goods. Much of Argentine productive equipment, such as the railways, was run down or worn out, but this was more an opportunity to modernize thoroughly than a handicap.

Perón himself and his advisers had many ideas about the needs of the community with which few people can disagree: the need to strengthen and extend basic industry such as steel, electrical power production, and fuel; the need to develop light engineering; the need to promote a more even development over the whole country instead of concentrating growth in Buenos Aires and the *Litoral*; the

184

need to improve education and alter its emphasis in line with the requirements of an industrial society; the need for increases in manpower through renewed immigration; the need for more comprehensive social services, designed to insure out of current income security in old age and sickness, and expanded to lift the level of the poorest and least organized sections of the community; and finally the need to find an independent position in the international community based on good relations with *all* nations.

Having the essential ingredients for success, i.e. substantial support in the community, the economic resources of capital and manpower, and the ideas, why did Perón make such a mess of governing Argentina? Why have his successors during the past thirteen years done little better? There is a temptation on the part of foreigners and of Argentines themselves to believe that their difficulties spring from some unique category of circumstances such as their remoteness from the advanced centres of production, or the fact of being Latin American, or their supposed underdevelopment, or their domination by a powerful class of rentier-landlords, or their subservience to foreign capital. There is nothing unique about Argentina. Argentine experience has lessons for all mankind, and for the advanced nations of North America and Europe even more than for those of Asia and Africa. What has happened in Argentina can happen anywhere, and may be doing so.

Perón and the movement he created were the revolutionary response of the Argentine community to the disasters of *laissez faire* capitalism which began with the depression of 1929 and culminated in World War II. This revolution changed profoundly the institutional structure, the productive organization, the decision-making apparatus, and the social relations of the Argentine community. And yet it was, like the fascist-Nazi revolution Perón sought first to imitate and the Labour-socialist revolution in Britain which next he copied, a half-revolution lacking the internal logic of the old *laissez faire* Argentina on the one hand and the new communist states on the other. The men who inherited the system made by Perón, whether conservatives like Aramburu and Guido or the Radicals like Frondizi or Illia, could neither dismantle the system, as the Americans dismantled the Nazi system in Germany and created a *laissez faire* state, nor learn how to run it better than Perón as the Gaullistes have in some measure learned to run the hybrid system in France. It is at first sight hardly credible, but there is a parallel in principle between the failure of the British Tories to run the system taken over from Attlee and the failures which have followed the overthrow of Perón in Argentina. There are many reasons for supposing that, perhaps, Onganía is learning how to operate the system produced by the Perónist revolution, and that, perhaps, Argentina has at last discovered the means of running a hybrid system for which traditional representative, democratic decision-making processes are not the appropriate and effective mechanisms for stable operation.

In his first message to Congress after his inauguration, Perón declared his intention to end the *laissez faire* state and make the state a central agency in directing and administering the economy. Until Perón emerged the central and provincial government of Argentina had a comparatively small direct part in productive processes. They provided certain public services, such as the postal services, the maintenance of public roads, education, municipal services, some docks, and they operated some small railways. The only major industry in government ownership was petroleum, but even this did not have a monopoly of refining and distribution. Even before his inauguration Perón began to change all this. The Central Bank was nationalized. Within two years the state had taken over the railways, the telecommunications systems, the gas industry, a substantial part of central electricity generation, and had established state enterprises in the field of coastal and deep-sea shipping and air transport. A state-sponsored mixed enterprise was set up to produce steel. The *Fábricas Militares* (industrial enterprises run by the armed forces) were extended, and a state-owned aviation industry was set up. Insurance was nationalized. Noises were made suggesting the nationalization of land. The main export business in grain and meat was not nationalized, but a state marketing agency took control of the export of all major commodities, the *Instituto Argentino de Promoción del Intercambio* (I.A.P.I.), with power to fix prices to producers and (it was supposed, during the period of mounting prices) to consumers. At the same time the pension system was extended to all industrial workers so that 25 per cent of the workers' wages (10 per cent from the worker and 15 per cent from the employer) was canalized into state pension funds. The pensionable age was set at the absurdly low age of fifty-five, and pensioners were geared to wages at the time of retirement and not to payments into the funds. The pension system was eventually extended to rural workers at lower rates of contribution.

In this way an enormous new complex of entrenched interests was created which constitutes a formidable political obstacle to change. Short of a devastating civil war it is hard to see how the revolution worked by Perón can be undone. For all practical purposes it is impossible to return to the *laissez faire* system and to restore the free market as the principal decision-making mechanism of the Argentine community. Given the facts of life as Perón created them, the only possibility would seem to be to discover the method of operating the system effectively, introducing elements of flexibility here and there as opportunity offers.

Indisputably Perón operated his system extremely badly. Like a spoiled child he wanted everything and he wanted it at once. He revealed himself totally incapable of making choices and establishing the priorities which are necessary for the operation of any economic system. Furthermore he taught the community to believe in the instantaneous and total pay-off, so that no one had any order of expectations. The infinite expectation is equivalent to zero, and that is what it has amounted to in Argentina. The Argentine community today is worse off than it was twenty-five years ago, and while much of the world has moved ahead in terms of material standards of living, Argentina has remained stationary and everyone runs harder in order to stand still. A high percentage of professional people, workers, and pensioners have to do two jobs in order to live.

In principle, there is no reason why Perón's system should not have worked. This is as true of Perón's brand of socialism as it is of a *laissez faire* system or a communist system. But this truth is conditional upon a number of elements which Perón either neglected or did not understand. When he announced his first five-year plan he set up an economic high command in the form of a National Economic Council under Miguel Miranda, an industrialist who had enjoyed great success under the *laissez faire* system mildly modified by the controls established during the 1930s. Señor Miranda may have created a temporary atmosphere of confidence among the private business interests, but it was soon demonstrated, as it so frequently is, that the techniques and the knowledge acquired in private business are no guarantee of capacity to handle a whole economy. In any case Miranda did not have a free hand, because every economic decision was conditional upon the political requirements of President Perón, and these soon made nonsense of the plans in general and of the details of their successful execution.

Perón's plans for the economy required the investment of large
sums of capital. His own first estimate of the cost of the first Five-
Year Plan was 1,500 million U.S. dollars; not much by modern
standards, but enormous by the standards of 1946 and enormous
compared with anything previously attempted. It was a sum greater
than the entire investment made by British capitalists in Argentina
over a period of seventy years. Where was this capital to come from?
Argentina had approximately this sum available in its foreign balances, and the domestic resources of capital were equally good.
There was nothing inherently absurd in what was proposed, provided the investment was made prudently in enterprises capable of
producing goods and services at a real cost sufficiently low to yield
the surpluses for fresh investment and for the development of production as an on-going process capable of renewing plant, improving
techniques, and increasing production. This was not at all what
happened.

Instead of increasing the capital of Argentina, Perón proceeded to
decapitalize the community while at the same time bringing into the
state structure productive enterprises which were either badly run
down or on the brink of technological development requiring more
not less capital. The transport and telecommunications systems provide an example of this mistake. The basic cause of the mistake was
political. Years of nationalist and anti-imperialist agitation had
created the popular myth that the sovereignty and independence of
the nation depended on its ownership as distinct from its control of
the productive resources of the community. Britain, for example,
owned a substantial part of the Argentine railways, therefore Britain
exploited Argentina and Argentines worked to provide profits for
British railway owners and holders of railway bonds and debentures.
The same argument was advanced about the Americans in regard
to the telephone system. What was not recognized, particularly in
the case of both the British- and the French-owned railways, was
that they needed more capital and a thorough reorganization if they
were to become a cost-reducing, efficient factor in the overall
economy of the country. Several options were open to Perón. He
could have taken over the railways with or without compensation,
and proceeded to invest capital in their reorganization and modernization. He could have invited the owners to undertake this programme
on their own, even threatening expropriation if they did not. Or he
could have joined with them in a joint programme. Some of the

options were not as possible as others. The British, for example, held the Argentine sterling balances, and could have continued to hold them if he seized British property without compensation. Furthermore they still bought Argentine exports, and might have closed their markets if their property was seized. The obviously most beneficial course would have been to extend the British and French railway franchises in return for a fresh investment of capital. This plan was tried, but in the end nothing came of it because Perón came to believe that the foreign railway interests were supporters of his political enemies, the conservatives, and that there was more political benefit to be gained by taking over the railways. In the end he agreed to pay £150 million, a sum considerably in excess of the stock-market value of the enterprises and greatly in excess of their inventory value. As a business deal, the purchase was thoroughly bad from the Argentine point of view, and in the long run equally so from the British, for it closed still further a British export market. In fact Argentina used a proportion of her assets to increase the capital stock of Britain, not to improve her own productive equipment. Such was the price of nationalism and indifference to economic reality.

The danger of foreign control had never had much substance, but what little there was was diminishing and this had been so for many years. The relative position of foreign investors in Argentina had been declining since World War I, so that the need for foreign capital was becoming marginal. Even if Perón had given the British and French railway companies £150 million, or even £200 million, on condition they used such sums to improve their properties, little difference would have been made to the overall situation. By doing what he did, he eventually made Argentina more, not less, dependent upon foreign investment, and this the last stages of his regime revealed.

If assets were frittered away on a large scale to satisfy ill-founded nationalist sentiment, this was nothing compared with the resources directed for political purposes to improving popular levels of consumption and for the re-equipment and expansion of the armed forces. Most politicians have to pay off their supporters in some way or another: either in the shape of policies producing recognizable benefits, or in the form of booty. Perón was pre-eminently a master of the pay-off, but this had two defects as far as the long-run viability of the community was concerned. Too much of his pay-off was booty – the direct transfer of assets from one person to another – and it was on too large a scale. He had won his way to power by conferring quick benefits on a limited number of people – the organized workers – and he had done this in circumstances of rising productivity and labour shortages in expanding industries. He was paying off in very favourable economic circumstances so that he was achieving results only slightly better than the market would have in any case produced. Once he was in power, he felt obliged – and easy economic circumstances reinforced his desire – to pay off everyone. There is a difference in paying off X and paying off X^3 in a population of X^4. The consequences are rather different, and this Argentina began to discover.

Without going into the effects upon the accumulation of capital of rapid absolute increases in real income as a result of favourable wage negotiations, the institution of compulsory payments of thirteen months' wages for twelve months' work, holidays with pay, pensions at fifty-five and generous welfare programmes, we need only look at the distribution of spendable funds in the public accounts during the years of Perón's power and at a comparison of this with distribution in earlier periods. It must be borne in mind that Perón vastly extended the public responsibility for providing capital for the productive services essential to the economy. During the period 1935–39, the public authorities of Argentina spent 21.3 per cent of the gross national product, and during the years 1940–44, this percentage fell to 19.5 per cent. During the first five years under Perón, from 1945 to 1949, the percentage jumped to 29.4 per cent and even in the last year of his government never dropped below 28.2 per cent. Keeping in mind the enormous expansion of the responsibility of the Argentine government for high-capital industrial services, this expansion of government spending was not great. In fact it was insufficient. The critical point, however, is on what the public money was spent.

It is popularly believed that Perón's first Presidency was his best. In fact the euphoria of his first three years in office was the foundation elements of all his later disasters. In economic terms his last years in office were his best, and if he did anything of value for Argentina it was between 1952 and 1955. Put briefly, he decapitalized and impoverished Argentina between 1946 and 1951 by overspending and misapplying resources. Perhaps sobered by the drought of 1952, he changed his economic policy and began to use resources more rationally and productively. Because, during these

later years, there was no pay-off, he lost political support. When the
going got tough, he became vicious, tried to turn his supporters
against one another, and was destroyed.

A quick look at the public accounts of Argentina will reveal the
measure of his improvidence during his first term of office. During
the years 1935–39, Argentine public authorities were spending 6.9
per cent of the gross national product on the wages and salaries of
public employees; 2.2 per cent on materials used by them in their
work; 5.7 per cent on pensions, interest on debt, and subsidiaries;
6 per cent on direct investment; and 0.5 per cent on indirect investment. During Perón's tenure of office the proportion of the gross
national product paid out to public employees grew steadily: 7.9
per cent in 1945–49; 9.1 per cent in 1950–54; and 9.2 per cent during his last year of power. The proportion spent on materials used
rose but not so greatly, from 2.2 per cent to a high of 3.5 per cent
during 1945–49, and declined thereafter to 2.5 per cent in 1955. The
proportion paid in interest on debts, pensions, and subsidies declined
from 5.7 per cent in 1934–35 to 5.1 per cent during 1945–49, and
then rose sharply to 9.9 per cent in 1955. What is most critical in
this expenditure pattern is, however, investment. The proportion
of public funds spent on investments inevitably declined during the
years of World War II from 6 per cent before the war to 4.6 per
cent during 1940–44. Investment then jumped to 8.7 per cent of
direct investment, but from zero to 4.2 per cent on indirect investment, i.e. the purchase of railways, telephones, etc. Then the proportion invested fell away to 8 per cent in 1950–54, and to 5.9 per
cent in 1955.

It may be argued that an increase in investment by public agencies
from a proportion of 6.5 per cent of the gross national product in
1935–39 to 12.9 per cent in 1945–49 is an impressive increase. But
in what was investment made? In 1935–39 6 per cent was made in
direct investment such as the building of roads and irrigation works,
and only 0.5 per cent in the purchase of enterprises and indirect
investment. In 1945–49, however, almost one-third of investment
was indirect, and was not investment in Argentina. It was a transfer
of assets to foreign capitalists, and there is no proof that they invested the assets they acquired in Argentina. Very likely they
invested them in Rhodesia or South Africa or Canada.

What was invested in Argentina was not predominantly used to
build up productive capacity. Of all investment during the years

1945–51 50.8 per cent was non-economic and most of it on conspicuous waste: 12.4 per cent on public buildings; 29.3 per cent on
the armed forces; and only 12.4 per cent on objects of some possible
use to the economy, i.e. on sanitary works. Transport and power
production, now almost totally the responsibility of the state, got
less than half the investment resources.

Only during the last three years of Perón's regime did this improvi-
dent pattern change. Transport and power production during these
years received 72.6 per cent of all investment funds, and non-
economic investment only 27.4 per cent. Investment on the armed
forces fell from 21.3 per cent to 9.7 per cent. But the damage was
already done. Perón was only an extreme instance of a state of mind
common among politicians everywhere which blinds them to the
facts of economic life. An industrial society, whether capitalist, socialist, or communist, requires constant attention to renewal, to technological improvement, and to expansion, and this involves dividing
current production between spendable funds for consumption goods
and spendable funds for the renewal of plant and expansion of
equipment. If this constant attention is directed too long and
resources are directed too completely to satisfying the desire for
immediate consumption, upon conspicuous waste, upon war or the
preparation for war, the productive system begins to run down, to
become less productive, and people have either to work harder or
go short. This happened on a great scale in Argentina under Perón,
and the nation has not yet recovered. The evidence is visible on
every hand: poor roads, poor railways, poor telephones, inadequate
electric power, indifferent municipal services, shabby schools, overcrowded and under-equipped universities, and a brain drain to
other countries. This has happened in a thoroughly modern community. It is not the result of some legacy of terrible poverty and
backwardness in the past. This is precisely why Argentine experience
is so important for others. It can happen in western Europe. It can
happen in the United States of America.

The economic mistakes made by Perón stemmed directly and
inevitably from his political character and *modus operandi*. He had
developed a pay-off strategy of rallying political support, and this
had brought him to power. Power he viewed in absolute terms much
as a soldier is likely to do, for he equated power with command. For
him power was not the means of enforcing decisions, but the means
of making decisions. Perón hated opposition, because opposition im-

plied the existence of interests he did not control and people he did not dominate, and opposition was incompatible with his view of power as command.

This disposition of the new President soon revealed itself in respect to the Supreme Court: a body which existed to contain the government within the constitution, and to bind it to the past decisions of the community stated as laws. Before his inauguration the Supreme Court had found unconstitutional some of the decrees of the military government. Perón intended to have no repetition. The president of the Supreme Court, Dr Roberto Repetto, resigned. This was a premature and unnecessary surrender which encouraged Perón to attack at once all opposition. Dr Ernesto Sanmartino, a Radical deputy, was suspended for criticizing the President. This set the temper of the new government. A great budget of reform followed, and parallel with this Perón led a great attack on all sources of opposition. The Supreme Court was investigated and purged. Radio stations were taken over. The government secured from the Congress the power to mobilize the whole nation for war, which involved the power to break strikes. This programme, designed to smash all opposition and build up presidential power, was carried forward by a gigantic pay-off: large wage increases for the workers; a large re-equipment and expansion programme for the armed forces; and plenty of jobs for the boys in the nationalized industries, the public service, and the expanded welfare services, and tariff protection for the industrialists.

By the end of 1948, the economy began to show signs of incapacity to support this vast strategy of pay-off. Foreign exchange reserves were exhausted. The price of Argentina's main exports, which were still the traditional mass produced commodities, meat, cereals, and wool, began to fall relative to Argentine purchases of fuel, machinery, and industrial raw materials. Large deficits began to appear, and these were met with increasing floods of paper currency and government borrowing. Meanwhile, the state monopoly of exports was being employed to squeeze the agricultural interest by extending the differential between the prices paid for commodities and the prices at which these commodities were sold. At the very moment when rural production needed to become more competitive in the world market and increasingly productive to meet the expanding demand in the home market, the ranchers, farmers, and processing industries were deprived of the means of improving efficiency by mechanization and access to the rapidly expanding technology of fertilization, plant-breeding and vegetable and animal hygiene.

The economic crisis of 1949 manifested itself as an inflationary rise in prices, a fall in real incomes, and a blight on popular economic expectations. Perón's response was an intensification of his determination to forge new weapons for more effective political control. A plan to reform the constitution was introduced at short notice. A new Perónista Party was organized and endowed with a new ideology labelled *Justicialismo*. An anti-Argentine activities investigating committee was set up, and it was made a serious criminal offence to insult the President or any of the public authorities. A plot to assassinate the President and his wife was discovered. Perón's old friend and ally, Cipriano Reyes, was flung into prison along with a selected panel of conspirators drawn in a representative fashion from the various sectors of the community: the Church, the armed forces, business, and the landed interest. In the case of the Church and the armed forces, a clever economy of effort was achieved; the men arrested were naval chaplains.

In the short run, totalitarian political mechanisms reinforced with popular propaganda can solve political problems by shifting opposition and imposing conformity to the sovereign will, but they cannot by themselves solve economic problems. A programme of industrialization such as Perón had proposed requires large stocks of capital, i.e. purchasing power in the national and international markets which is not earmarked for consumption expenditure. He had already wasted a substantial volume of the necessary purchasing power buying badly depreciated capital equipment and non-productive equipment such as military jet aircraft. While he did not imitate Stalin in liquidating kulaks he attacked the landed interest ideologically while he milked them dry economically by his system of differential payments and exchange control. The agricultural and ranching interests, being the largest and richest interests in Argentina, were one of the best potential sources of investment capital, but the attack upon them not only ended the possibility of them investing in industry, but destroyed their inclination to invest in their own business. Their surpluses began clandestinely to flow abroad or into static assets like more land and urban house property. Informed guesses by economists estimated that by 1965 there were more Argentine assets outside the country than in Argentina, and if this was so (and it was so to some degree) this process was initiated by

Perón's attack on the landed interest. Furthermore, this impairment of accumulation and investment had serious secondary effects because the dependent middle class, where investment capacity, individually small, is globally large, were rendered so frightened that they, too, started investing not in growth but in secure assets such as land and house property and other forms of hedges against inflation. Foreign capital Perón disdained to use even if foreign investors could be persuaded of his capacity to secure their investments and ensure a return upon them.

Thus the crisis of 1949 produced an intensification of the drive towards totalitarian political control without at the same time producing any real change in the economic policies of the government. Demagogy and tension mounted together. Attacks were made on the press, and in 1951 *La Prensa* was seized and transformed into a trade union paper. In August 1951, a great gathering of Perón's supporters calling itself, in imitation of the revolutionary gathering in 1810, a *Cabildo Abierto*, proclaimed the candidature of Perón for a second term as President and the candidature of Eva de Perón as Vice-President. This was a truly revolutionary departure. The old constitution of 1853 prohibited an immediate second term for a President. The new constitution permitted this, and so did it allow for the candidature of a woman, for women had been enfranchised by Perón. Suddenly the armed forces and the Church, the two leading secondary organizations supporting Perón, had it forcibly brought home to them that Perón and his wife were not only impoverishing Argentina but changing its social character.

A common liberal leftist misconception about Argentina is based on the notion that the armed forces and the Church are allies and/ or tools of the economic élite, whether the landed interest or the capitalists both native and foreign. This belief is out of line with reality, and thus it is an obstacle to all analysis and understanding. Both the officers and the ecclesiastics of Argentina have repeatedly demonstrated their almost total ignorance of the economics of the nation and of the material problems which require solution and management. Professionalization in the army and the immigrant and ultramontane character of the Church have so narrowed their understanding that they have been as much taken in by spurious nostrums stemming from social envy and fear as the simplest and most illiterate workers and gauchos. Rosas, Mitre, Roca, and Justo were military men, but they were landowners, entrepreneurs, and

economic planners first and military men second. So were the Catholic apologists of the late nineteenth century. The new breed, of
which General Perón and Cardinal Copello are conspicuous
examples, have not more, but less, understanding of fundamental
economic questions than the most narrow-minded and self-absorbed
businessmen or trade unionists. It is necessary to say this in order to
understand why the secondary organizations behind Perón supported
him in the first place and then remained so long the basis of his
power. They were just as much taken in by him as anyone else, and
they only turned away from him when he began to gore their ox.

This started to happen as Perón's economic failures obliged him
to move towards full totalitarianism and to attempt to impose ideological and administrative controls on all aspects of community life.
Up to the point where the economy began to fail, Perón had made a
revolution on the cheap, much as Castro later did in the early 1960s
in Cuba. Argentina was not a broken-down society as Russia was
when the Bolsheviks seized power, nor was it even a temporarily
prostrate society as Germany was when Hitler took over from the
frightened German bourgeoisie. Perón's was a revolution of incoherence in which in the first stage he was able to offer something to
every established interest and always enough to weaken their
solidarity and understanding of their group requirements. He never
destroyed interests as the Bolsheviks did. He never cleared the
ground in order to build anew. Like all opportunists he acted on the
maxim 'sufficient unto the day is the evil thereof', and by 1951 this
day was coming.

The proposal that Argentina should elect Perón to the Presidency
for a second term and his wife to the Vice-Presidency provoked a
serious tremor in the armed forces, somewhat in the way that
Stalin's anti-semitism finally shook the most craven Bolsheviks. The
possibility of a woman succeeding to the Presidency and becoming
the Commander-in-Chief of the armed forces outraged the officers,
and disturbed their psychological equilibrium in somewhat the same
way that the thought of a woman on the throne of Spain had driven
the Carlists of Spain mad. There is a 'thing' about women in
Spanish culture, and enough of this remained among the officers and
clerics of Argentina to produce what might be called the Carlist
syndrome. Eva Duarte de Perón was a woman well calculated to
exacerbate this disease. Perónista propaganda was already depicting
her as a well-dressed saint, as if she were simultaneously the Duchess

of Windsor and St Frances Cabrini. Advertising and propaganda can work miracles but one they could not work, at least among the Argentine armed forces, was the transformation of the President's wife into the Virgin of the Calle Corrientes. A new delegation came to Perón from the Campo de Mayo. Evita must be put away not as a mistress this time but as a vice-presidential candidate. This time Perón bowed to another authority, and this was the beginning of the end.

But not quite. He had another four years of power. In September 1951, there was a military rising which was put down partly by pro-Perónista officers and partly by mass action by the workers. The election followed. Perón secured 4.6 million votes compared with 2.3 million for his Radical opponents Balbín and Frondizi. The people were still on his side.

But was Divine Providence? Almost simultaneously a severe drought afflicted Argentina. This revealed how completely Argentina was still dependent on the products of rural industry. To feed the people cereals had to be imported! Meat production declined catastrophically. In July 1952, Eva Perón died.

Death is a central event in the Spanish traditional culture, and no less so in Argentina than in Spain. The cities of the dead reflect and symbolize the cities of the living. The Recoleto cemetery is the *Barrio Norte* of the dead as the Chacarita is a middle-class suburb of the Hereafter. A funeral is no less important than a wedding in the ritual life of Argentina. Perón took full advantage of this. The funeral of Eva Duarte de Perón was an event on a scale never before witnessed in Argentina. The outpouring of sentiment was unprecedented and people who did not wear mourning lost their jobs. The Perónista machine organized an attempt at instant canonization. A vast mausoleum in the style of a Greek temple was built in the old working-class area of Buenos Aires. It began to look as if Perón was going to take over the ritual and merit system of the Church as a political weapon, much as Rosas had done when the *Mazorca* induced the display of Rosas' portrait on the altars of the churches.

There were already causes of dissension between Perón and the ecclesiastical interests. His welfare programmes together with his wife's personally controlled charitable organization, the Social Aid Foundation, had usurped the Church's place in the charity movement; nor had the Church taken too kindly to the enfranchisement of women, a mistake on their part because women in Argentina, as elsewhere, tend to be more pious than men, and potentially a favourable factor for the Church in the equations of politics. But the Church did not see the matter this way at this time. The paganism of the Perónistas disturbed the clerics.

Another interest began to move against the government: the students. As in many other fields of endeavour, Perón had some good ideas on the subject of university reform. He made admission to the universities free so that higher education was available to all. He also believed that university teaching should be made a full-time occupation and should cease to be an amateur enterprise adding to the prestige of the rich and to the income and professional kudos of the lawyers, engineers, and doctors. But equally, as in so many other cases, Perón's good intentions were corrupted by his political requirements. Perónistas took over the direction of the universities, and soon were using them as a means of employing their supporters and as a transmission belt of their ideology. Students were increasingly instructed by oafs and indoctrinated by fanatics. Perónista supporters became professors of engineering, who scarcely knew any arithmetic; professors of literature, who could not spell; and professors of physics, who understood the Perónista constitution better than the constitution of matter. This was a fatal proceeding, because the Argentine students, being mostly poor and ambitious, were serious-minded and determined to acquire the skill and understanding needed in their careers. They developed first contempt and then hatred for the institutions of higher education, and they had no inhibitions about protesting against the state of affairs in the universities. Arrest and torture did not cow them. Thus Perón, through the inexplicable stupidity of his policy towards intelligent youth, created an opposition among the very people whom he aimed originally to help and whose assistance as intellectual workers his industrializing intentions required.

By the end of 1952 the economy of Argentina was in such bad shape that Perón was obliged to consider a change in economic policy. Politically he was not yet in a position to turn the screw on the wage-workers, and to find there the means of bolstering up his investment programme. The landed interest and the farmers were hit by drought and steady decapitalization. There remained only the foreign capitalists, and to these he turned. In August 1953, a negotiation was opened with the Standard Oil Company of California. Not only petroleum extraction but industrial development in

engineering was opened up to foreign enterprise. From 1953 onwards American and European industrial firms began to take over
the major sectors of Argentine industry which Perón's previous
economic and educational policies had made it impossible for
Argentina to finance or to staff at the top. With the aid of the
Perón government, given in the form of tariff protection, American,
Italian, and German firms developed profitable but high-cost auto-
mobile and tractor plants and a chemical industry. From Perón's
point of view this influx of capital was politically helpful, for,
although it denied his nationalist pretensions, it made jobs for the
only segment of society still actively friendly to him. He began, too,
to improve the infrastructure. In electricity this was possible by
building large power stations, but in the case of the railways
modernization and the reduction of costs was very difficult because
the railways were an enormous political pork barrel supplying job
opportunities and feather-bedding for workers of all kinds. As it
was, he faced a great railway strike, the breaking of which did not
lead to improved management.

By 1954, there had developed a new alignment in Argentine
politics. Unable to break totally or control completely the secondary
organizations such as the armed forces, the Church and the
universities, Perón found himself in an alliance of workers, foreign
capitalists, and government office-holders and hangers-on. In a
sense this was a situation congenial to himself inasmuch as it located
in one camp all the people he hated because they had the organization and intelligence to limit his power. That they were divided
among themselves was likewise an advantage. The foreign capitalists
he did not have to take too seriously because they tended to confuse
power with authority, and the Americans, Italians, and Germans
tended, in any case, to prefer 'strong' men to strong institutions.
Through 1953 and 1954 Perón persisted in the illusion that he could
continue his attack on the major secondary organizations so long as
he kept control of the trade unions. In December 1954 he hammered
the Church with a law making divorce legal, and for good measure
authorized the reopening of brothels. This he followed with a
decree banning religious holidays, and downgrading Christmas and
Good Friday to the category of secondary holidays.

While one cannot but admire the boldness of Perón's political
manoeuvres, one must acknowledge that he exhibited an unprinci-
pled coarseness, insensitivity, and lack of respect for other people's

courage and intelligence which is too often characteristic of a weak and neurotic character. His manoeuvres *vis-à-vis* the landed interests particularly illustrate this. The old oligarchy had never liked Perón and few of the traditional élite had supported him. He had treated them with contempt and violence. In 1953 his goon squads had burned down the Jockey Club and robbed or destroyed the magnificent library and art collection of that institution. And yet he believed then that by easing their financial burdens they would somehow not only increase food production but come round to his side. They did neither.

In June 1955, there was a great Corpus Christi demonstration, which turned into a mass demonstration against the government. Perón replied by kicking the Papal delegates out of Argentina. On 16 June, a formation of the air force swept over the Plaza de Mayo in Buenos Aires, bombing the Casa Rosada. This ill-conceived attempt to kill Perón only succeeded in killing several hundred citizens. Perón went temporarily to pieces, and had to be carried to the deep bomb shelter he had had prepared for such a contingency. He soon recovered, however, and gave ground. Angel Borlenghi, his Minister of Interior, was relieved of his Cabinet post, and Perón went on the air to declare he was now the President of all Argentines and not simply the leader of the government party. He pleaded for co-operation.

This was but a ruse. On the night of 31 August gangs of trade union hooligans started burning churches. The noble churches of San Francisco and Santo Domingo were put to the torch. Their great domes exploded from the heat, seeming to herald the end of the world. The rumour went round that arms were being handed out to the workers. Perón declared that five enemies would be killed for every Perónista slain.

But this was the end. In Córdoba the garrison rose under the leadership of General Eduardo Lonardi, and there was a great popular demonstration of support. This time no significant element in the armed forces came to the President's rescue. The students and middle class as well as workers came out into the streets. Perón sought refuge aboard a Paraguayan gun-boat, and was taken into exile.

Chapter 8

The Failure of Neo-Democracy – Part One

THE OVERTHROW of Perón as President was a simple operation; the elimination of Perónism was quite otherwise. It may indeed be doubted that this has yet been achieved. Perón still lives on in Spain, but he lives on, too, in Argentina. For at least ten years after his flight into exile he was the most important figure in Argentine political life: the leader of the opposition *extra muros*; the shadow President. Although he is no longer the black king on the Argentine chessboard, he is still more than a pawn. General Rosas from his place of exile in Hampshire exercised no influence in the community he so long dominated. Perón did. Why?

Some of the continuing fascination with Perón was attributable to the memory of past benefits conferred on the forgotten people of Argentina and to the charm and force of his personality. Many Argentines regardless of political allegiance remember the late 1940s as a time of excitement and popular well-being when the expansive generosity of the government obscured its serious failings and the chorus of gratitude and approval silenced the apprehensive murmurs and individual indignation of the regime's opponents. By 1960 the benefits which it was popularly believed that Perón had brought to the people were but dimly remembered, and a new generation was growing up which knew not the master. Perón's charm was personal, and this, too, was unfamiliar to or unremembered by more and more people as time passed. When, in 1965, he sent his young wife Isabel to Argentina with tape-recordings of his voice, this exercise in propaganda was regarded more as a joke than a message from across the water. And yet even in 1965 Perón was a presence in Argentina, and an important one.

The explanation is to be found not in the messages he sent, but in the organizations he left behind in Argentina and in the interests connected with them. Every leading Argentine politician since 1955, elected or military, has tried either to destroy these organizations or to enter into alliance with them. Until General Onganía took power in 1966 no one succeeded in either strategy, and it is not yet clear whether Onganía's steel hand in a sponge rubber glove has got a controlling grip on the Perónistas.

At the expense of repetition, it must be restated that Perón re-shaped and expanded the trade union movement, and that he attracted to this core movement the support of a wide range of unorganized people through his welfare and pension systems. Furthermore, he taught the masses to participate in public life not just by voting but by striking, demonstrating, wrecking, and burn-ing. Like Rosas he developed a technique of control through partici-pation in ways which gave the illusion of power, freedom, and release. The masses themselves as an aggregate of individuals neither benefited individually nor acted on their own initiative, but a minority of adventurous organizers, of whom Perón himself was the most conspicuous example, learned manipulative techniques, institu-tionalized them, and constituted a substantial interest group which used, and to a degree still use, the masses in much the same way that employers use workers or ecclesiastics use believers. Of all those who learned and developed manipulative skills under Perón the most enduring, because the most solidly based, were the trade union leaders. From 1955 to 1966 they were an autonomous factor in the power equation.

The departure of Perón and the shattering of the *gleichgestaltung* which he had imposed on the trade unions produced a number of superficially fissiparous tendencies. Some trade union leaders re-mained loyal to Perón, abasing themselves at his feet and declaring their intention to follow his path. Others made a distinction between the fallen saviour and his doctrine, and declared themselves for 'Perónism without Perón'. Others became openly anti-Perónistas. What the trade union leaders had in common was, however, much more important and powerful than what divided them: i.e. common problems of organization, the interdependence necessary to maintain their several empires, and their common need to maintain the mystique of their *conquistas sociales*. Out of the wreckage of the Perónista regime there emerged a trade union élite equipped with manipulative techniques, organization, and financial resources com-parable with the military élite, the ecclesiastical élite, the business élite, and the landed élite. In many respects they were better equip-

ARGENTINA RESOURCES

ped to exercise influence and affect decision-making than the business and landed élites.

An analysis of the sources of power of the trade union élite is necessary for any understanding of the course and character of the Argentine economy as well as Argentine politics since 1955. As the result of developments during the military dictatorship of Ramírez and Farrell and the subsequent regime of Perón trade union leaders ceased to be a group of skilled negotiators who depended for their existence on their capacity to negotiate with employers on behalf of their own employers, the wage-workers. They had become masters each of his own empire whose clientele were dependent on them not only for the rate of wages they earned, but, in the major industries, for their jobs. An Argentine employer could no longer discharge a worker with a week's pay. The discharge of a worker made an employer liable for a substantial capital payment in the shape of severance pay. In industries like electricity, the railways, telecommunications, and petroleum, which were wholly or substantially state-owned, the trade unions themselves exercised a large control over employment policies, and these controls were designed to maximize the numbers of workers employed through artificially inflated or wholly unnecessary rules governing the need for stand-by shifts, over-manning, and under-working in dangerous and dirty jobs and so on. There were few negotiations at plant level. Wages were fixed politically for whole industries or the nation as a whole, and were unrelated to the costs, profits, or productivity of particular enterprises. The trade union leaders were interested in employing the maximum number of men and women, but they were concerned only emotionally, not operationally, with the fact of persistent high levels of unemployment. Argentine private employers were afraid to expand their labour force because it was financially disastrous to contract that labour force in response to changes in techniques or in market conditions. Only very small enterprises had an escape route via bankruptcy. Public enterprises were subject to a law of expanding labour forces because in this sector financial burdens caused by large work-forces could be transferred to society as a whole by deficit financing and inflation. In the case of large industrial employers they could and did protect their position by insisting on and getting high tariff protection to ensure non-competitive, captive markets for their products.

Inflation was inevitable in this set of circumstances, but inflation itself became an indispensable element in the preservation of the empires of the trade union élite. The rapid erosion of real incomes by rising prices required annual wage increases in the range of 25–30 per cent in order that the wage-workers could stand still or fall back only slightly in their real standards of life. Occasionally real standards fell as much as 6 per cent in one year, but in general the large increases in money wages effected by trade union pressure were sufficient to preserve the mystique of *conquistas sociales* and to impart to the sacred drama of the class struggle a faint flavour of reality.

The secondary consequences of these wage increases were important for the trade union élite and constituted a major factor in their power and their financial strength. Until the practice was stopped by President Illia the central organization of the trade unions, the C.G.T., took one day's pay for every member of every affiliate in the form of a May Day offering. This was a sizeable sum amounting to approximately .35 per cent of the total wages of the organized workers. The affiliates on the other hand were empowered by law and did in practice take the entire wage increase for one month. With wage increases running at 25–30 per cent this was an enormous sum, which the union officers, like all others holding currency rapidly deteriorating in value, invested in safe hedges against inflation such as land, hotels, and house property. These investments in turn enabled them to sell services to their members in the form of house mortgages, flats, holiday facilities, hospital services, and consumer goods sold for cash and by hire purchase. The bank employees, for example, operate one of the large department stores in Buenos Aires as a shop exclusively for bank employees and their families, and the light- and power-workers operate one of the largest luxury hotels in Mar del Plata as a holiday centre. Argentine trade unions are big-business enterprises with captive markets and large capital resources. Some were crooked enterprises with big rake-offs by the leaders, but many were, and still are, well managed and provide a wide range of good service which cannot be faulted in terms of what they provide and how they provide it. The really disastrous consequences arose not from the dishonesty or bad management of the trade union élite (for this was by no means true of all union leaders) but from the effects which their *modus operandi* had on industry as a whole and the inflexibility and high costs which they had institutionalized, the vested interest in inflation they created, and the impairment of capital accumulation and its channelling towards hedges against inflation rather than towards industrial expansion.

Although the trade union élite owed most to Perón and stood by him longest, it must not be supposed that they were the sole interest group with a natural involvement in Perónism. Perón in his struggle for power had combined in an effective alliance the armed forces, the Church, and the trade unions. The élites of these interest groups were non-capitalist and some of them were anti-capitalist. All three had a common characteristic, viz. that they depended for their existence upon belief systems capable of convincing large numbers of people of the credibility and hence the value of the services they had to offer: security and order in the case of the armed forces; comfort and salvation in the case of the Church; and social dignity and redemption from poverty in the case of the trade unions. Because everyone needs security, comfort, and dignity the problem of credibility, in the case of these interest groups, was much simpler than it was for the capitalist interest groups – the industrialists and the rural interests. From Rosas to Ramírez the capitalist interest groups had depended for credibility upon performance and upon a liberal ideology which is not easy to understand and, being rational, was not rooted in massive, general emotions. In the ideological game the liberal capitalist interests had long since not only lost but lost their nerve.

The men who led the *Revolución Libertadora* declared their intention of restoring an open, democratic, and liberal political process. Declaration of intention was easier than performance. The two major interest groups which had overthrown Perón were the army and the Church, and neither of these was liberal in principle nor were the numbers among its leaders large who were convinced of the advantages of a liberal political order as distinct from a liberal society. The capitalist interest groups were confused, bewildered, and afflicted with self-pity. Their political thought never rose above the level of narrowly asserting their own interest or harking back to the past. Although the services they could render in the sphere of economic life were absolutely essential for the solution of the problems left behind by Perón, they were peculiarly ill-equipped to 'sell' themselves to the community at large in competition with the armed forces, the Church, and the trade unions. The possibility of allying themselves with the other interest groups was limited because the military officers, the clergy, and the trade union leaders were not as groups completely sympathetic to the capitalist and landed élite. On the contrary Perón's 'class struggle' style in politics and his appeal to the *descamisados* had owed as much to the radical, anti-capitalist tendencies at work in the Church and the armed forces as it had done to the Marxist socialist and anarchist tendencies in the trade unions. The strong medicine fed to these interests by Perón had only attenuated not eliminated a disposition to rely on slogan-mongering and ideologically biased agitation among the 'people'. Nationalism preached in the armed forces and Christian Democracy agitated in the Church were the respectable manifestation of the anti-capitalist, class struggle style in post-Perón politics, far more important obstacles to the solution of economic problems than the extremist agitation of the *Tacuará* on the right and the *Trotskistas* and would-be guerrillas on the left.

Given these tendencies in the major interest groups it is in no way surprising that the suppression of the Perónista constitution and the restoration of the liberal constitution of 1853 did not lead to the re-establishment of a stable, democratic political process capable of solving economic and social problems. The leaders of the *Revolución Libertadora* called a Constitutional Convention intended to restore and renovate the constitution of 1853. In accordance with the best tradition of liberalism they planned that the people as a whole should by election and ordered argument legitimize a participatory system of government expressive of the general will and renewed and guided by it. The elections for the Constituent Assembly revealed how far the major interest groups and the people at large were from accepting and working a liberal system. The Perónistas cast over 2 million blank ballots – about one-fifth of those voting. The trade unions called a general strike. There was an unsuccessful revolt in the armed forces in June 1956. It speaks well for the faith in liberalism of the leaders of the *Revolución Libertadora* that they pressed on in spite of such formidable discouragement and the fairly obvious fact that the old Argentina of the days before the Great Depression and World War II could not be restored.

It is the belief of this writer, derived from both the contemplation of Argentine history and analysis of its recent and contemporary condition, that the Argentine community lives best both in a material and spiritual sense when it produces abundantly and pushes to the furthest possible limits its capacity to buy and sell cheaply and efficiently in world markets. The Argentines are by tradition and temperament a world-class people and are only at peace with themselves when they are present in the great world and the great world is present in Buenos Aires. This need for distinction and association with the recognized best cannot be satisfied by military prowess or commanding economic power or religious or spiritual leadership. And it cannot be suppressed by a xenophobic search for separation from the world. Experience suggests that it can only be satisfied by economic success such as Argentina once enjoyed and is now the basis for the world prestige of the Japanese, the Germans, the Dutch, and the Canadians.

The leaders of the *Revolución Libertadora* aimed at restoring Argentina to its past paths, but they did not know how to go about this. They appeared to suppose that a generous dose of liberal democracy would somehow serve as a sovereign remedy. It had been easy enough, when General Urquiza overthrew General Rosas, for the victor to inaugurate a liberal political process because General Rosas had already firmly entrenched a capitalist economic process. When General Lonardi and General Aramburu overthrew General Perón pure capitalism, competitive markets, private enterprise, economic decision-making based on individual or corporate bargaining were no longer normal features of Argentine economic life. State power was a factor in all major branches of the economy. The vast web of interests feeding on each other or on third parties was beyond the wit of the liberal-minded officers and their advisers either to manage or to destroy. The policy of the provisional President Aramburu in respect to the economy amounted to little more than an assault upon the superstructure of the Perónista economic system. The abolition of direct state participation in the marketing of the main exports was more a declaration of intention than a change which caused the economy to function differently than it had done under Perón. During the time which elapsed between the *Revolución Libertadora* in September 1955 and the elections in February 1958 the beneficiaries of Perón's system were given time to plan their response in the new democratic setting.

It is now pretty clear that Aramburu made a mistake in supposing that the re-establishment of an open, democratic political process was a necessary condition for the re-establishment of a liberal capitalist economic process. The vested interests created by and dependent on the Perónista state were able to take advantage of the inevitably competitive situation created by a democratic election to make bargains with the aspirants to political office, and thus to ensure their own perpetuation. The partisans of a democratic system, on the other hand, were badly divided among themselves. The temptation, in some quarters, to seek Perónista support was therefore very great.

The conservative liberals, of whom Aramburu was the best example, could be counted on not to yield to this temptation. No other group, save perhaps the doctrinaire socialists, could be so trusted. This was particularly true of the largest political grouping, the Radicals, which had managed to survive Perón. The Radicals split into the *Unión Cívica Radical Intransigente* and the *Unión Cívica Radical del Pueblo*: the first supporting as presidential candidate Dr Arturo Frondizi and the second Dr Ricardo Balbín. The differences were personal. Both Frondizi and Balbín had made their reputation as defenders of men and women persecuted by Perón for opposition to his regime. Both were partisans of an open society, free elections, and people's democracy. But both were seeking the same office. In the end the competitive situation in which victory tends to go to the most unscrupulous determined the conduct of the contenders. Dr Frondizi declared that he could 'out-demagogue' the demagogues, and this he proceeded to do. As a result Argentina was plunged into a fresh round of hubbub, hysteria, and political neurosis.

Dr Arturo Frondizi is a very intelligent man with a good knowledge of economics and a fine capacity for the imaginative and practical solutions of economic problems. He would have made an excellent Minister of Economy. As a President he was a disaster. No matter what technical capacities any political leader may have, an indispensable requirement for success is moral authority which enables both his friends and his enemies to know where he stands and what he stands for. In the days of Perón, Dr Frondizi had identified himself strongly as a liberal, democratic, reformist opponent of Perónism. He had likewise established himself as a nationalist and a protagonist of Argentine economic independence based on industrialization. Above all he had spoken out again Perónism and defended in the courts the victims of Perónist repression and injustice.

In his bid for power, Dr Frondizi undermined his moral authority. In office he further destroyed this authority so that in the end no one knew where he stood on anything. He believed he could be the friend of everyone and of every interest, and he ended up with no friends and no support. When the soldiers asked him, and then compelled him, to resign no one lifted a finger to save him.

Dr Frondizi's basic mistake was his clandestine deal with Perón in which he promised to readmit the Perónistas into the Argentine political process in return for Perónista support in the election. The election for the Constituent Assembly had revealed that there were roughly 2 million voters willing to indicate their support for Perón by casting blank ballots. Obviously Perónista support would assist victory if any politician could command it. Simple realism would suggest this, and Dr Frondizi was good at realism. Furthermore he believed that the positive things done by Perón and the restructuring of life achieved under Perón could not be abandoned. And so he went right to the fountain-head of Perónism, to the *caudillo* himself, and reached an agreement which he kept quiet and subsequently denied. The result was Frondizi's victory. In the election of February 1958 the number of blank ballots fell from roughly 2 million to 750,000, and Frondizi had a comfortable victory over his Radical rival: 4,370,000 votes out of 10 million and 1,300,000 more than the candidate of the *Unión Cívica Radical del Pueblo*.

But it was also the beginning of his difficulties. The day of his inauguration in May, the commanding officer of the military parade before the President refused to salute him. Characteristically, Frondizi did not at once act to deal with this insubordination. He started to play chess with the military officers, so that the armed forces, instead of being the support of the President, were turned more and more into a cockpit of politics. This happened not just because Frondizi played upon their internal dissensions, but because his friendliness to the Perónistas destroyed all confidence elsewhere in the community. The anti-Perónistas were the majority, but like the armed forces they were a divided majority. Frondizi played on these divisions, too. As a result none of them trusted him, because all of them feared he would let them again become the victims of Perón.

The continuous and bitter uproar created by Frondizi made it impossible for him to bring to fruition his many sensible notions about the reformation of the economy. Perón had destroyed the internal capacity of the Argentine community to finance itself, discipline itself, and co-operate within itself, and he had turned in his last three years of power to foreign capital and foreign entrepreneurs to carry forward his plans for industrialization. Frondizi followed essentially the same tactic. In spite of his nationalism he made contracts with foreign oil companies to expand the search for and processing of petroleum. He reached agreements with the International Monetary Fund, and revived the flow of foreign capital into the light-engineering industry, into the financing of electric power production, and the re-equipment of the transport system. All this looked like a solution, but it was not. By 1961, the Argentine economy was in just as much difficulty as it had been when he took power.

Attempts have been made in Argentina and elsewhere to blame what happened on the bad advice given by the experts of the International Monetary Fund (e.g. the Oxford economists Eshag and Thorp). This is neither here nor there. Frondizi's deals with foreign bankers and foreign capitalists represented an avoidance of the real problems of the Argentine economy, which is not the need for foreign capital and foreign confidence, but the need for internal capital accumulation and investment, the creation of opportunities for Argentine technologists and managers, the need for greater flexibility in the use of resources, and the deployment of labour. None of these real problems could be tackled so long as Argentines were encouraged to hate one another and suspect one another. This was the central defect of Perón's policies, and having made an agreement with the Perónistas, this became the central defect of Frondizi's policy.

Frondizi did not himself become a Perónista. On the contrary, he did nothing more than promote in the Congress and secure an amnesty for the Perónistas. In the end he engaged in the suppression of their militants. What he did do, however, was create uncertainty about his intentions, which encouraged them and depressed their enemies. Guerrilla outbreaks of violence occurred in Salta, Jujuy, and Tucumán. Terrorism spread in the cities, and Frondizi was himself a target of attack. And yet always confident in his capacity to play off one force against another, he invited Che Guevara to the Casa Rosada for a talk. He may have thought he was outwitting Guevara, but he was outwitting himself. The tragic flaw in Frondizi is his cleverness: too clever by half.

In the end he was removed from office by the armed forces. It would be entirely wrong to suppose that this action was the product of monolithic patriotism and understanding of the soldiers. During the whole of Frondizi's Presidency the officers of the armed services were at each other's throats, and this confusion and political turmoil had passed well beyond the realm of innuendoes, insults, and duels to the point where bombers were flattening army barracks, tanks were flattening air bases, and men were being killed and imprisoned. That a combination could be found sufficiently co-ordinated to dismiss the President amounted almost to an accident. The internal dissension in the armed forces prevented the re-establishment of a military dictatorship on the pattern which had led to Perón's ascent to power. General Aramburu still had some prestige and influence among the soldiers, and he it was who caused a decision to be made against military dictatorship. Dr Guido, the president of the Senate and a non-partisan politician, was installed as President to prepare for fresh elections.

Chapter 9

The Failure of Neo-Democracy – Part Two

P RESIDENT FRONDIZI was deposed at the end of March 1962. President Arturo Illia was elected in July 1963. During this time there was a civil war within the armed forces, the outcome of which *may* prove to be a turning point in Argentine history and the beginning of better days.

Because of their long and progressively more intensive involvement in politics the armed forces had become, during the Frondizi regime, a focal point of all the dissensions which divided and paralysed the Argentine community. If, under Frondizi, there was no clear moral and political authority in civil society, there was equally no final authority in the armed forces. They were split, of course, into three services: the army, the navy, and the air force; and they were split politically so that the officers and N.C.O's themselves admitted the existence of parties: the *Azules* and the *Colorados*. It was, and is, easier to pin the labels than to define their meaning. The *Azules* or blues have been described as a group soft towards Perónism and the *Colorados* or reds as stern anti-Perónistas; but this description is almost meaningless, because many *Colorados* were partisans of military dictatorship and numbered among them officers of a strong Perónist disposition. On the other hand there were *Colorados* who were anti-Perónistas and nothing more. Their opposition to Frondizi, to Guido, and to Illia was based on the belief that the politicians were too soft on the Perónistas and particularly on working-class Perónistas. *Colorados* of this type were particularly numerous in the navy. The *Azules*, on the other hand, were for the most part anti-Perónistas and conservatives, but some, not all, were partisans of liberal political processes. An important element in identifying the *Azules* was a belief in the need to make the armed forces non-political and professional, and thus bring to an end the role of the armed forces as arbiters in the political process. A still further complication was the comparative distribution of *Azules* and *Colorados* in the services. The *Azules* were strongest in the cavalry and motorized units of the army; the purely anti-Perónista *Colorados* in the navy. The air force tended to be less defined, while the *Colorados* of a dictatorial and Perónist inclination were strongest in the engineering and supply services and in provincial garrisons.

The connections of these several groupings with the political and economic interest groups in civil society are not susceptible to easy description. The probable reason for this is the absence of any stable relationship of any kind. The armed forces, like all the other components of society from the family, through the Church to the business corporations and trade unions, had been split by the manipulation, reorganization, and stimulus of Perón. Hence, it is as unreasonable to suppose, as it is difficult to prove, that any one group of officers was indubitably connected with any one group in civil society. The most that can be said is that the disposition of most *Azules* to take the armed forces out of politics was in line with the hope of non-Perónist and anti-Perónist elements in all segments of the community that a viable democratic society free of Perónist totalitarianism could be restored.

The confusion and anarchy in the armed forces was exacerbated by the removal of Frondizi. He had stirred up the antagonisms in the armed forces, but he had also played upon them. This Dr Guido was either incapable or indisposed to do. As a consequence there developed a struggle for power in the services unimpeded and unguided by outside political influences, but having at the same time profound implications for the civil government. The most that the civilian politicians could do was to look on and deplore with gestures of despair the warfare within the armed forces. Dr Federico Pinedo, recalled to the government service after a quarter of a century in the wilderness, resigned in protest against the conduct of the officers. Others did the same. The President deplored and the Church prayed, but nothing could stay the struggle, which, fortunately for the nation, was conducted as a sort of private civil war not seriously destructive of the community as a whole.

As the disputes developed about who should be recommended to hold the defence secretariats, and by implication whether the officers should establish a dictatorship, or allow elections and what sort of elections, three leading personalities emerged: General Carlos Severo Toranzo Montero, an extreme anti-Perónista of an authoritarian disposition, inclined to favour, but never bold enough to advocate, a military dictatorship; Admiral Isaac Rojas, an anti-Perónist conservative who favoured the outlawing of Perónism root and branch as a condition for holding elections; and General Juan Carlos Onganía, an *Azul* advocate of non-participation in politics.

In the first stages Toranzo Montero made the running. He forced the government to accept his candidates for the defence posts and became briefly Commander-in-Chief until he found he did not have an absolutely free hand to appoint and dismiss officers under his command. He was successful in forcing the government to impose further restrictions on Perónista organizations. Toranzo Montero, however, was never able to assert himself fully, perhaps because he was not clear in his own mind what his objectives were. As it was, he never succeeded in getting control. In August 1962 his brother, General Federico Toranzo Montero, raised a rebellion in the garrison in the sub-Andean province of Salta. This provoked an outcry among the civilians about the conduct of the officers, and obviously alienated conservative liberals of all kinds.

At this stage General Onganía entered the struggle. He was a cavalry general in the Campo de Mayo outside Buenos Aires. He proclaimed himself a supporter of the civil power who desired to take the armed forces out of politics. He was able to assert this view with a force of Sherman tanks. When the government troops, commanded by the *Colorados*, attempted to check him his tanks smashed through them at La Plata and took up positions in all the key points in Buenos Aires. The President welcomed this revolution on his behalf.

A few weeks later the navy under Admiral Rojas attempted to reassert the authority of the *Colorados* and the air force came to his assistance. Onganía and his officers deployed their forces with some skill and speed. The naval base at Puerto Belgrano was overrun and destroyed. Airfields were overrun by tanks and put out of action. Altogether 600 officers and 1,600 N.C.O's were rounded up and put under restraint or forced to flee to Uruguay or Chile.

It is possible to argue that General Onganía's rebellion is one of the most formative events since the overthrow of Perón. Following the triumph of the *Azules* under Onganía's leadership no faction in the armed forces was able successfully to assert itself against the officers connected with or appointed by Onganía. Since his rescue of provisional President Guido from the *Colorados*, the course of politics has been determined by Onganía and his friends: from 1962 to 1965 negatively by pursuing a constitutional neutrality and since then positively by organizing and carrying out a seizure of power which in June 1966 placed Onganía in the office of President.

Like the officers who organized and led the *Revolución Liberta-dora* of 1955, Onganía is a conservative with a strong hankering after the old Argentina, where, it is imagined, everyone had his place, knew it, and kept it. Probably influenced by Aramburu, Onganía and his friends decided to repeat an experiment in democracy, believing that the restoration of an open political process would lead to the solution of the economic problems left behind by Perón. The only restraint imposed was the prohibition of a Perónista candidate for the Presidency. The Perónistas were, however, left free to organize their own party and to participate in the election of members of the Congress and of the provincial governments.

The electoral contest revealed the extreme fragmentation of political life which had come about. Over forty parties entered the field. Of these four were major groupings which the electorate could recognize in terms of their records and their personalities, and there were five lesser parties such as the Socialist Party, the Christian Democrats, and the communists whose meaning the voters could identify. There were now two clearly separate radical parties: the Intransigent Radicals of Arturo Frondizi and the People's Radicals who put up a modest doctor from Córdoba, Dr Arturo Illia, as their presidential candidate. The Perónistas appeared under the title of the *Unión Popular*. The conservatives under the name of the *Unión Democrática* nominated General Aramburu. These were the large parties capable of getting more than a million votes each. The lesser parties were in the half-million vote class. The thirty-odd remaining parties represented persons or localities or ideologies rather than trends of opinion and groups of interests.

This time only the Christian Democrats endeavoured to do a deal with the Perónistas. This overture was treated with contempt because the Christian Democrats were not big enough to serve the Perónistas' purposes. With no deals to obscure the result the 10 million-odd voters went to the polls in the winter of 1963. The People's Radicals came out easily the largest minority with 2,440,000 votes or 26 per cent of the total. The Intransigent Radicals' vote was only 1,592,000, compared with the 1,694,000 blank ballots cast by the Perónistas. General Aramburu was able to command only 1,339,000 votes. Thus, 70 per cent of the voters who had opted to support the candidates of the major national parties, were manifestly split, and split in a way calculated to maximize uncertainty about the political future of the country. The other 30 per cent were so fragmented that none of the fragments were large enough to serve as building material in an alliance.

If President Frondizi had shown himself too willing to abandon pledges and principles, President Illia revealed an opposite tendency – towards an excessive pedantry in the adherence to his pre-election promises and declarations. He rejected all thought of forming a coalition of parties, which was understandable, and of interests, which was incomprehensible. He gave the principal offices in the government to his faithful followers, and he sought to avoid the possibility that some of the stronger characters in his party, such as Dr Ricardo Balbín, might impose their policy on him. He did this by placing them in posts of prominence in a Cabinet which he seldom or never called together.

In this way a nation whose problems required general solutions ramifying through the whole structure of government and the economy, was obliged to submit to the control of isolated Cabinet officials presiding over departments and policies many of which were still what they were in Perón's day.

President Illia appeared to believe that the troubles of his country derived solely from the fact that it had lacked for too long free and honest elections. To him democracy was an end in itself, not an effective means of generating the information needed by responsible leaders for the just and acceptable solution of the vast range of social, economic, and moral problems of a complex industrial society. He therefore gave to purely political problems the first order of priority and most of his attention, and relegated to a secondary place the economic and social problems which his administrative arrangements were ill designed to consider, let alone solve.

Shortly before his deposition he pointed with legitimate pride to the fact that no citizen of the Argentine Republic was in jail for political reasons and only one in exile. The tolerance he exhibited towards the Perónistas was not part of a plan to ally with them but a strategy for their destruction. He believed that if they were obliged to take full responsibility for the affairs of provincial governments where they held legitimate power they would either expose the emptiness of their pretensions, or they would become legitimate parties playing a constitutional role.

This reasoning was sound enough as far as it went, but the anti-

Perónista majority were naturally uneasy about what might happen if the Perónistas won power by election in the large province of Buenos Aires. President Illia was able to prove to his own satisfaction that this would not happen, but this satisfaction was not widely shared. In fact President Illia's doctrinaire liberalism created almost as much apprehension and uncertainty among anti-Perónistas, and as much hope and optimism among the followers of the dictator-in-exile, as Frondizi's policy of clandestine alliance.

In the matter of the relations of the government with the major interest groups, President Illia attempted a policy of even-handed neutrality. In effect, this amounted to a policy of refusing to interfere with the abuses inherited from the past while at the same time alienating and depressing those who wished to do better and knew how to. He shared a lower middle-class suspicion both of the working class and the upper class. He attacked the trade unions, but only to a certain extent. He attacked foreign business, but only to a certain extent. He attacked the landed proprietors, but only to a certain extent. This may have heartened the lower-middle class, but it disheartened everyone else. It irritated the major interest groups without disarming them.

President Illia's moderate, tolerant, and conservative political style was partly the product of a modest, tolerant, and conservative temperament, and partly the product of a belief that the Argentine people needed some relief from the hysterical, exaggerated rhetoric which had flourished since the seizure of power by the officers in 1943. This was a sensible view, but unhappily inappropriate in the circumstances of stagnation and decay which prevailed. The cartoonists depicted the President as an immobile, quiet, figure with the dove of peace nesting in his hair. There was a real grain of truth in the satire. Argentina could very well have done without rhetoric, but required an active, radical reorganization of the economy and the public services.

Some of the economic measures initiated by President Illia were admirable and some were disastrous. He quite rightly rejected the view that massive foreign assistance was necessary to put the economy right. In order to encourage the accumulation of investment funds in the country, his government began to finance its deficit with bonds written in terms of U.S. dollars and payable in that currency. The same spirit of national self-reliance produced, however, a major disaster: the destruction of Frondizi's principal economic triumph, i.e. the expansion of the petroleum industry. Frondizi's concessions to foreign oil-capitalists had been brilliantly successful and the heavy weight on the balance of payments of a growing fuel bill, owed to foreign importers of petroleum products and coal, had been eliminated within the space of four years. President Illia, however, was pledged to save Argentine oil from the imperialists. One of the first acts of his government was to cancel the oil concessions and to commence paying compensation: a sum of £145 million. He thus repeated the economically insane mistake of Perón which consisted of making massive transfers abroad to foreign interests of capital which Argentina needed for growth. Ironically, compensation was paid not only to foreign companies lucky enough to have struck oil but also to those whose luck had failed. The executives of one of these enterprises remarked on one occasion: 'The Government's policy suits us very well. Our big problem is to convince the cynics that we haven't bribed the President and his friends.'

In another instance the President's devotion to justice and equality led him to sponsor policies destructive of Frondizi's work. Frondizi had very sensibly endeavoured to put farming and ranching on a business basis by separating the income of the farmer from the income from the farm as an enterprise, in order to work a system of depreciation allowances in relation to income tax. Illia's government ended the system and reimposed flat income taxes on total income. One big farmer in the Pergamino district said to the author in April 1966: 'The Government has decided to take 50 per cent of my annual receipts over and above expenditure as income tax. Fine, I can live well on what is left, but if the Government refuse to regard my farm as a business enterprise, then I won't either. Things just tick over, and that is how it is going to remain.'

President Illia's government pursued a neutral policy *vis-à-vis* labour and the trade unions which neither induced co-operation nor destroyed their power to obstruct. On the one hand the government tried to weaken the autonomous power of the trade union bureaucracy by diminishing their sources of income, e.g. the right of the central congress of the C.G.T. trade union to take one day's pay from every worker for the finance of the central office was abolished; closer inspection of accounting procedures in trade unions was imposed; and stricter verification of membership was required. On the other hand, the government gave no leadership at all on the subject of labour legislation about severance pay. A bill was introduced into Congress to increase the already large rights of workers to severance pay, amounting to significant capital payments. This legislation was depicted as a new *conquista social*, and for electoral reasons the President's party as well as other politicians feared to resist a thoroughly bad piece of legislation which would render the labour market increasingly inflexible and make it harder and harder for men to get jobs and change jobs. The old Perónista demagogy seemed to be returning. The employer pressure groups raised a great opposition. In the end the President vetoed most of the bill, having made enemies both among the union bureaucrats and the employers simply because he had no policy and had given no leadership.

After two years of Dr Illia's government there was still no easily visible evidence of change for the better in Argentine circumstances. Knowledgeable and intelligent citizens of the Republic declared to the author that, as far as economic policy was concerned, Perón in his last two years as President had a better idea of what needed to be done than Illia, and that men of good intentions without policies might be less preferable than evil men who know what to do. The grounds for this discontent were to be found in the economic stagnation visible everywhere: dirty streets; broken pavements; dirty, delayed trains; wrong telephone numbers; undelivered letters. Everyone could see and experience these evidences of disorder. More informed observation revealed unemployment at 7–8 per cent; prices rising at $2\frac{1}{2}$–3 per cent per month; little or no private or public capital investment; a thriving black market in foreign currency; little movement in the stock market; continuing heavy deficits in the budget; incapacity for price competition in world markets for industrial goods; a continuing decline in the Argentine share in the world market for food products. The government of Dr Illia did nothing wicked, and some of the things which it did were good, but it did little and that little was insufficient.

As the Argentine winter of 1965 drew to a close the discontent of the major interests coupled with the apathy of the public at large promised ill for the government. Rumours of a *golpe* began to grow. The shrewdest observers recognized that General Onganía was the key to the political solution, not because he was a pillar of the government, but because the armed forces were the pillar of the state. He occupied the non-political post of Commander-in-Chief of the Army, and he was committed to the principle of the supremacy of the civil power; at least that was presumed to be the case in view of his leading role in the victory of the *Azules* over the *Colorados*. Onganía himself had never expressed any views with respect to policies not directly concerned with his profession. During a large part of his time as Commander-in-Chief he travelled abroad, visiting the United States and Europe where he engaged in a study of professional problems. At West Point in the United States he made a speech in which he underlined the importance for good public policy of obedience to the civil power.

The shock to the government was, therefore, the greater, when in November 1965 he resigned his post as Commander-in-Chief and retired from the service. When and under what influence General Onganía decided thus to turn against the President cannot yet be stated with any certainty. It is evident, however, that he did so with deliberation on a carefully selected issue. He let it be known that he disagreed with the President's policy of refusing actively to support the United States intervention in the affairs of the Dominican Republic, and that in this matter he sided with the Foreign Minister, who wished to swing the Organization of American States solidly behind the American policy of rapid response to the alleged dangers of another communist take-over in the Caribbean. President Illia was firm in his determination to preserve Argentina's traditional neutrality, and he won praise not only from the leftist minorities everywhere in Latin America but also from the moderate supporters of the O.A.S. who believed that it had a legitimate function provided it was not required to respond unthinkingly every time the United States blew the bugle with panic firmness. In choosing this issue General Onganía was not necessarily doing himself any political good in Argentina, nor with the United States, which at that time, and as late as June 1966, regarded the government of Dr Illia as a sound, democratic, middle-class regime of which there were too few south of the Río Grande.

In the light of what happened between November 1965 and June 1966, it is now pretty clear that Onganía and his friends had decided to end the policy of submission to the civil power which had been dominant in the armed forces since the *Revolución Libertadora* and which had been the norm to which all successful *golpistas* after Perón had tended. Onganía himself was the most conspicuously successful of this school of thought. His turn-about was, therefore, the more revolutionary. Whether Onganía appreciated to the full the

implication of what he was doing is doubtful, but he did know one
big thing – namely, that he was abandoning the conventional wisdom
of a decade which said that Argentina had only the alternative:
either Perónism or the liberalism of the constitution of 1853.

Once Onganía had resigned, the tide of rumours swelled prodigiously. Every interest began making contingency arrangements
which were exceeded in their urgency only by their inconsistency.
President Illia remained calm. He toured the country, belying his
appearance of premature senility and extreme langour by feats of
physical endurance which left his secretaries and military aides exhausted in spite of their comparative youth. He was in fact a tough,
tolerant, nice old man, but Argentina was too sick for his doctoring.
He approached his country like the general practitioner which he
was, believing that nature cures most ills provided the patient can be
comforted and kept quiet. Even in medicine the management of in-
fluenza or diarrhoea differs, however, from that of arterio-sclerosis.

The President's appeal to the people to preserve democratic institutions ran parallel with an endeavour to play upon the ambitions
of the officers in the armed forces in order to divide them. The consequences of Onganía's victory in the war between the *Azules* and the
Colorados were evidenced in the incapacity of the President to find
anyone in the armed forces capable of serving him effectively. The
Minister of Defence, Dr Leopoldo Suárez, met the Secretary of the
Army, General Castro Sánchez, and General Manuel Laprida, for
a nine-hour conference late in April 1966, to see what could be done
to retain the loyalty of the armed forces to the civil power. Castro
Sánchez and Laprida were both *Azules* and both devoted to the
principle of civilian authority, but neither could conceal the fact that
now the men of their own views were changing course. Castro
Sánchez decided to stick with the government. If this decision meant
anything, it required that he find the means within the armed forces
of enforcing his will and the will of the government. This involved
forming a party. He turned to the commander of the garrison in
Rosario, General Caro, whose brother was a Perónista. It was then
revealed how strong the *Azul* party was. The Commander-in-Chief,
General Pascual Pistarini, declared that he no longer recognized and
would have no further communication with the Secretary of the
Army. Information reached Pistarini that General Caro was meeting
a delegation of Perónistas. Caro was at once arrested. President Illia
ordered the removal of Pistarini as Commander-in-Chief of the

Army and appealed to the nation to support democratic institutions. He was too late. The commanders of the three armed services acting together evicted the President from his office and proclaimed the 'Argentine Revolution'.

The story of this eviction from a reliable source suggests something of the temper of Argentine politics and the almost conventional character of a *golpe* as a part of the political process. On the night of 27 June, President Illia was working late in his office in the Casa Rosada having, as he thought, just sacked General Pistarini. The great doors at the end of his room opened, and there appeared General Julio Alsogaray. He said to the President, 'In the name of the Armed Forces which I represent, I order you to leave.' The President stood up, looked at the General, and said, 'You represent no one. You are a burglar. Get out!' This was the first time General Alsogaray had been given an order by his Commander-in-Chief. He hesitated, and then obeyed. President Illia then sat down at his desk and resumed his work. An hour or so later the door opened again, and a colonel appeared with two N.C.O's. This time the army man said, 'In the name of the armed forces which I command, I order you to leave.' President Illia said nothing. The colonel hesitated. He dared not shoot the President or otherwise injure him. He ordered the N.C.O's to assist the President to leave. Outside the President's office and in the corridors of the Casa Rosada there was a great milling about of the followers of Dr Illia and soldiers, and much shouting and shoving. Eventually one of the 35,000 taxis of Buenos Aires was summoned, and the ex-President left for the house of his brother, a secondary-school master in a suburb of the federal capital.

The fifth successful *golpe de estado* in thirty-six years had obviously been planned with care and skill. Unlike the other *golpes* it did not appear to be the work of a secret society of officers, nor the work of colonels, majors, and captains. It was the product of a decision taken by the top commanders of the three armed services who constituted themselves as a revolutionary committee. In the most general political sense this *Junta* had well-defined intentions – carefully prepared plans for the organization of the government and clearly identified support from people associated with the major interest groups. Within a few hours of the departure of Dr Illia from the Casa Rosada the *Junta* of commanders proclaimed a Charter of the Argentine Revolution, which declared that the new government 'represents all the people of the Republic', that it 'commands the support of the Armed Forces, and also of the other security forces and the police; and that it therefore commands sufficient power to maintain public law and order and to protect the life and property of the inhabitants'. As to the government itself, it was to consist of a President nominated by the *Junta*; a Ministry constituted in accordance with a law which it was proposed to proclaim; and a Supreme Court enjoying immunities and independence set out in article 96 of the constitution. All legislative powers except that relating to impeachment of judges, were to be taken over by the President. All provincial governors were to be appointed by the national government to operate under the provincial constitutions and were guaranteed permanency of tenure. Judges and provincial governors were to be removed only on impeachment procedure carried out by a jury system to be established by law. The Charter undertook to respect all international obligations entered into by the Argentine Republic. The Congress was suspended *sine die*; the political parties dissolved; their property seized.

Immediately following the proclamation of the Charter, General Juan Carlos Onganía was named President. In his broadcast to the nation General Onganía declared that the revolution 'is not directed against any public figure or any political group. . . . We are embarking on a process of reconciliation and reconstruction. . . . I shall govern for all Argentines indiscriminately, and I ask for the co-operation of everybody.' He promised no quick solutions of problems. The most general problems, he said, were the moral and physical diminution of the country and the chronic frustration that was incomprehensible in the circumstances of the wealth of Argentina's moral and physical resources. He suggested that this frustration arose not from the wickedness and stupidity of any one part of the community but from the selfish antagonisms of interests which had been taught for too long to look exclusively to their own advantage at the expense of the co-operation from which all benefit.

The generalities of General Onganía were admirable enough, in as much as they indicated an intention not to adopt the militant class-struggle, political style of Perón and Frondizi or the doctrinaire, moralistic, democratic style of President Illia. But what framework did he intend to provide for decision-making? Who were going to participate in decision-making? What underlying moral ideas, apart from a corporative, patriotic, and authoritarian temper, would give directions to decision-making?

The Charter of the Revolution provided some answer to the first question, but only a sketchy one. Further clarification was provided by a law concerning the Ministry. This established a centralized but collective authority made up of five Ministers under the chairmanship and guidance of the President: a Minister of Foreign Affairs, a Minister of Defence, a Minister of the Interior, a Minister of Economy, and a Minister of Welfare. These formulators of policy and managers of the community were backed up by a Council of National Security which was the Ministry plus the heads of the armed services.

Some light was thrown on the second question by the swearing-in ceremony of the new President. The representatives of all the major interest groups were present: the landed interest, industrial organizations, trade unions, the Church. Only the party politicians were missing. The concept of dialogue was much publicized. The President and the government would discuss anything with anybody, but in private and through existing organizations.

Since June 1966 those discontented with the policies and character of the Onganía regime – and they are many and drawn from all major interest groups including the armed forces, the Church, business, the landed interest, the trade unions, and the professional politicians – have lived in the expectation of a new *golpe*. In December 1966 one was hoped for, and again in August–September 1968, but nothing happened. In the first instance President Onganía sacked two of his three key Ministers; in the second, he retired prematurely the three commanders of the armed forces. Whatever else may be said about the President, it cannot be said that there is doubt about who runs Argentina. The armed forces and the government have been integrated so that power and policy-making are concentrated in a single centre. There are no longer autonomous power centres – actual or potential – in the Argentine community, and the state is now organized so that formal power and real power are in the same hands – a condition of affairs which has not existed in Argentina since the election of Yrigoyen to the Presidency in 1916, save, perhaps, during the Presidency of General Justo from 1932 to 1938. Perón wrestled with the problem, but made so many mistakes that he failed calamitously. Onganía's success is not much to the liking of many of the several élites, but it is a fact with which the Argentine community, for better or for worse, is now obliged to live.

Chapter 10

An Experiment in Authority:
the Regime of Onganía

ALTHOUGH IT WAS clear enough that the structure of the new government involved a revolutionary concentration of executive and legislative power in the hands of the President and policy-making in the hands of a small Cabinet of five Ministers over which the President presided, it was far from clear to the public and to the new government itself what its policy would be. Policy is a matter of choices and priorities, no matter what mechanisms may be established for making them. The revolutionary *Junta* had established new mechanisms which it was possible to suppose were more responsive than those which had existed since the fall of Perón, but the question still remained how to operate them and to what purpose. During the first six months of the new regime it became increasingly evident that General Onganía was not much better than Dr Illia at finding answers. The concepts of peace, order, and patriotism which came easily to soldiers are necessary but not sufficient for effective government and especially for the government of a community afflicted by problems as complex as those of Argentina.

The conflict of interests and the incoherence of goals were not suddenly resolved by the *golpe*. In order to make the revolution Onganía and his friends had drawn elements from every major interest group into the movement, so that after the shouting had died down and the federal capital had reopened for business the problem of policy formation was just about as difficult as it had been at any time in the past.

Like Dr Illia's, General Onganía's style as a leader was low-key and modest. He had dignity and he wore an appearance of dour resolution. He had no public charm and no talent for rhetoric. This was all to the good, for Argentina had for too long been frazzled with sentimentality, hysteria, demagogy, and empty slogans. He promised very little except an effort to restore Argentine pride and self-respect, and to do so in a spirit of conciliation necessary for national unity and social co-operation.

Shortly after the President's first message to the nation, there appeared over his signature a policy statement which may be described as an ideological pronouncement. The position of Argentina in the international community was described as 'Americanist' and Christian. A special reference was made to the mother country, Spain, which seemed a hint of admiration for General Franco, but the hard core of definition with respect to foreign relations was a traditional determination to cultivate good relations with other nations based on a reciprocal respect, with a view to achieving economic and commercial expansion. The largest proportion of the statement was devoted to an exposition of economic policies. The first proposition promised the establishment of an economic system free of totalitarianism, which stifles energy and initiative, and free also of the deformations of the free-enterprise system which conspire against justice, competition, and social progress. The new system was to be based on the principle of free choice for consumers and producers within the limits of monetary, fiscal, exchange, and tariff policies, which were to be the responsibility of the state. Private property was declared to be the basic factor in the economy because it was the basis of individual freedom and the source of legitimate human incentive and endeavour. 'All that can be done by individuals and private enterprises, within the framework of the common good, shall be their responsibility.'

While asserting thus a doctrine of free, competitive enterprise, the state was considered to have the duty of eliminating violent economic fluctuations and assuring the full employment of labour and resources through 'a sustained and persevering effort towards the achievement of monetary stability'. It was also specifically asserted that 'contrary to what is advocated by certain schools of extreme liberalism in such matters, the State's role in the face of economic problems should not be a mainly passive one'.

The policy statement referred briefly to the intentions of the government *vis-à-vis* the trade unions and the labour movement. A minimum of interference in the legal rights of trade unions was promised, and reform was to be directed towards maintaining 'a just balance between the interests of the country, of labour, and of management, maintaining the various organizations within the framework of their respective functions'.

On the subject of health, welfare, and social security the statement pledged the government to a reform and extension of the existing system and the improvement of housing through new building.

On the subject of defence the statement committed the government 'to develop the military potential in accordance with the real possibilities of the country in this respect and with needs implicit in the pursuit of the political objectives envisaged'.

This cautious yet positive policy statement was based on a realistic knowledge that a successful *golpe* had not extinguished the capacity of the heterogeneous opposition, if goaded, to come together and employ the one weapon which they possessed: a general strike and mass demonstration of the kind which had defeated the attempt of the soldiers to remove Colonel Perón from the Vice-Presidency in October 1945. The specific repudiation of 'extreme liberalism' was directed at two men who had helped to make the revolution: Lt-General Julio Alsogaray and his brother Ingeniero Álvaro Alsogaray. The latter was a successful businessman who preached a doctrine of total free enterprise, which as a Minister he had vainly endeavoured to implement during the last days of Frondizi's regime. Lt-General Alsogaray was briefly the secretary of the Presidency under Onganía, and his was the first politically motivated resignation. He was made Commander-in-Chief of the Army, while Álvaro Alsogaray was sent as ambassador to Washington where he was free to advocate free enterprise in the congenial atmosphere of Wall Street and the Shoreham Hotel.

Onganía's side-tracking of the Alsogaray brothers was necessary because a revolutionary abandonment of all controls, worthwhile as this might be as an ultimate goal, was objectionable as an immediate policy on two grounds: its inhumanity and its impracticality. On strict grounds of cost-efficiency a strong case would be made by doctrinaire free enterprisers for the immediate closure, to take only one impressive example, of the Argentine railways. The railways of Argentina are more a welfare system than a transport system. When Onganía's government raised the passenger and freight rates by 70 per cent, the increase in income was only 10 per cent, a proof, if any was needed, that there were better alternatives to the railways. But closure would have deprived of their income over 160,000 railway employees. These employees were organized, and not unacquainted with militant tactics in politics.

If the railways provide an extreme example of the impracticality of a sudden and rigid application of doctrinaire principles of *laissez faire*, the economy as a whole was deeply afflicted with the parasitism generated by a superabundance of regulations, high tariffs designed to promote industrialization, and administrative devices designed to overcome economic deficiencies caused by fundamental errors of economic policy-making. A vast class of hard-working parasites lived off the existing arrangements. What, for example, would have happened to the Argentine motor-vehicle industry if the government had suddenly decreed the free sale of vehicles manufactured in the U.S.A., Britain, Germany, Italy, and Japan? What would have been the consequences of suddenly abolishing all export controls, export taxes, and price supports for agricultural products? What might be desirable and beneficial in 1970 would have produced chaos and uncontrollable disorder and misery in July 1966. The extreme liberals like Álvaro Alsogaray were asking that Argentina devastate itself as the Allies had devastated Germany in order that a *laissez faire* economic miracle might take place. President Onganía was neither rash nor ruthless enough to adopt such a policy.

The rejection of a revolutionary liberal course of action involved real dangers of the *immobilisme* which had afflicted the regime of Dr Illia. By December 1966 men well disposed to the new government were openly asking 'In what way does Onganía differ from Illia?' Dr Illia himself said to the author in October 1966: 'Onganía does not know how many and how difficult are the problems of Argentina. There will be another revolution within a year.'

While the basic decision concerning the course of the government was taken by the President, what would be achieved by that course depended on the men chosen to execute it. The leading positions were for the most part occupied by political Catholics – some right-wing Christian Socialists and some left-wing Christian Democrats. The Ministry of the Interior which controlled the police, justice, education, and relations with the provincial governments was put in charge of Dr Martínez Paz, a professor of constitutional law in the University of Córdoba who had measured up to at least one of the criteria of Catholic orthodoxy by fathering seven children. The Ministry of Economy, which very sensibly included trade union affairs and wage determination, was given to a Christian Democrat businessman, Dr Jorge Salamei. The determination of the government to maintain good relations with the trade unions and with the Perónistas was expressed not by placing any of their representatives in the government but by appointing as a secretary in the Ministry of Social Welfare Dr San Sebastián a civil servant who had won their confidence not as a partisan but as a fair-minded negotiator and auditor.

Below the first level of appointments it was not so easy to discern an underlying pattern of preference or intention. The men put into executive positions in the state banks, the under-secretaryships of the several departments, the state enterprises, the government of the federal capital, and so on were a very mixed crew. Some were men of exceptional talent and character, but at the other extreme were men of quite exceptional stupidity, having regard for the tasks they were expected to perform. None of them were obviously rascals, but some were petty moralists and fools. The best of the appointments tended to be drawn from those who had developed their attitudes and understanding of community problems technically and without reference to generalized political value-systems. For some years before Onganía came to power there had grown up a movement among the educated groups in business and agricultural life, and to a lesser degree in the trade unions, who, disillusioned with all political programmes and slogans, concentrated their attention on problems and techniques of scientific management. In agriculture this was exemplified by CRFA (*Consorcios Regionales de Experimentación Agrícola*) which aimed at practical action for agricultural improvement by forming groups of farmers and ranchers to employ agronomists and veterinary scientists to guide them in technical matters of farm management. In industry and commerce there was IDEA (*Instituto por el Desarrollo de Ejecutivos Argentinas*), which organized courses in management studies designed to bring to business executives a knowledge of methods of quantitative analysis and of the behavioural sciences as they related to management problems. The machine-tool manufacturers and designers association devoted itself to advertising the quite unappreciated and unsupported talents of Argentina in this area of industry. Another group of technologists committed themselves to co-operate with any government willing and able to provide the means of building thermo-nuclear power stations, with the result that Argentina has now established the first thermo-nuclear power plant in South America, and is developing the means of autonomously equipping such plants.

Men drawn from what may be called the pragmatist movement had a chance to prove themselves, but their intelligence was sadly obstructed by the intellectual shortcomings, narrow prejudices, and inadequacy of the leaders. President Onganía seems himself to have been sympathetic to the narrowest kind of petty Catholic phobias on the subjects of sex, communism, and the arts. Police zeal on the subject of long hair on men and short skirts on women suggested to all but the most blinkered and pious little men and women that the government had an inadequate idea of what was important and serious in the Argentine situation. Raids on the houses of accommodation, called *Hoteles Alojamientos*, and the reporting of errant husbands to wives and vice versa created the impression of a peeping-Tom mentality, amounting to perversion. The prohibition of the performance of the opera *Bomarzo* in the *Teatro Colón* by the *intendente* of Buenos Aires led to a correspondence between Ginastera, the composer, the librettist, and the government and press which revealed the farcical fact that the leading members of the government were unaware that the so-called 'topless opera' was the work of one of the few Argentine composers of international distinction, that the opera had been paid public honours in the United States and Brazil, and that in one case an Argentine ambassador had joined in the tributes to the genius of one of the most famous citizens of the Republic.

Silliness of this description might have been overlooked had it not been for the disastrous mistake made in dealing with the universities. On 29 July 1966 a decree was issued ordering a reform of the universities. Police and troops closed the University of Buenos Aires. In the Faculty of Exact Sciences students and teachers were alike given five minutes to get out of the buildings. The police then assaulted them and arrested a number. Among them was an American professor of mathematics whose beating was the subject of a Note delivered by the U.S. government to the Argentine government.

This ill-conceived act of stupidity was completely without justification, an example of Perónism at its worst. No one in Argentina – university students, university teachers, or the general public – doubted the need for a reform of the universities. One of the worst aspects of Perón's regime was his intervention in the universities, his imprisonment and torture of students, and his installation of second- and third-rate hacks to take the place of teachers driven into private life or into exile. After Perón's fall the damage had been only partly repaired. Teachers were ill-paid and without secure tenure. Most were obliged to do two jobs to live. Students studied in dirty, overcrowded buildings without adequate equipment. In the University of La Plata, for example, 220 students of veterinary science had eight elementary microscopes available for their studies of animal tissues. In order to enable his students to look through microscopes, the lecturer was obliged to repeat his lectures eight times. In spite of poor physical conditions for work, inadequate equipment, and political disorder, which came into the universities from the surrounding society, a surprisingly large number of Argentine teachers and students managed to achieve the highest intellectual standards and to accomplish much that could be respected by anyone anywhere. Viewing the difficulties of their Argentine colleagues and remembering their own abundance and security, North American and European scholars could not help but feel both admiration and guilt. Of course, the students protested. Of course, they went on strike. This was the only method by which they could bring to the attention of the government the betrayal of the intellectual and spiritual welfare of the community.

General Onganía and his colleagues were persuaded, however, that student unrest was the work of communists. After the assault on the University of Buenos Aires, the Rector, Dr Hilario Fernández Long, spoke out. Ordinarily he was a mild, devout Catholic engineer whose principal interest was the translation of the papers of Heisenberg into Spanish. Dr Long declared that of course there were communists in the University of Buenos Aires, and this could be expected in any free institution of learning. He then resigned. More than a thousand teachers followed his example. The departments of mathematics and physics almost disappeared. The brain drain – already serious – swelled, and the United States, Canada, France, Germany, Venezuela, Chile, and Mexico benefited from the folly of the Argentine government. In alarm the officers of the armed forces began to tell the departing teachers that it was all a mistake and that opportunities would be made for those who had quit.

This piece of barbarous idiocy had a purgative effect. Onganía began after this episode to change his course and to search for better men and better policies. The influence of the fanatical right began to wane. Several episodes illustrate this change. In October 1966 a group of armed youths seized an *Aéreo Líneas Argentinas* plane in flight from Buenos Aires to Comodoro Rivadavia in the far south. At gun-point they ordered the pilot to fly to the Falkland Islands and land there. Aboard was the governor of the province of which the Argentine government claims the Falkland Islands to be a part. The object of the hijackers was to proclaim Argentine sovereignty over the Falkland Islands and thus to embroil the government openly in a quarrel with Great Britain for nationalist purposes. A Perónista newspaper, *Crónica*, had sent along a photographer and Frondizi praised the heroism of the enterprise. A nationalist magazine, *Azul y Blanco*, published a great appeal illustrated with a pathetic flock of twenty-six sheep, underneath which was the legend 'The wealth of which the imperialists have robbed us'.

The unofficial Argentine army of liberation consisted of sixteen armed men and a woman. In true Perónista fashion the command was in the hands of a man and a woman, but it was unclear which of the two was in charge. The pilot had skilfully landed the heavy plane on the racecourse outside Port Stanley. When the liberators emerged they were confronted by a police sergeant who had at his disposal a force of seven, of which two were full-time and four part-time policemen. Thus the British were not only surprised but out-numbered. When it was finally explained to the commander of the imperialist forces that the army of liberation was intent on proclaiming Argentine sovereignty, he burst out laughing. This upset the liberators, and they climbed back into their plane to reconsider their position. Meanwhile, the British governor had got in touch with his superiors and the Argentine government. A Catholic priest was sent to talk to the liberators. The outcome was that the army of liberation were taken off by an Argentine ship, removed to Ushuaia in Tierra del Fuego, charged there with the theft of public property, and so passed into history.

This plot to embarrass President Onganía and raise a nationalist commotion was matched by an attempt on the part of the *Tacuara* (a small youth organization which daubed walls with a symbolic Indian lance and slogans such as 'For God, home, and country' and 'Kill a Jew a day') to seize the government of La Rioja, a small Andine province. They occupied the public offices in the capital. The governor, Commodore Julio César Krause, did not live up to his name. He sought advice from Buenos Aires, but unfortunately the Chief of Police acted. He chased the young delinquents out of the buildings, and with the tact usually displayed in the matter of crime by right-wing hooligans he permitted them to flee to Chile. Commodore Krause was told in Buenos Aires that his business was to govern, not to play politics.

*

When President Onganía had resigned as Commander-in-Chief during the Presidency of Dr Illia he had suggested that the principal defect of the Illia government was its softness on communism. A belief in the 'Communist danger' appears to have inspired his mistakes in the matter of the University of Buenos Aires and to have motivated his appointment as the under-secretary of labour of Dr Juan Pedro Tamborenea, a Christian Democrat who professed to find the spectre of communism lurking everywhere. It is, therefore, important in understanding the errors of President Onganía to estimate the reality of the fears which appear to have motivated him.

The possibility of Argentina 'going communist' is about the same as in any community which allows itself to live for a long period of time without stable government capable of solving the economic and social problems which a complex society continuously generates. In the Argentine case, this possibility was considerably reduced because the official Communist Party, ideologically and politically affiliated with Moscow, was an old, bureaucratic, and orthodox Marxist organization. Señor Vittorio Codovilla, the leader of the Argentine Communist Party, was the oldest communist leader in the world. In fact, Perón had long since seized the leadership of the revolution from the communists, and they never solved the problem of recapturing it from him. Revolutionary enthusiasts had for many years recognized this state of affairs, and they moved in on Perón. The 'bad men', like Juan Cooke, who surrounded Perón in his last days of power, were militants much influenced by Marxist analysis. Like Perón, they were believers in mass propaganda, mass action, and organization of the masses in depth. Unlike Perón, they advocated a workers' militia; and the possibility of arming the workers was at the heart of the crisis which led to Perón's overthrow.

After his overthrow, the revolutionary left was fragmented, but not extinguished. It is fortunate for Argentina that Che Guevara did not remain in his native country. As it was, Juan Cooke filled something of the gap left by Guevara. In 1959 he inspired an insurrectionary group, the *Uturunko* (the tiger men of Quechua), which operated briefly in Tucumán province. As late as 1966 troops were stationed daily in the central square of Tucumán and police checkpoints operated on all the roads going in and out of the city. But the *Uturunko* came to nothing.

The victory of Castro in Cuba in 1959 showed what could be done by inventive, determined, revolutionary militants in spite of the existence of a bureaucratic, collaborationist Communist Party. During the whole of Frondizi's administration, acts of terrorism were perpetrated in the main cities of Argentina. After his overthrow, a guerrilla movement was organized in the north-western province of Salta and Jujuy under the name of *Ejército Guerrilla del Pueblo*. Perhaps it was over-organized. Arms and food supplies were assembled, and a training camp established by young dissidents from the Communist Party. When the police descended on it, it had yet to fight anyone or do any damage. A dozen were arrested and six were shot. By the time President Onganía came to power, any real danger of a replication of Cuba in Argentina was at an end. Any diagnosis of the Argentine situation which sees in the declared revolutionary militants the principal source of danger is very wide of the mark. These militants can have effect only if there exists in the community widespread disorganization in the government and even more importantly in the secondary organizations of society. The real merit of President Onganía has been his capacity to recognize this fact, and after some initial errors to turn to the task of encouraging and assisting the secondary organizations to knit themselves together and join in supporting the state.

General Onganía emerged on account of his victory in the armed forces, and the order he imposed there. While he was making a great mistake in the universities and exacerbating their problems, he was at the same time moving to a solution of problems in another direction. In October 1966 his Foreign Minister, Dr Nicanor Costa Méndez, negotiated a new agreement with the Church. This agreement ended the interference of the state in the affairs of the Church, and left the Church free to appoint its own officers in its own way. The government reserved the right to make representations to the Church on matters which concern it. No one can say with certainty what informal and political understanding underlies this formal agreement; but events since the 'concordat' suggest that the hierarchy has agreed that in exchange for freedom it will confine itself to religion and education, and that authority will be exercised to keep priests and bishops out of politics, and end their agitation for social reform and their expressions of partisanship. The bishop of Avellaneda, who specialized in preaching the need for new *conquistas sociales*, has been dismissed; worker priests have been sent home to Spain; the governor of Tucumán has publicly told priests to mind their own business in the matter of the sugar-workers' union – and this is all to the good. Religion is an essential catalytic agent in Argentine society, but taken straight and in large doses it is a terrible poison. It is enough for the Church to teach men to love one another and worship God, a full-time job if ever there was one, but Argentine experience has demonstrated that priests and bishops are totally unqualified to tell men how to vote, how to distribute wealth, how to manage enterprises, and how to establish productive work-relationships. President Onganía seems to have got the Church out of politics and helped it to re-establish its unity, authority, and function.

He has equally made some progress in this direction with the trade unions. President Onganía has accepted the fact that the trade unions are permanent elements in the social and economic life of Argentina. Judging from his relations with them, it would appear that he considers them agencies of social stability and economic development, provided they can be de-politicized and encouraged to fulfil their function as part of the communication system of a complex industrial society. In approaching the problem this way, he is working towards a goal which more and more union leaders recognize explicitly as desirable. Political methods may have been important in bringing some of the unions into being and creating their present structure, but fifteen years of economic stagnation have provoked in some of them the thought that investment, productivity, and economic expansion are important for them and their members, and that they, as leaders, are as likely to become victims of revolutionary disorder as archbishops, landlords, or industrial magnates. They are now part of the élite structure and therefore have to make the system work.

The task of integrating the trade unions into the socio-economic structure is by no means complete, but some progress has been made. In the first months of his regime, President Onganía made two things plain: that his government would discuss anything and everything with the trade unions, at the same time as it would fight any infraction of the law whether by fraud or violence. His first clash came with the most crooked and indefensible of all the unions – the port-workers. As a result of weakness on the part of management and the government, and of union power and abuses, the Argentine ports had become the highest-cost ports in the world. All consignments to Argentine ports carried an automatic freight surcharge to bear the costs of delays in unloading, excessive charges, theft, and general uncertainty. As a means of increasing wages the 'dirty cargo' racket was worked so hard that in Buenos Aires 80 per cent of all cargoes were declared dirty and in Bahía Blanca 100 per cent. If dockers worked ten minutes longer than their shift, they were paid for a second shift, so that naturally all jobs tended to require one shift and ten minutes. The union leaders, and not the port managers, hired and fired the dockers. No one worked without the union's permission, and the rake-off on wages was high. Ship-owners knew, too, the power of the union leaders and the cost of getting it used on their account.[1]

President Onganía's government dealt with the situation in the ports by direct action which began in October 1966. Port captains were appointed with full powers to manage ports; to ensure that any-one who wished to work could work; that workers were employed directly by the port authority; that they were paid at the agreed rates for the work they did; that the classification of cargoes was standardized in accordance with objective criteria as to dirt and danger. All entry into the port areas was barred except to workers and the police were mobilized to enforce the law. There were shrieks of rage from the union leaders but nothing happened. The head of the port-workers, Eustaquio Toloso, went to Europe in October 1966 to raise an international dock strike against Argentine ships. When he returned to Argentina he was charged with conspiracy and crimes and was sentenced to five years in prison. (He was released in January 1969.) Other trade union leaders have protested, but their heart is not in the protests. Buenos Aires is now a low-cost port. In 1967 port costs in Buenos Aires were reduced by $125 million and the turn-around time of grain-ships was reduced from 12.5 days to 2.1 days. There are now no dirty cargoes in Buenos Aires.

A similar situation, but a more intractable one, existed in the state-owned railways. Feather-bedding was widespread, and the *Unión Ferroviara* was determined to resist the ending of a system by which the locomotive drivers were paid six hours' wages for three hours' work. An interventor was installed in the union and the

---

[1] The author's experience in May 1966 of sending one cubic metre of books from Buenos Aires to Birmingham, England, illustrates the cost of the port regime, and his experience could have been multiplied a million-fold. The cost of packing the books, transporting them 6 miles to the North Dock, and putting them in the hold of an Argentine ship was $70. The cost of transporting them 7,000 miles from Buenos Aires to London, unloading them, passing them through the customs, transporting them 110 miles to Birmingham, unloading them at a private residence, and insuring them was $40.

union's funds were taken over; but again nothing happened. Unfortunately, feather-bedding is not the only problem of the railways. Indeed, it is a minor problem compared with over-staffing, poor equipment, poor maintenance, and almost total absence of management as distinct from mere administration. No amount of reform of the railway unions can cure the malaise of the Argentine railways. This is a much bigger problem which is draining away the life blood of the economy.

After the first dialogues with the government the more militant leaders decided on a test of strength. Their *plan de lucha*, announced in February 1967, involved widespread strikes. These strikes were a fiasco. The government stood firm. The union's pension funds were separated from their operating funds. Political expenditure ceased. As a result some of the largest and best organized unions have decided to co-operate with the government. For them there is no pay-off; simply a role to play, a function to perform. The leader in this movement among the trade unions is Juan J. Taccone of *Luz y Fuerza*, the light- and power-workers' union. Taccone like other union leaders has forced over-manning in industry and has worked the 'danger' racket as ably as any, so that the giant new Costerana thermal-electric plant in Buenos Aires requires 60 per cent more men to operate than a similar station in Britain and 80 per cent more than Japan. But Taccone is a man of long-range views and some knowledge of economics. He and his union have negotiated an agreement with the electricity industry which has placed decision-making with respect to organization and manning with managements, and has affirmed and strengthened the union's role as a negotiator of agreements concerning wages and hours. Taccone, of course, is in a more favourable position to move as he has done because power production is an expanding industry, and the Onganía government's main effort in capital investment is directed to building at least one giant power complex at Chocon-Cerrado. Hence it will be easier for *Luz y Fuerza* to protect its members and move towards economy in the use of manpower than it is, say, for the metallurgical union of Augusto Vandor to welcome rationalization in the motor-vehicle industry or the railway union to do the same in the transport industry.

The trade unions on the whole are confused, largely because most of the trade union leaders, trained under Perón and expert in working the rackets possible under the conditions of uncertainty which obtained after the *Revolución Libertadora*, have had almost no experience of real negotiation with employers. This is equally true of employers. Very few employers or trade unionists in Argentina have had any experience of wage bargaining as a central fact of labour relations in plants and factories. Under Perón and since then wage increases have been events which happened to employees and employers alike; they were not events which they themselves made to happen by their relations with each other within the limits of the enterprise's relations with the rest of society through the sale of its products or services.

The absence of this experience of decisive labour relations at industry and plant level has helped to perpetuate among the trade union leaders a faith in political solutions of their problems. About what political solution they cannot agree, and therefore none has worked. The central organization, the C.G.T., has split into two factions: one of which wants to be moderate and to collaborate with the government but does not know how; and the other which wants to take advantage of the government's difficulties to rally the masses to action. Every challenge flung down before the government and particular employers has failed. When the militants called out the petroleum-workers at the Y.P.F. refineries at La Plata in September 1968, the government stood firm and backed up the management which dismissed all those absent from duty. After six weeks the strike collapsed, largely because petroleum-workers elsewhere in the country did not respond to an appeal to paralyse the industry. And why should they have done so? The La Plata workers in the nationalized industry worked six hours a day. The workers elsewhere in private refineries and in Y.P.F. plants elsewhere in the country worked eight hours a day. The La Plata workers refused more pay for eight-hour shifts, which the management required for efficient working, in order to enable the majority to hold two jobs. There was scant sympathy for a racket established by feeble management, political pressure, and aggressive trade union opportunism.

A more fundamental cause of the weakness of the trade union movement than the government's firmness in the face of militancy is the slowing down of inflation. Inflation has been essential to the trade unions. The need to push money wages up by at least 25 per cent a year has been both their *raison d'être* and their means of building up the resources at the disposal of the leaders. As a result of Dr Krieger Vasena's policies prices have ceased to rise so rapidly as hitherto. In fact prices in the federal capital were actually falling slightly late in 1968. The idea of a wage freeze no longer excites revolutionary talk. The real crisis of labour in Argentina is no longer between the labour movement and the government or between the labour movement and the employers, but within the labour movement itself. Unless the leaders of the major unions are willing to imitate the Taccone approach to labour problems and to recognize that henceforward there are great benefits for their members in direct negotiation with management at the level of the plant and the firm, the trade union movement as present constituted is going to die away.

The simple-minded enthusiasts among the investing class who rushed to the Stock Exchange to buy shares and securities in the confident expectation that the right kind of revolution would solve at once all economic problems were sorely disappointed. Economic problems grew worse during Onganía's first six months in power. Inflationary pressures grew. Budget deficits mounted. The purists of the International Monetary Fund had cautiously approved the economic policies of Frondizi and they might even have loved Illia if he had let them. Of Onganía they soon learned to disapprove. The trouble was not his economic policies, but their absence. The tenure of Dr Salamei in the Ministry of Economy proved beyond doubt that modest business success, religious orthodoxy, and the right connections are insufficient qualifications for the direction of a complex economy afflicted with deep distress.

The climax of confusion in economic policy came in November 1966. On 8 November President Onganía announced personally in a speech of some length and generality that the peso would be freed of all controls and that the control of exports would be done away with. This was a step in the direction of liberalism of the kind desired by the Alsogaray brothers. But was it? The President's speech was plain enough. But the decrees issued implementing his declared policy ordered almost the opposite. The peso was devalued to the point where the official rate roughly equalled the black, or parallel, market rate. Taxes on exports remained and control was only modified, not abolished. It was pretty plain that either Onganía did not know what he was doing or Salamei did not. This was incompetence such as Argentina had not witnessed since the Presidency of General Ramírez after the *golpe* of 1943. Dr Illia and other banned politicians spoke out, and people began to listen.

Onganía responded to the situation with a clever political move inside the power structure. General Pascual Pistarini, the Commander-in-Chief of the Army, was retired and General Julio Alsogaray was promoted in his place. A few weeks passed; and on the day of the Holy Innocents, 1966, President Onganía slaughtered his Cabinet. All the Ministers were invited to hand in their resignations. Those of Costa Méndez of the Foreign Office and Petracca of Social Welfare were refused. Those of Martínez Paz of the Interior and Salamei of Economy and Labour were accepted. The Defence Ministry was already vacant.

But this was not Alsogaray's victory. He was firmly placed in a spot where he had to obey orders. The President had the power of appointing his Ministers, and this he proceeded to exercise in a way which did not alter the balance in his Cabinet between the liberal extremism favoured by the landed classes and the *dirigisme* favoured by the business and labour interests which had grown up since Perón's time. The political Catholics were ditched, and much abler men than Martínez Paz and Salamei were brought in. Dr Adalberto Krieger Vasena was appointed Minister of Economy and Labour and Dr Guillermo Borda Minister of the Interior.

Krieger Vasena is an able economic technician strongly oriented towards a free enterprise system of economic organization, but cautious and in no way disposed towards 'the rich cow pasture' concept of Argentina. He had served General Aramburu and President Guido and was therefore identified as a conservative. His main virtue consisted in knowing what needed to be done and how to do it.

Dr Borda was an ex-Perónista. He had been a member of the electoral college which had formally elected Perón in 1946, after the popular poll had been taken. Perón had appointed him to the judiciary, where he made a reputation for honesty and fair dealing – something of an achievement in the days of the dictator. Unusually lucky or prudent, he had contrived to be on leave when the will of Perón's brother-in-law, Juan Duarte, had come before his court for probate. After Perón's fall, he had continued on the bench. Onganía, when he came to power, appointed him to the Supreme Court. As the Minister of the Interior, he was a standing promise to the Perónistas that there would be no victimization, but he was also a warning that the law would be enforced and justice done.

Krieger Vasena quickly implemented a balanced economic policy. Balance in this context meant that he moved to end inflation by a once and for all massive devaluation while at the same time taking measures to prevent large windfall profits for those who could not be counted on to invest in productive enterprise. The peso was devalued from approximately 280 on the parallel or black market to 350 to the U.S. dollar. This was declared to be the last devaluation. At the same time taxes up to 25 per cent were placed on all the major exports so that the landed interests and holders of stocks of cereals and meat would not reap instant fortunes. As a result capital from abroad, much of it Argentine, began to flow into Argentina to earn the high interest rates there, to take advantage of the favourable rates of conversion into pesos, and to seek the investment opportunities which the prospect of political stability and intelligent economic policies promised. To provide opportunities for investment and for the absorption of labour from manpower-intensive industries like the railways, Krieger commenced the organization, as distinct from the mere planning, of a large development of the infrastructure of the economy: power production, steel manufacture, roads, and housing, financed substantially but not entirely by internal capital resources. He cut tariffs on industrial products. Argentine tariffs were among the highest in the world, and a means of feather-bedding industry in a way parallel to the feather-bedding practised by labour unions. Increasingly Argentine industry has to compete in its own markets. Government assistance to industry is now given conditional upon a revealed capacity to export. Bank credit has been reorganized and expanded to enable industrialists to borrow on productive records and viable plans for production. Rent control has been done away with under a system which obliges the landlord either to use his land productively or sell it to the tenant who will do so. A petroleum law has opened up investment opportunities to international capital. The state-owned oil enterprise Y.P.F. (*Yacimientos Petrolíferos Fiscales*), which is the fourth largest oil enterprise in South America, has been reorganized so that the management manages in response to changing commercial and technical conditions instead of administering in accordance with government directives, and the men who manage are paid at professional rates so that it is necessary no longer to staff a large and complex business with men who had to be either saints or rogues to live on the low salaries prescribed by an egalitarian philosophy.

But political caution has slowed Dr Krieger Vasena down. The railway problem is still there, and railway deficits are still a serious drag on the economy. Large enterprises like the hydro-electric-irrigation scheme *El Chocon-Cerrado-Colorados* have been slow to organize because the Minister of Economy has wisely tried to rely heavily on domestic investment and to scatter foreign holdings, thus reducing the possibility of over-dependence on any one interest. Anti-communism notwithstanding, a serious effort has been made to involve the Soviet Union in the enterprise.

Political caution and a determination not to let the landed interest regain control of the country has prompted Dr Krieger Vasena to refuse to yield to the pressure of the agro-pecuarian lobbyists. They and their publicists and political pressure boys have loudly denounced export taxes. These the Ministry of Economy has reduced step by step so that they are down from 25 per cent to 6–10 per cent, but the Minister has been plain and firm that the landed interest bear its fair share of the tax burdens of the community and that taxes be levied more on the profits of ownership than on productive activity. A land tax has been devised which will hit the non-productive, speculative, and under-productive owner and will become a diminishing proportion of the total income of the man, or firm, which increases his receipt by increasing production. In order to show the landed interest that it is possible to do at least as well as the Australian agricultural and pastoral industry, the government has launched a large-scale experimental scheme for the improvement of marginal pastures – the Balcarce plan, embracing 220,000 hectares in the southern part of Buenos Aires province.

The traditional selfishness and short-sight of the landed interest has not left them in spite of all their bitter lessons. Their organs of public opinion still hammer away at the need to restore liberal democracy and inaugurate a regime of unrestricted free enterprise, not eventually but immediately. In spite of the almost total expulsion of the Christian Democratic influence from the government, the oligarchic liberals are still alleging that the government has a 'communitarian' philosophy and is too much addicted to planning. In July and August 1968 fresh rumours of a *golpe* were put in circulation. Onganía struck again. The commanders-in-chief of the three services were retired, and three new men were put in their places. Lt-General Alsogaray was thus out, and his brother soon resigned as ambassador to the United States.

It is now abundantly clear that President Onganía cannot be overthrown by playing politics with the armed forces. Since March 1968, they have been in the control of a civilian Minister, Señor Emilio van Peborgh, a young, professional businessman who helped to launch the *Instituto por el Desarrollo de Ejecutivos Argentinas.* Van Peborgh, an immensely tall man who stands head and shoulders above the soldiers over whom he presides, is forceful, of incisive intellect. He listens more than he speaks, but when he does it is a pleasure to hear him briefly and powerfully sweep away the sentimentality and cant of nationalist and do-good politicians. He was first appointed by Onganía to run the *Banco Industrial.* This he did with conspicuous success and imagination. He sees clearly in precise economic terms what Argentina needs, but he sees equally that Argentina needs social and political peace. In his view it will be another six or eight years before Argentina can afford to run the risk of attempting to select its government by democratic election. In the meantime he is committed to seeing that there is no risk of *golpes.*

Even Álvaro Alsogaray now admits that he cannot say who is appointed to the government, and that there is no alternative to President Onganía and his team. The Perónistas, the trade unions, and both the wings of the Radical Party have lost all prospect of upsetting the government. The Christian Democrats have lost their influence. The liberals, however, have now turned to applying pressure through public manifestation of support for a return to open political processes. In September 1968 a great dinner attended by 1,200 guests was organized to celebrate the anniversary of the *Revolución Libertadora.* The main speaker was Admiral Isaac Rojas, whom Onganía crushed in the struggle between the *Azules* and the *Colorados.* Generals, scholars, and lawyers of the liberal establishment abounded. General Aramburu sent a message of rather ambiguous support. Amerigo Ghioldi, the socialist ex-congressman and editor of *Vanguardia,* was there. In his speech Admiral Rojas asserted that there had only been three genuine revolutions in Argentine history: the revolution against Spain; the overthrow of General Rosas; and the overthrow of Perón. The Onganía regime was described as a threat to freedom. Rojas made a spirited attack on planning, high taxation, and state enterprise. All this is to the good. The greatest danger facing Argentina in its present circumstances is that the government will become rigid, over-authoritarian, and over-addicted to making a superabundance of rules and regulations. The natural inclination of soldiers is to administer and not to lead – especially officers of an army which has never fought against real enemies for ninety years. Onganía is one of the rare Argentine officers who has actually conducted a successful military operation, but as he has himself publicly acknowledged, it is easy for people in office to think they are doing their job when they get through the papers in front of them. Argentina needs peace, but it also needs creative tension. This is why it is to be hoped that the ex-generals, the trade unionists, and the students will continue to stir things up. A whiff of fire is good for a general, and that is what President Onganía is. He has proved he can take it.

To say that he has proved his capacity for survival and his capacity for the exercise of power does not imply that he has solved all of Argentina's problems. He has only solved the most important one, and that solution will soon become negative, if he and the leaders chosen by him cannot solve the secondary problems, relating to economic and social organizations and performance. The central questions of the Argentine economy are still as they have been since 1945 – concerned with whether or not the purchasing power of the community is spent more on production than on consumption, and, of equal importance, whether that portion not spent on consumption is hoarded in some form or other (either by investment in land and buildings, or in the purchase of saleable foreign capital assets) or is spent in Argentina on Argentine productive activity. By creating a continuous political uproar in the community and by stimulating hatred, suspicion, and fear under the guise of preaching the emancipation of the shirtless workers and the quick inauguration of Utopia, an unbalance in the disposition of spendable resources has been established as a seemingly permanent characteristic of Argentine life. Argentina has explored the depths of this condition for rather long and rather more deeply than most modern civilized communities. There are some signs that Dr Krieger Vasena's policies are lifting Argentina out of the morass. But when we see nations like Britain, France, and the United States moving towards a condition in which the propensity to spend exceeds the disposition to save, we may well wonder whether Dr Krieger Vasena and President Onganía can teach wisdom to people as naturally hedonistic, sensuous, and luxury-loving as the Argentines.

After its initial and mistaken attempt to create an atmosphere of anti-communist terror, the regime seems to have recognized that terror, no matter at whom directed, creates a sense of insecurity in everyone. Terrorism by definition terrifies, and thus erodes the psychological foundations of human co-operation. The two socially formative regimes of Argentine history suffered from the same fundamental faults which rendered them in the end unworkable as long-term agencies of development and worthwhile life. The regime of General Rosas, which consolidated the position of the landowning class, and the regime of General Perón, which consolidated the position of the urban industrial interests, both employed terror, mass agitation, and intrusion into private life to achieve the changes which their supporters wished. Working on the foundations laid by Rosas, the *laissez faire* liberals erected a social and economic structure which demonstrated its capacity for growth and the creation of a life worth living for the majority of the Argentine people. A similar task faces the successors of Perón: to create a system sufficiently open and tolerant to make possible social co-operation and a worthwhile life for individuals. In spite of a lingering disposition to intrude into private life, to bully artists, and to inflict on society a small-minded puritanism, the present regime appears to be moving towards liberty based on law and towards a society organized by inclusive rather than exclusive decision-making processes. As yet one cannot discern the full shape and character of the new institutional structure, but the indications are that flexible and inclusive techniques of government will be found.

*

Argentina is a remote community. When one leaves a plane from Europe at Ezeiza one feels strongly that one has reached the end of the earth and that one can go no farther away. Argentines feel this too. One young Argentine sociologist has developed the concept of marginality to explain Argentine society and to identify it: Argentina on the edge. But feeling and location and circumstance in international political life do not fully identify Argentina. The historical record suggests beyond a doubt that Argentina was born of the great revolution in world society which we describe as the industrial revolution, the rise of a capitalist, *laissez faire* economy, the creation of representative government, and the participation and interdependence of the mass of mankind in the processes of political, economic, and cultural life. The great crisis of this society, which began with World War I and culminated in World War II with the dissolution of empires and the emergence of great power blocs, afflicted and transformed Argentine society as much as any community in the world. Argentina has experienced the fever of that crisis and has survived it. Slowly order, authority, and liberty are being restored. Slowly Argentina is finding a viable economic and political relationship with the international community which incorporates the new into what, for want of a better word, we may describe as the permanent. It is the central fact of the human condition everywhere that men can only live in society and, hateful as they are, they must learn to love one another and care for one another. Perhaps the Argentines are once more asserting, however feebly, the primacy of this imperative.

*

Since these words were set up in type violence and disorder have developed in the major cities of Argentina during May–June 1969. The police and armed forces are arrayed against students and a substantial body of trade unionists. The most likely result of this clash will be the strengthening of the regime and renewed emphasis on its authoritarian character. Paradoxically, it is likely that it will become more liberal in its economic policies. On the central question of the power and authority of the state President Onganía is both clear and determined, and he possesses the means to implement his will. On the other side there is indignation and bitterness; but these are not the ingredients of an alternative.

Chapter 11

Argentina in the International Community

I N THE DISCOURSE of the western world it is conventional to speak and think of Latin America as a category of communities having certain characteristics (e.g. underdevelopment or a tendency towards dictatorial forms of government) and a certain kind of relationship with what are called the advanced industrial nations (e.g. a semi-colonial or neo-colonial relationship). Argentina is included in this category. Latin Americans have come to speak and think in similar terms, and Argentines in some degree also. An inclusive category need not, however, imply either homogeneity of substance or continuous and dense interconnection.

Latin America from the Río Grande to Tierra del Fuego is not as well integrated in terms of the division of labour and the organization of trade, nor even in terms of culture, as, for example, the United States and Canada or western Europe. In some respects it is not as well integrated as Europe including the U.S.S.R. The patterns of connection one discerns in Latin America are less continental than oceanic. To travel by motor-car or to transport goods by land between Buenos Aires and Rio de Janeiro is an enterprise of some difficulty which the man who drives from Nome, Alaska, to New Orleans or from Edinburgh to Athens would not care to undertake without some careful study and much preparation. South America may be rich and populous, but it is not an easy continent to get about in, nor to use and enjoy.

The object of stating the obvious is to emphasize the first truth one must keep ever in mind when one thinks about the place of the Argentine Republic in the international community and its relations with the states of South America and overseas. There is a powerful geographical determinant in the national independence of Argentina; a combination of land, climate, and location that acts as a reinforcing factor in the socially and politically generated value-systems of the Argentines. The values inform their lives and actions in many diverse ways, but all of them are influenced by or stem from the importance which the overwhelming majority of all classes and all origins attach to their national identity and national independence. They are so anxious about their independence that one suspects they cannot take it for granted.

And this is so. Located at the end of the world the Argentines thrive best connected with its centres. With the human and natural resources to do great things, Argentina has not enough to stand alone and impose its will on others. But contrariwise Argentina can if need be stand alone. A combination of location, resources, and human inclination has enabled the Argentine community since colonial times to resist and destroy the power of three European imperialist nations to control the River Plate and its hinterlands, while at the same time depending on first one and then the other two for the means of growth and material prosperity; to resist and defy the strongest power in the Americas without the full material means to do so; and while benefiting from their connections with both the European powers and the United States to convince themselves that they are victims rather than equals.

This lively concern with national independence which animates the people of Argentina and has always set the course of their government's policy in international relations is a product of geopolitical and economic factors. Buenos Aires is the commercial and political key to the richest, most easily accessible, and largest temperate and semi-tropical zone of the Americas south of the Río Grande. But so is Montevideo. The Spaniards may have located the capital of the Viceroyalty of the Río de la Plata at Buenos Aires, but they selected Montevideo as the strong-point of their empire in that part of the continent. The control of Montevideo was a critical matter for the English invaders in 1806–07, and for the revolutionaries against the Spaniards. The revolutionaries lost Montevideo to Portuguese-Brazilian imperial control. Once the revolution was over the regime in Buenos Aires made the recovery of Montevideo and the hinterland of the *Banda Oriental* (or Eastern Bank) the first item on the agenda of international politics. But prematurely so, as it turned out. Revolutionary tactics reinforced with military backing were insufficient to incorporate Uruguay into the 'Argentine family'. Equally, military and administrative effort by the Brazilians was insufficient to maintain Brazilian control. The result was a stalemate manifest in the form of Uruguayan independence.

In Argentina at least, this result was then and still is attributed to the machinations of the British and particularly to the British minister in Buenos Aires, Lord Ponsonby. In fact the settlement was born of the exhaustion of the parties to the dispute, and was reached as a result of mediation by the Colombian government and not the British government. For nearly a quarter of a century the government in Buenos Aires sought in one way or another to get control of Montevideo but with no success. Just as the creation of an independent Uruguay was blamed on the British, so its survival was blamed on first the French, then the British, and finally on both. Whatever British or French policy may have been, the salient political fact was the rivalry of the two commercial entrepôts and the incapacity of the politicians and revolutionaries in Buenos Aires to gain control of Montevideo. The possibility of Montevideo controlling Buenos Aires was never worth considering once the Brazilians left the field of contention.

A factor in the overthrow of General Rosas in 1852 was his persistence in the clearly unprofitable and debilitating endeavour to seize Montevideo. More effective than eliminating or incorporating a rival were the policies of economic expansion put in train by the liberal successors to General Rosas. Montevideo left to itself had a very limited potential. Buenos Aires, on the other hand, had a hinterland of immense size, variety, and riches once the community had organized itself to find the people and the capital to render it productive. Argentine primacy in South America until the depression of the 1930s stemmed, not from military power employed to threaten or conquer its neighbours, but from peace and economic development. After the close of the war with Paraguay in 1870, Argentina fought no wars except against the Indians of the southern pampas and Patagonia. Border disputes with Paraguay and Chile were resolved by arbitration and in the case of the Argentine-Chilean frontiers arbitration became an institutionalized and a reoccurring procedure for resolving the consequence of expansion into uninhabited and unsurveyed territories in the Andes region.

Although one of the largest and the richest of the communities in South America, Argentina has for nearly a century adopted the policy of accepting her neighbours, Chile, Bolivia, Paraguay, and Uruguay, as independent communities with which there are no irresolvable problems. In the case of Brazil, with which Argentina shares a comparatively short boundary line, relations have been peaceful but not always harmonious for 140 years. Argentina was an ally of Brazil during the hideous war of attrition against Paraguay, but the defeat and near obliteration of Paraguay revealed the unwillingness of the allies to accord any great territorial extensions to each other. Indeed, it is possible to suppose that Paraguay like Uruguay exists because Argentina and Brazil are rivals for the control of at least part of a continent. This rivalry is deeply rooted both in the history and the conscience of the two communities. For many years Argentina was obviously the more thriving and up to date of the two, with the result that the Brazilians both feared and envied Argentina. During the last thirty years the comparison between them has been to Argentina's disadvantage. Brazil has advanced rapidly in terms of industrial and economic power, while Argentina, since the military *coup d'état* of 1943, has floundered around in a swamp of its own making. The Argentines tend to attribute this comparative success of Brazil to 'American backing'. Undoubtedly, the Brazilians, like the Mexicans, took full advantage of the fears and anxieties of the United States in the dark days after Dunkirk and Pearl Harbor and benefited enormously from the American desire to strengthen the economy of the Americas as well as the United States, but this was an option open to Argentina and one which no leading Argentine except Federico Pinedo was willing to exploit.

The comparative rates of development between Brazil and Argentina, which prompted the supposition that Brazil will dominate South America and become, perhaps, the Latin American equivalent of the United States, are no longer so different as they were in the 1950s. Brazil is a much disturbed society with some massive and unresolved social problems. Argentina, on the other hand, looks as if its darkest days are over, and is about to resume the rhythm of development broken by World War II. This change in the relative positions of the two powers need not be the substance of a tragedy, but it could be.

The reasons for this are connected with development. Neither Argentina nor Brazil is any longer what they were until the 1930s: nations organized economically and commercially as exporters of primary products. They are both industrial states, and are both increasingly bent on becoming mature industrial societies. That there exist in both societies – and now more in Brazil than in Argentina – obstacles to intensive industrial development contributes to the possibility of difficulty rather than otherwise. Industrialization and

the need and will to intensify the rate of this development are creating a new range of problems requiring a political solution. The
River Plate system, for example, is one of the greatest undeveloped
sources of hydro-electric power in the world. Improvements in this
river system for flood control, irrigation, and navigation are urgently
needed. The demand for electric power in Rio Grande do Sul and in
the *Litoral* regions of Argentina and Uruguay are growing enormously. The development of the full potential of the region requires
the co-operation of Argentina, Paraguay, and Brazil and Uruguay,
and the participation of Bolivia in any scheme of development is
highly desirable. Will such co-operation be forthcoming? There are
talks and talks about talks, but there are also some ominous signs of
differences. The possibility of an oil-field beneath the waters of the
River Plate has prompted the Uruguayan government, desperate for
new sources of revenue and in need of some basis for developing its
stagnant economy, to demand a revision of the agreement between
Argentina and Uruguay governing the use and management of the
great rivers and the estuary. The potential for oil, power, and water
is there; the need for development is there; but one finds no clear
evidence that the political foundations are there. Several kinds of
solution are possible and all are being explored, but some more than
others. The Argentines have begun to strengthen their hand by
planning a home-based armaments industry relying on national self-
sufficiency in steel, petroleum, nuclear energy, and the industrial production of armaments. It must not be supposed that a resolution to
develop in this way will lead into a blind alley as far as the stimula-
tion of the economy is concerned. A big factor in the solution of the
problem of stagnation in the United States, Germany, and Britain
was rearmament in the 1930s, and the impetus behind Stalin's
industrialization programme was the conviction that the Soviet
Union must defend itself against its enemies. We may very well be
witnessing the beginning of a similar process in South America.

Instead of a co-operative development of resources in accordance
with the ideals of the Latin American Free Trade Association, a
process of establishing alliances of client states can develop. The
notion that the United States, the Organization of American States,
or the United Nations can prevent this is not well founded. The
United States may complicate and inflame the situation by endeavouring to do so, but the expectation of their success is much less than
the danger of their intervention. While no one need yield to

unrelieved pessimism, it is prudent to face candidly the explosive as well as the benign possibilities connected with the pressure for development.

This pressure is manifesting itself elsewhere than in the Plata-Paraná river system. One of the first acts of the Onganía regime was to proclaim the extension of Argentine sovereignty from 3 miles from the shore-line to 200 miles. The object of this endeavour to revise international law is control over the fishing resources of the continental shelf and over the petroleum and gas resources which may very well exist there. So far Argentina has had little success in finding agreement to their proclamation, and the Soviet Union is a great power which has refused to recognize the Argentine claims. It must be borne in mind, however, that the capacity of Argentina to assert her authority in the south Atlantic is not negligible and will become greater in the future. The purchase of second-hand aircraft-carriers, new and used submarines, and strike aircraft is not just a gesture of appeasement of a military President to his brother officers, but part of a policy which has at least as much possibility of working as the policies of Israel in the Middle East or the Soviet Union in Czechoslovakia. It is likewise pretty unlikely, if the experience of the Kennedy and Johnson regimes is any guide, that the United States can impose its will so far from Washington.

*

The Argentine concern with resource potential along and beyond its boundary lines affects Anglo-Argentine relations. The islands in the south Atlantic which the British call the Falklands and the Argentines Las Malvinas are a subject of dispute between the British and Argentine governments. This dispute has been in progress since 8 August 1829, when the British Foreign Secretary, the Earl of Aberdeen, instructed the British consul-general in Buenos Aires to protest against the Argentine occupation of the islands and the appointment of a governor 'done without reference to the validity of the claims which His Majesty had constantly asserted to the sovereignty of the islands'. Since January 1833, the roles have been reversed. Argentina has been protesting against the British occupation of the islands. No shots have been fired in the dispute, but an abundance of paper has been discharged by the parties at each other. Currently the battle is raging quietly, and the dispute has surfaced in the House of Commons and in the Argentine press.

On the British side there are probably not more than fifty persons in Britain and in the islands themselves who know what is involved in the dispute or were even, until recently, actively aware of its existence. On the Argentine side the matter is a popular issue: a massive generality about which large numbers feel strongly but no one can precisely define why. The British presence in the Falklands-Malvinas is for the Argentine nationalists a physical proof of the myths about imperialism which are part of their political stock in trade and, like other non-problems, a means of stimulating latent paranoia. As a non-problem the islands have the power to touch British neuroses as well. The reaction to the mild rationality of Lord Chalfont, the British Minister of State at the Foreign Office, on the subject has demonstrated that it is no more possible to talk sense about the Falkland Islands in Britain than it is in Argentina.

The object of the dispute is a group of islands in the south Atlantic located approximately 350 miles off the coast of Argentina and about 250 away from the entrance to the Straits of Magellan. In the group there are two large islands, one slightly more than 2,000 square miles in area and the other about 2,600 square miles. Dotted about them are some 200 tiny islands. Although they are located in the shallow seas which extend from 50 to 400 miles out from the shore-line of Argentina from the River Plate to Tierra del Fuego, the islands are geologically more part of Africa than South America. They are rocks raised above the surface of the sea, their hollows and flat surfaces filled or covered with peat and soil. The winds blow fiercely, as they do in Tierra del Fuego and Patagonia. Rains fall moderately and the temperature seldom rises above 70°F, and the long winters limit the range of vegetation to grasses and vegetables. The indented coasts provide sheltered harbours, but the remoteness of the islands has frequently disappointed hope that they might play a large part in international maritime shipping. Britain thought briefly in 1899–1905 of establishing a naval base in the islands, but abandoned the idea in favour of an unfortified coaling-station and fuel depot, which served its purpose in World War I and in World War II.

Lacking commercial minerals and petroleum, the economic activity of the inhabitants is limited to sheep-farming, sealing, and fishing. At one time ship-repairing offered some employment, but the days when distressed vessels sought the islands for repairs, rest for their crews, and supplies have long since passed. The total population is only slightly more than 2,000, of whom half live in Port Stanley, the only town. There is on balance a migration from the islands, and supplies of labour for the sheep-farms are short. The native-born show a tendency to migrate; contract labour from Britain has proved unsatisfactory; and recently labourers from Chile have been imported.

In several important respects the economy of the islands closely resembles that of the Argentine provinces of Chubut and Santa Cruz, except that they possess no petroleum. The sheep-farms are owned mainly by absentee landlords who operate their properties through managers and hired labourers. The farms are very large in area and ownership is concentrated. The Falkland Islands Company owns about one-third of the area devoted to sheep, and the trend has been towards large commercial exploitation rather than small-scale farming. As in Chubut and Santa Cruz the sheep-station managers are frequently Scottish, Australian, and New Zealand professionals. The only way in which the Falklands proprietors differ from the proprietors in Santa Cruz and Chubut is that all of them are British, whereas in the Argentine provinces only some of them are.

The economic history of the islands has been one of steady exploitation of resources and men rather than development, and this has been more so than in Argentina. The cattle were ruthlessly killed off in the first half of the nineteenth century. The attempts of the British authorities to prevent total destruction of the herds were much more feeble than the Argentine efforts in similar circumstances, and for the very good reason that in Argentina the landed proprietors controlled the government and had an interest in the permanence and preservation of the economy, whereas in the Falkland Islands the government was the agency of a remote bureaucracy capable of knowing what was needed but with no political means of enforcing a policy.

When the cattle were gone, sheep took their place, but the same process of exploitation persisted. The pastures were over-stocked. Little attention was paid to animal hygiene, the renewal of pastures, or the scientific management of the environment. In the early 1890s the sheep flocks exceeded 800,000, but have declined since then. Today they number about 600,000.

From the proprietors' short-term point of view the economy is sound. Exports amount to over £1 million a year or about £500 per head, and imports amount to half this figure. This suggests that the level of investment and the incomes of the people are low. Profits, on the other hand, are high. There is little infrastructure and few social services to maintain. In some respects the Falkland Islands are a miniature paradise from the bankers' and owners' points of view. The balance of payments is extremely favourable. There are 1,850 bank accounts in the Falkland Islands although there are only 2,000 inhabitants.

Why is there a dispute about these unattractive, windswept rocks and bogs? There is no substance whatever in the argument of the Argentine nationalists that the imperialists have robbed them of great wealth. The five largest *estancias* in the Chubut are larger and more productive than the Falkland Islands. Britain could give up the Falkland Islands and not suffer the slightest loss. Correspondingly Argentina could acquire them, and gain no noticeable benefit. If all the inhabitants of the Falkland Islands were added to the population of Argentina they would only increase the number of British passport-holders resident in Argentina by 10 per cent. If the Argentine government compelled all the inhabitants of the Falkland Islands to become Argentine citizens they would be in no different position than the Welsh settlers in the Chubut, who have lived and thrived in Argentina for more than one hundred years. It is extremely difficult to see how, in economic or human terms, the transformation of the Falklands into Las Malvinas would alter anything and equally how a refusal to do so will change anything.

This is so if one looks only at the Falkland Islands themselves. In a wider frame of reference the transfer of the Falkland Islands to Argentina will have an immense benefit. There is no substance nor has there ever been any substance in the popular Argentine myths about British imperialism. It is useless, however, to assert this. It is so, but it must be seen to be so. The Falkland Islands are no longer of any use to Britain. They can be transferred to Argentina without any injury to the inhabitants. If this is done a myth will be destroyed and energy given to the movement to end imperialism and myths about imperialism everywhere in Latin America. If Britain behaves rationally in this matter, the United States will be under strong pressure to behave equally rationally in the matter of the Panama canal zone and its naval base in Cuba. The effect of justice and rationality will be immense and achieve far more than financial aid, peace corps, and do-good programmes.

This dispute about the Falkland Islands-Malvinas has its origins in the imperialist rivalries of the eighteenth century. Unless one is obsessed with history and legality, no purpose is served by examining the claims of Spain based on the Bull *Inter Caetera* of 1493 or the Treaty of Tordesillas of 1494. After the Seven Years War the British government developed a policy of trying to penetrate the Spanish empire from free ports off shore in the Caribbean and elsewhere. The foundation of a settlement on West Falkland was part of this policy. It was countered by the French who established a colony in East Falkland and then transferred it to Spain. The Spaniards drove the British out of West Falkland, and the British threatened to go to war. The French advised the Spaniards to back down. Knowing they could not successfully fight Britain without the help of France, the Spaniards yielded. They acknowledged the British claim to West Falkland, but the acknowledgement of the British claim to East Falkland was ambiguous.

As it turned out, political difficulties in Europe and elsewhere obliged both the British and the Spaniards to leave the Falkland Islands. With the coming of the American Revolution, the British never re-established their settlement in West Falkland. The Spaniards continued in East Falkland, but with the outbreak of revolution in the Spanish dominions, the garrison in East Falkland was withdrawn in 1811. For nine years there was no authority of any sort in the islands. Sealing- and whaling-vessels, mostly American and British, anchored in the islands to hunt seals, take on fresh water, and hunt wild cattle for food. In 1820 a vessel flying the Argentine flag captained by Daniel Jewitt asserted the authority of his government, but this did not amount to more than warning the sealing captains that Argentina claimed sovereignty. Three years later a governor was appointed, and grants of land and fishing rights were made. One of these grantees, Louis Vernet, was a serious man of business who established a considerable settlement, and was made the Argentine governor of the islands.

As governor he asserted his power to grant licences and charge fees for sealing and anchoring in the islands. Some American sealing captains recognized his authority, but some did not. These Vernet arrested. When news of their arrest reached the U.S. consul in Buenos Aires he protested. An American warship, U.S.S. *Lexington*, was sent to the islands late in 1831. The Americans landed, spiked the Argentine guns, blew up the powder magazine, seized a stock of seal-skins, put the leading men in irons, and carried them away to be tried as pirates. The Argentine government broke off relations with the United States, and was still arguing about the American behaviour as late as 1885.

The Americans destroyed a viable settlement and declared the Falkland Islands free of all government. The aftermath of the events of December 1831 was observed by the Captain of H.M.S. *Rattlesnake*, who reported to the Admiralty. As a result an instruction was issued by the British government to assert the sovereignty of King William IV in the islands, and to this end H.M.S. *Clio* was despatched to the south Atlantic. Meanwhile the Argentine government sent to the islands the warship *Sarandí* for the purpose of establishing a penal colony.

When the H.M.S. *Clio* arrived the captain and officers of the *Sarandí* had just finished putting down a mutiny. When requested to haul down the Argentine flag, Captain Pinedo refused and protested against the demand. He then embarked and returned to Buenos Aires. British marines landed, hauled down the Argentine flag, and ran up the Union Jack.

At this stage there existed on the islands a state of chaos. American and British sealing- and whaling-vessels were coming and going. The remainder of Vernet's colony were endeavouring to re-create a life for themselves under the leadership of Vernet's lieutenant, Captain Brisbane, who fortunately for the Argentine myth-makers was an Englishman. Apart from these colonists there were the Argentine escaped convicts – some gauchos and some Indians under the leadership of a gaucho named Rivero. A struggle familiar enough in Argentina developed between the mercantile employees under Brisbane, and the gauchos and vagabonds under Rivero. Rivero and his band murdered Brisbane and destroyed the remains of the Argentine colony. To the Argentine nationalists Rivero is a hero. Brisbane, his victim, was an Englishman. Unfortunately for the myth, Brisbane was the agent of Vernet, the Argentine governor, who had been carried away in irons by the Americans. In fact Rivero murdered Brisbane because Brisbane insisted on paying the gauchos and Indians for their work in Argentine money and not in British money or some other hard currency.

When the British proceeded to assert their authority as distinct from their sovereignty they hunted down Rivero and his gang and transported them to Britain. There their trial presented such insoluble legal problems that they were turned loose in Uruguay.

Vernet was deprived of his concession on the legal ground that he had received it from a government which had no rights in the islands. Ironically an officer of the Royal Navy, who had been granted a large holding by Vernet, was also deprived on similar legal grounds. Eventually, after years of litigation and petitioning, Vernet's widow was paid a small sum as compensation for moveable property belonging to her husband.

The Argentine government, of course, protested strenuously about the British action. General Rosas tried to do a deal: to surrender all Argentine claims if Britain would write off Argentina's defaulted bonds held by British subjects. This the British refused. For many decades the dispute was left in abeyance. During the past thirty-odd years the issue has been revived in Argentina partly as a result of political agitation by nationalist extremists and partly because development in southern Argentina suggests, if it does not prove, that the Falklands-Malvinas may have some importance in the growth of off-shore petroleum production, as a nucleus of a fishing industry, and as a staging-point for development in Antarctica.

From the British point of view there is much to be said both politically and economically for settling the dispute by transferring the islands to Argentina. Unfortunately what is rationally desirable is frequently emotionally unacceptable. The Argentines have behaved throughout with exceptional foolishness. Always determined to argue their case on legal grounds, they have rigidly refused to recognize the British presence in the Falklands. To admit any living connection with the Falkland Islands involves, in their view, the weakening of Argentina's legal position. As a result the inhabitants of the Falkland Islands are more remote from Argentina than they are from Britain or even Australia. All their connections with South America run through Uruguay. Who can blame the inhabitants of the Falkland Islands if they fear Argentina? They have never had an opportunity of knowing any Argentines or of visiting Argentina or of learning that ten times as many British people live in Argentina as live in the Falkland Islands or of knowing that British communities in Argentina are frequently more British than the British. If they are totally ignorant and therefore opposed to Argentina this is the Argentines' own fault and a product of the obsession of the upper classes with legal argument and of the lower classes with their xenophobic myths.

If the problem of the Falkland-Malvinas Islands leads to tragedy, the disaster will be a prime instance of the effects of non-communication all round; of a national dilemma rendered lethal by separate and total ignorance from which the political neuroses of the parties prevent escape. The combination of ignorance, patriotism, and devotion to the dogma of self-determination on the part of the British is perhaps more dangerous than Argentine legal pedantry and nationalist zealotry, because the British government has no political support in its community for resolving the conflict and the government is too frightened or complacent to give the British public a lead. And yet it could. The international treaty of 1959 concerning Centarctica, to which both Britain and Argentina are parties, provides many suggestions for a solution. As events are shaping up, however, it is possible to foresee a situation in which Argentina will force the solution, as it can, with the support of the United Nations, the Organization of American States, and the United States, and thus do something the Argentine government has no wish to do, i.e. to humiliate Britain. If this happens the British will have no one to blame but themselves.

*

If Anglo-Argentine relations terminate their present phase, with both a bang and a whimper, what of Argentina's relations with the United States? Argentina and the United States were both born of a revolution, and both cherish a revolutionary tradition. For these reasons they are antagonists, and have been since the first Pan-American Congress held in 1889. Until the Americans produced this confrontation by summoning a gathering designed as a step towards a larger United States of America, the Argentines and Americans had little to do with each other. Revolutionary sympathy signalized by an early recognition of the United Provinces of the Río de la Plata as an independent state was matched by the casual brutality of the American intrusion into the Malvinas. Until the Americans became entirely absorbed in continental expansion after the Anglo-American War of 1812–14, American shipping was a big factor in trade from the River Plate, but thereafter the American interest declined proportionately to that of other nations, but did not disappear. When the Argentines embarked on a policy of expansion through the importation of foreign labour and capital, they turned to Europe, and particularly to Britain and France, for money, and to Spain, Italy, and Germany for men and women.

In their relations with European states, the Argentines resembled the Americans, except that in the matter of capital requirements the Americans, after their great civil war, were autonomous or nearly autonomous in their capacity both to meet their own capital needs and to produce capital equipment. At the same time and until the 1890s the Americans were attending to their own business and were not a very likely source of capital to meet Argentine needs.

This might not have been entirely so, had vested interests of the United States not stood in the way of the development of American-Argentine trade. From the 1840s onward Argentina depended much on the sale of coarse wool, largely used in the manufacture of carpets, and the carpet manufacturers of the north-eastern United States were good customers. Bit by bit the American wool interests pushed up the tariffs and made foreign competition in the American market difficult. Argentine exports of wool were diverted increasingly to Europe. When the chilled- and frozen-meat industry developed, it too, was a competitor with the American meat interests, and Argentine products were handicapped or excluded from the American market. Ironically the first large-scale American participation in the Argentine economy came about as a result of this, for the big American meat-packers established themselves in Argentina in order to strengthen their position in the European markets for meat products. As far as cereals were concerned the United States and Argentina were competitors in world markets.

Until the Great Depression of 1929 the economic contacts between Argentina and the United States were not as extensive nor as well balanced as they might have been, and this was due to the selfishness of American vested interests and the unwillingness of Americans to practise the free competition they professed to believe in. On the plane of politics there was antagonism but not rancour. The Argentines resented the American barriers to trade and resisted the American endeavours to claim and to organize through the Pan-American Union the leadership of the United States in the Americas. American policy in Mexico, the Caribbean, and Central America found little sympathy in Argentina, but on the other hand the Argentine government did not go out of its way to denounce or expose American endeavours to teach the Latin Americans to elect good governments. Their settled policy was one of neutrality vis-à-vis all conflicts and all states. This was joined with efforts to get established in international law the principle of non-interference of states in each other's affairs and to assert the doctrine, named after the Argentine Foreign Minister, Luis Drago, that no state has the right to resort to political sanctions on behalf of creditors. This was a manifestation of anti-imperialism of a polite, rational, and practical kind.

The Argentine policy of neutrality was tested by World War I. Argentina remained neutral throughout. This was good business and good politics from the Argentine point of view, but it was not so regarded by the Americans after they entered the war. After the war was over Argentine-American relations worsened as Argentine-American economic intercourse increased. American films, American automotive equipment, farm machinery, and industrial enterprises began to enter Argentina on an increasing scale, but, on the other hand, Argentine economic opportunities in American markets were not improved. American intervention in the Caribbean and Central America, and the American special position in Cuba, began to generate a consciousness in all segments of Argentine society of an 'American problem' which increasingly came to be described by the pejorative shorthand 'Yankee imperialism'. When President Franklin Roosevelt attempted to refurbish the American image in Latin America by proclaiming the 'Good Neighbour Policy', he chose Buenos Aires as the platform from which to project this new conception. The occasion itself was loaded with ambiguities best illustrated by a little-known episode during the opening ceremonies of the meeting of the Pan-American Union – 1 December 1936. President Justo, as host, presided over the gathering. When Roosevelt rose to speak there was a loud cry from the back of the chamber – 'Down with Yankee imperialism'. There was a scuffle, a few thuds, and then a silence which allowed the American President to launch upon his speech. When the meeting was over and the platform party was leaving President Justo whispered to a police captain, 'Was that my son Liborio?' And the answer was 'Sí, Señor Presidente'.

Not all Argentines were so inclined as Liborio Justo to give embarrassing expression to their views, but the opposition to American attempts to lead and control the political life of Latin America became a settled disposition in Argentina. This was a big factor in the political crises during World War II. For a variety of reasons, some of them suggested in early chapters of this book, the Argentine government was never able to reach decisions which would have enabled them through co-operation with the Americans to take advantage, as the Mexicans, Canadians, and Brazilians did, of the desire of the United States to increase the general economic power of the Americas in the presence of the prospect that Germany and Japan might dominate Europe and Asia respectively. When, after the war, Perón endeavoured to establish for Argentina a 'Third Position' in world affairs there was no material or political base for such a policy. Like much else that Perón did, his foreign policy was all sail, little keel, and no cargo.

The Argentine government seems now to have accepted the fact that there is nothing to be gained by endeavouring to stand forth as the leader in the resistance to American pre-eminence in the Americas. This can be safely left to Fidel Castro, and he can be left alone to carry the torch of anti-Yankeeism. The power, both economic and political, of the United States is a fact, but not necessarily an eternal fact. In any event, why oppose American influence? It is becoming clear from the Canadian experience that more real independence and influence can be achieved in the political sphere by intelligent and close collaboration with the Americans than by adopting totally intransigent policies which weaken the one fact that all nations tend to respect, i.e. capacity for effective economic performance. It will be a long time before Argentina can put a man on the moon. In the meantime there are advantages in having an intelligent man in Washington. And also in London, Paris, Bonn, Rome, Moscow, and Tokyo. Once these advantages are reaped, Argentina can think finally of having an intelligent man in Peking, and so get back to the traditional Argentine policy of friendship with all and alliance with none.

Appendix

Presidents of Argentina
(dates of birth and death in brackets)

Bernardino Rivadavia	1826–27	(1780–1845)
Vicente López y Planes	1827–28	(1785–1856)
Juan Manuel Rosas, Governor and Captain-General of the Province of Buenos Aires	1829–33, 1835–52	(1793–1877)
Justo José de Urquiza	1854–60	(1800–70)
Santiago Derqui	1860–62	(1846–91)
Bartolomé Mitre	1862–68	(1821–1906)
Domingo Faustino Sarmiento	1868–74	(1811–88)
Nicolás Avellaneda	1874–80	(1837–85)
Julio A. Roca	1880–86	(1843–1914)
Miguel Juárez Celman	1886–90	(1844–1909)
Carlos Pellegrini	1890–92	(1846–1906)
Luis Sáenz Peña	1892–95	(1822–1907)
José Evaristo Uriburu	1895–98	(1831–1914)
Julio A. Roca	1898–1904	
Manuel Quintana	1904–06	(1835–1912)
José Figueroa Alcorta	1906–10	(1860–1931)
Roque Sáenz Peña	1910–14	(1851–1914)
Victorino de la Plaza	1914–16	(1840–1919)
Hipólito Yrigoyen	1916–22	(1852–1933)
Marcelo Torcuato de Alvear	1922–28	(1868–1942)
Hipólito Yrigoyen	1928–30	
José Félix Uriburu	1930–32	(1868–1932)
Agustín P. Justo	1932–38	(1878–1943)
Roberto M. Ortiz	1938–41	(1886–1942)
Ramón S. Castillo	1941–43	(1873–1944)
Arturo Rawson	1943	(1885–1952)
Pablo Ramírez	1943–44	(1884–1962)
Edelmiro J. Farrell	1944–46	(1887–)
Juan Domingo Perón	1946–55	(1895–)
Eduardo Lonardi	1955	(1896–1956)
Pedro Eugenio Aramburu	1955–58	(1903–)
Arturo Frondizi	1958–62	(1908–)
José Maria Guido	1962–63	(1910–)
Arturo U. Illia	1963–66	(1900–)
Juan Carlos Onganía	1966–	(1914–)

For Further Information

THE FOLLOWING BOOKS are suggested as a means of finding one's way towards an understanding of Argentine society through analysis and description of several kinds: historical, economic, sociological, literary, political, or ideological.

Some books originally in English or translated into English.

Robert J. Alexander, *The Perón Era*, New York, 1951.

George I. Blanksten, *Perón's Argentina*, Chicago, 1963.

Miron Burgin, *The Economic Aspects of Argentine Federalism, 1820–1852*, Cambridge, Mass., 1946.

H. S. Ferns, *Britain and Argentina in the Nineteenth Century*, Oxford, 1960.

Aldo Ferrer, *The Argentine Economy, an Economic History of Argentina*, Berkeley and Los Angeles, 1967.

Tomás R. Fillol, *Social Factors in Economic Development, The Argentine Case*, Cambridge, Mass., 1961.

Alec G. Ford, *The Gold Standard, 1880–1914; Britain and Argentina*, Oxford, 1962.

Jean Franco, *The Modern Culture of Latin America: Society and the Artist*, London and New York, 1967.

Julius Goebel, *The Struggle for the Falkland Islands*, New Haven, 1927.

Ricardo Güiraldes, *Don Segundo Sombra*, trans. by Harriet de Onis, London, 1948.

José Hernández, *The Gaucho, Martín Fierro*, trans. by Walter Owen, Buenos Aires, 1960.

R. A. Humphreys, *Latin American History: A Guide to the Literature in English*, London, 1958.

R. A. Humphreys, *Liberation in South America, 1806–1821*, London, 1952.

Preston E. James, *Latin America*, New York, 1959, chapter on Argentine geography.

John J. Johnson, *The Military and Society in Latin America*, Stanford, 1964.

John J. Kennedy, *Catholicism, Nationalism and Democracy in Argentina*, Notre Dame, Ind., 1958.

268 ARGENTINA

F. A. Kirkpatrick, *A History of the Argentine Republic*, Cambridge, 1931.
John Lynch, *Spanish Colonial Administration, 1782–1810*, London, 1958.
J. C. F. Metford, *San Martín, the Liberator*, Oxford, 1950.
Thomas F. McGann, *Argentina, the Divided Land*, New York, 1966.
Thomas F. McGann, *Argentina, the United States and the Inter-American System, 1880–1914*, Cambridge, Mass., 1957.
George Pendle, *Argentina*, London, New York, and Toronto, 3rd edition, 1963.
J. D. Perón, *Perónist Doctrine*, Buenos Aires, 1952.
Ysabel F. Rennie, *The Argentine Republic*, New York, 1945.
José L. Romero, *A History of Argentine Political Thought*, Stanford, 1963.
James R. Scobie, *Argentina, a City and a Nation*, New York, 1964.
Carl C. Taylor, *Rural Life in Argentina*, Baton Rouge, 1948.

Some books in Spanish.

Walter M. Beveraggi Allende, *El Servicio del Capital extranjero y el control de cambios*, México, 1954.
A. J. Pérez Amuchástegui, *Mentalidades Argentinas (1860–1930)*, Buenos Aires, 1965.
Francisco de Aparicio, *La Argentina: suma de geografía*, 9 volumes, Buenos Aires, 1958–1963.
Sergio Bagu, *El Plan Económico del Grupo Rivadaviano 1811–1827*, Buenos Aires, 1966.
Jorge L. Borges, *Aspectos de la Literatura Gauchesco*, Montevideo, 1950.
T. Halperin Donghi, *Historia de la Universidad de Buenos Aires*, Buenos Aires, 1962.
Ezequiel Martínez Estrada, *Radiografía de la Pampas*, Buenos Aires, 5th edition, 1961.
Gino Germani, *Politica y sociedad en una época de transición*, Buenos Aires, 1962.
José L. de Imaz, *Los Que Mandan*, Buenos Aires, 1964.
Raul Scalabrini Ortiz, *El hombre que está solo y espera*, Buenos Aires, 1935.
Jorge M. Mayer, *Alberdi y su Tiempo*, Buenos Aires, 1960.
Juan V. Orona, *La Logia Militar que enfrentó a Hipólito Yrigoyen*, Buenos Aires, 1965.
Raul Scalabrini Ortiz, *Fl hombre que está sol y espera*, Buenos Aires, 1931.

Jorge A. Paíta (ed.), *Argentina, 1930–1960*, Buenos Aires, 1961.
José M. Rosa, *Historia Argentina*, 5 volumes, Buenos Aires, 1964.
Torcuato S. di Tella, Gino Germani y colaboradores, *Argentina, Sociedad de Masas*, Buenos Aires, 1965.
United Nations, *El Desarrollo Económico de la Argentina*, 3 volumes, México, 1959.

Books from the past.
Thomas Faulkner, *A description of Patagonia and the adjoining parts of South America*, London, 1774.
R. A. Humphreys, *British Consular Reports on the Trade and Politics of Latin America, 1824–26*, London, 1940. (Camden 3rd Ser. vol. 63)
F. Bond Head, *Rough Notes taken during some Rapid Journeys across the Pampas and among the Andes*, London, 1826.
Charles Darwin, *Diary of the Voyage of H.M.S. Beagle*, ed. by Nora Barlow, Cambridge, 1933.
J. P. and W. P. Robertson, *Letters on South America*, 3 volumes, London, 1843.
Woodbine Parish, *Buenos Aires and the Provinces of the Rio de la Plata*, London, 2nd edition, 1852.
Domingo F. Sarmiento, *Life in the Argentine Republic in the Days of the Tyrants: or Civilization and Barbarism*, trans. by Mrs Horace Mann, New York, 1868.
V. Martin de Moussy, *Description géographique et statistique de la Conféderation Argentine*, Paris, 1861.
A. Martínez and M. Lewandowski, *The Argentine in the Twentieth Century*, London, 1911.
W. H. Hudson, *Far Away and Long Ago*, London, 1918.

Index

231; gains control in Uruguay, 79,
war with Argentina, 80–1; possibility of war overcome, 98; signs
treaty of free navigation, 98;
modern Argentina's rivalry with,
251–2
Bright, John, 107
Brisbane, Matthew, 258
Britain, British, 17, 23, 78, 88, 90,
95, 104, 119, 127, 128, 167, 229,
238, 245, 250, 252, 256, 260;
policy in Latin America, 9; importance of Argentina to, 9–10; war
with France, 32; relations with
Portugal, 33; effects of blockade
on Buenos Aires (1796), 45;
alliance with Spain against France,
44–5; resumes war with France
(1803), 45; policy towards Spain
after 1805, 47; surrender in
Buenos Aires, 47; change in policy
after abandonment of conquest,
58; factor of naval power of, 58–9;
commercial activity, 76; beliefs
concerning opportunities in Argentina, 77; recognizes independence
of Argentina, 80; relations with
Rosas, 84; intervention in Argentina, 89; admits mistakes in Argentina, 90; heavy investment, 95;
inaugurates free trade, 97; treaty
of free navigation signed, 98;
recognizes power of U.S. in
Americas, 104; does not object to
taxes, 109; proposals for intervention, 115–17; intervention in
Venezuela, 117; policy with low
political cost, 119; Argentine
preference for, 119; complementary trading policies, 128; Anglo-
American economic rivalry, 150;
D'Abernon proposals, 150; refusal
to train Argentine army, 151;
impact of depression on, 157;
abandons gold standard and free
trade, 160; theories of exploitation
by, 188; tactical advantages in
business negotiation, 189; disadvantage of railway sales by, 189;
dispute about Malvinas, 253–61;
number of passports in Argentina,
256; asserts rights in Falkland
Islands, 258; advantages of trans-

ferring Falklands to Argentina,
259
Brown, Guillermo, 81, 82
Buenos Aires, city of, 25–6, 94, 100,
184, 208, 223, 231, 232, 237, 248;
becomes capital of Viceroyalty,
37; mercantile character of, 41–2;
trade affected by blockade, 45;
union of city and province for
independence, 48; British decision
to reconquer, 51; Brazilian blockade of, 81; differences between
city and province, 93–4; wealth in,
120; beautification of, 134; restrictive social customs in, 138;
chief of police assassinated, 141;
socialists elected in, 143; distribution of political support in, 143–4;
capital market in, 162; October
1945 in, 176–7; *Azul* troops
occupy, 215
Buenos Aires, province of, 87, 169;
estancias in, 73; control by Indians,
79; land grants in, 86; Rosas and
interest of, 91; isolation of by
Urquiza, 98; policy of foreign
borrowing adopted, 99; guarantees
railway investment, 101; sells
assets, 106; Radical victory in,
159; prospective elections in
(1966), 218; agricultural experiment in, 243
Bullion, 26, 81; *see also* Silver
Bustos, Juan Bautista, 83

Cabildo, 29, 36, 37, 38, 50, 51;
Cabildo Abierto, 61, 195
Cabot, Sebastian, 25
Canada, Canadians, 17, 20, 95, 103,
121, 125, 127, 132, 146, 191, 208,
232, 248, 262, 263; obliged to
stand on own feet, 104; pattern of
development in, 126
Cape Town, 45
Capital, capital investment, 19, 119,
189, 220; changes during Brazilian
war, 81; landlords' need of, 94;
large British investment, 95;
autonomous accumulation versus
foreign investment, 98–9; conditions for, 100; role of private, 101;
chronology of flows, 102; conditions for renewed investment, 111;

Printed in Great Britain by
Western Printing Services Limited, Bristol

4/27/70

DATE DUE	
DEC 1 1 2003	
DEC 1 2 2003	